UNDER AS

'Under Asian Skies'

by

Sam Manicom

Australia to Europe by Motorcycle - Lands of Colour & Contrast

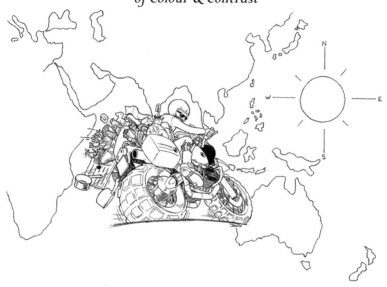

"Adventure is a path. Real adventure – self-determined, self-motivated, often risky – forces you to have firsthand encounters with the world. The world the way it is, not the way you imagine it. Your body will collide with the earth and you will bear witness. In this way you will be compelled to grapple with the limitless kindness and bottomless cruelty of humankind – and perhaps realise that you yourself are capable of both. This will change you. Nothing will ever again be black-and-white."

Mark Jenkins (Adventurer and Travel Writer)

ISBN   978-0-9556573-0-6

Cover design by Fil Schiannini and Sam Manicom
Layout by Fil Schiannini and Birgit Schuenemann
KDP layout by Mike Fitterling
Photos by Sam Manicom, Birgit Schuenemann, Sarah St George
Photos in this Amazon KDP print on demand version are black and white.
Motorcycle Line Art by Jez Cooper
Line art by Sam Manicom
Published by Sam Manicom
Although every effort has been made to trace the present copyright holders, we apologise in advance for any unintentional omission or neglect and will be pleased to insert appropriate acknowledgement to individuals in any subsequent edition of this publication.

Reviews

Under Asian Skies

'A unique and wonderful adventure.'
Ted Simon – Author of Jupiter's Travels
'Engaging from the off; a terrific read'
Overland Magazine
'Accessible and well written, this will prod anyone with a bike license to take off and do something amazing!'
Adventure Travel Magazine
'Why buy it? Inspiration!'
Motorcycle News
'Highly recommended.'
Motorcycle Monthly
'Sam has the skills of the story teller and this book easily transports you into three years of journey across Asia. He manages to bring the sounds, scents and heat of Asia to life without wordy overkill and he has obviously researched his historical facts carefully. ... In places Under Asian Skies is sad, and in others it's outrageously funny - look out for his battle with the Sydney port officials and the bus ride in Indonesia. All in all this is a really good read, whether you have been across Asia, or are planning a trip. This is true travelling on the cheap and not your everyday story.'
Horizons Unlimited.com
'We...are treated to what must be the most bizarre and hilarious entry into a country anyone has ever experienced! Sam's enthusiasm for biking, for exploring and for meeting new people jump off the page and even a serious back injury or nearly dying of Dengue Fever can't stop him. All these challenges seem to urge him on and don't dent the author's endless fascination for the world one bit.'
Bikersweb.co.uk
'Sam's ability to write in a compelling and funny (style) makes this book a compelling read. His ability to captivate the audience makes this book very hard to put down.'
motorbikesearchengine.co.uk
'...This is one helluvan adventure!'
Canyon Chasers.com
'A narrative of a world far different from the one seen on the evening news'
Zen Motorcyclist USA
'...the thing I most enjoyed about this book was the feeling that I was there with him as he went through everything. I've travelled a bit myself in this part of the world, and the feeling of the hustle, the smells, the people, the smiles the bartering, Sam's account brought it all back to me. '
London Bikers.com

Contents

"Stop worrying about the potholes in the road and celebrate the journey."
Fitzhugh Mullan

Acknowledgements

Making a travel book happen is very much like being on the road. Each challenge turns into an adventure, and success is never achieved without the help of others. I hope that everyone who has helped me already knows how grateful I am to them for their advice, critiques and hands-on assistance.

My partner Birgit, as ever, has been a tremendous support and enthusiast for the idea of *'Under Asian Skies'*. As a seasoned traveller herself, by both bicycle and motorcycle, her experience and her passion for the world have helped me to tell this tale.

I owe great thanks to Peter Henshaw – motorcycle magazine editor, and author – who edited the manuscript. Without his talent plus skilled cutting and polishing, it would not have worked.

Paul Blezard – motorcycle journalist – has meticulously added the finishing touches and has made sure that nothing went to print without being exactly the way it should be. His fresh eyes and experience made the difference.

The cover of *'Under Asian Skies'* is the brainchild and work of my friend the designer Fil Schiannini who also needs to take the credit for dealing with the page formatting, and promotional work – many thanks Fil – looking good!

Chris Scott – Motorcycle adventurer, Desert Specialist and Author (www.adventure-motorcycling.com), Motorcycling friends Les Madge, Glynn Roberts, Stewart and Dave from CW Motorcycles (www.cwmotorcycles.co.uk) are the ones to take credit for helping me decide on the title. Thanks guys – the skies over Asia are enormous and they cover a fascinating part of our world.

The lead cartoon is courtesy of Jez Cooper who has a magic touch with the cartoonist's pen.

I've been allowed to use some of the photos – the better ones – by Sarah St George and Birgit Schuenemann.

5

I must acknowledge and thank all the people I have quoted in the book. I apologise for the cases where I have not been able to make contact, and hope that you are happy to see your words in 'Under Asian Skies'.

I need to thank all the people I met along the way. You guys are the people that have made this adventure so vibrant. I have changed some of your names so as not to put you at risk. Thanks for sharing so much with me.

And my Guardian Angel too – thanks for working overtime to keep me rolling through all the adventures!

And finally, many thanks to everyone who bought and posted a review on Amazon, or reviewed 'Into Africa' on forums and in the press.

Without your generous feedback and enthusiasm, this book would not have been written – may you all have amazing journeys.

Prologue

Motorcycling, people and adventure are the inspirations for 'Under Asian Skies'.

When I set off to spend a year riding the length of Africa on a motorcycle, I'd no idea if I would like travelling by bike, or whether I would survive; I've an active imagination, and I'd been riding a bike for just three months. At times the roads made me feel like I was some sort of motorcycling accessory, not the person who was supposed to be in control. I learned lessons the hard way - falling off hurts, and jail in Africa should be avoided at all costs.

The bike acted as the connecting factor between adventures. It got me into and out of trouble. It gave me time to myself when I was on 'intake overload' from life on the road. It gave me the freedom to explore on the spur of the moment, and to take advantage of opportunities as they presented themselves. Travel on two wheels took me from gentle mellow cruising days, to full-on adrenaline-packed adventure and my bike frequently broke the ice between myself and strangers.

It's the people that make a trip like this into a success. They may wish to live your dream with you, or find empathy with some aspect of your nomadic adventure. Landscapes, climates and histories enthral, but it is people who make every day significant. For the traveller, people bring joy, frustration, and warm generosity. It was people and the act of riding a motorcycle 22,000 miles through the magic that is Africa that changed me. By the time I'd made it to Southern Africa, I was an addict; I wanted more. It felt as if the journey had barely begun, and that I had only just discovered how to look at the world. On impulse I shipped across the Indian Ocean to Australia, and headed for Asia.

There's a magical, captivating, buzz about being on the road under Asian skies. As I motorcycled across the continents, I was constantly challenged by things I'd never dreamt could happen. Things I thought I knew well were changed by the adventures. The stunning beauty of the land enthralled, and the people were an enigma; they were fascinating. There was no end to the adventures I could have and I either sought them with my eyes wide-open, or they came to me!

This world of ours is amazing and biking is a stunning way to see it. I'm incredibly lucky to have been able to share, though briefly, other people's homes, their dreams, their lands, their cultures and their travels.

'*Under Asian Skies*' is written to share the fun with those who dream of or plan adventure.

The Route

Chapter 1
"Sorry mate, I didn't see you."
'The more I travelled, the more I realised that fear makes strangers of people who should be friends.'

Shirley MacLaine

The heat of the day was intense. The sky above me was a clear blue and the grass under me, brittle and spiky. It was too early for pain to surface and though stunned, I lay thinking, 'I hope the first people here aren't smokers.' Something fast moving had flashed as a blur of blue in the side of my visor, and within an instant it had slammed into me!

The Pacific Highway was dual carriageway and just after a set of traffic lights, I'd stopped on a hard shoulder lay-by to have a drink and check my map. My plan was that when the lights were on red, I could ease on out with no traffic to deal with. Moving out onto the road, while I was looking in my right hand mirror to check what was happening at the lights, the blue van smashed into the bike from the left. It hurled us across to the central reservation, and I ended up wedged under the bike with petrol pouring out of the carburettors onto my legs. It happened in the blink of an eye, and after a long moment of stunned silence, suddenly all my senses were working on full power. The reeking petrol was stinging my skin through my trousers. The earth and grass by my nose, heated by the midday sun, smelt dry and held the tang of pollution. On the other side of the reservation cars sped past, just by my head. I could hear them and feel their draft, but trapped under the bike I couldn't twist enough to see them or get further away.

The first three people to get to me roared up on bikes. They were Australian Hell's Angels, and thankfully they weren't smoking. The one closest to me was astride a gleaming but very battered black and gold chopper that had forks so long the bike must have been a pig to get around corners. From where I was lying it was natural to start from the ground and work upwards towards his face; he sat impassively, looking down at me. He was wearing scuffed and oil-soaked square-toed bike boots, and equally oil-soaked black denim jeans that looked so stiff with filth that they'd probably have stood up on their own. He wore a filthy blue denim waistcoat that was decorated in front with embroidered skulls, crossbones and the like. His belly, which seemed to be instantly forming a sheen of sweat, stuck out between the unbuttoned front of the waistcoat. His arms were tattooed with age-faded blues and reds, and around his neck he had a skull suspended on a bike chain that still had oil on it. The chain left a dark mark around his neck, and a greasy pendulum shape on his chest where it must have swung back and forth as he rode. His chin was unshaven with about four days' growth, and his eyes were hidden by the darkest black wraparound shades I'd ever seen. On his shaven head, he had a German Second World War army helmet with a cow's horn sticking out of each side.

I had no sense of fear as I lay there, just the irreverent thought that he looked like an extra from a Hollywood biker movie. He leaned down, without getting off his bike, and said, "G'day mate, how's it going?" Though it was getting rather painful under the bike, and the heat of the exhaust was beginning to burn through my jeans, I was delighted by this absolutely perfect piece of pure Australian. I as a Brit replied, "Not too good actually". "I can see that mate", he said with a tone in his voice that made it perfectly clear that finding a Brit under a motorcycle in the middle of a dual carriageway was an everyday occurrence. He and the other two Angels got off their bikes, lifted my bike off me, and without a further word roared off in a triple Harley-Davidson blast. Until that moment, the van driver hadn't realised that it wasn't a Hells Angel he'd hit, but was walking bravely, honourably and very scared down the road from where he had parked up.

His first words to me were the classic, "Sorry mate, I didn't see you." He went on to explain, "I live just off the lay-by – down the hill a bit. I can see the lights from my drive, and when they go to red I shoot out. I was late today, and you were hidden by the bush – I never expected to see you there. I'm really sorry mate."

Once again I'd been lucky in my misfortune. I was a little shocked and I was sore, but unhurt. My left leg had been protected by

11

the gap between the bikes engine protection bar and my luggage pannier, and my bike gear had saved me from the worst of the fall. My leather jacket was covered in deep scratch marks, and my jeans and gloves had been torn open, but I hadn't collected a single mark. My helmet had an unhealthy dose of gravel rash and would have to be replaced, but I was glad I'd been wearing it.

Libby had taken a hammering though. She had slid across the asphalt at speed and had slammed hard against the kerb of the central reservation. She'd lost a lot of paint, her indicators were ripped off, and a mirror was broken. Both the plastic fairing and the windscreen were shot, which was very sad. They had been made for me by a man in a mud hut at the edge of the desert in Namibia after my accident there. They were souvenirs I'd hoped to be able to keep. The bash bars were mangled on both sides of the bike – the one side from hitting the ground, and the other from the impact of the van. My panniers had received just about the finishing touch – they were ready to be binned, though they had never been a good buy. From the time I had fallen off hard the first time in Sudan, they had let dust and water in, the locks could no longer hold the lids closed and I knew that they would have to be replaced before I shipped out of Australia. Other than that, the forks had twisted in the yokes, and the clutch and brake levers had bent and swivelled on the handlebars, which were also bent a little. I thought that all could be put back into line without too much work.

At that moment, as I surveyed the damage, I wasn't angry, but even if I had been, the driver would have calmed me straight down with his words of apology. Much later, I wondered if I would have been angry if I'd not been so shocked, but I decided that I wouldn't. Accidents in one form or another are inevitable on a trip like this, and it makes more sense to put energy into getting the situation sorted out, rather than wasting it on rage.

The driver lived close by and took me straight home for a cup of sweet tea. Peter's insurance, he was sure, would cover the damage. Once I had cuppa in hand he was straight on the phone, and within half an hour the insurers had agreed to pay up and told us it was up to us to find a garage to work on the bike. It was going to cost a lot more to put the van to rights – a loaded up 800cc BMW does a lot of damage to a vans panels.

Peter drove me to South African friends of mine who lived nearby, and agreed to pick me up the next day. He duly did so, and with the bike strapped to his trailer, took me on a tour of the five local bike shops until I found one that I liked the look of.

This delay was a pain in more ways than one, and I'd no idea if damage other than visual injury had been caused to the bike. The garage assured me not, and I simply had to trust them. A key issue was that the delay was going to eat into money-earning time, and that could be a problem, though I wasn't worried. Delays so far had nearly always turned into adventures that had real value.

Arriving by container ship from Africa into Australia had been one such adventure, with a wonderfully unique event attached to it. I'd just spent a year riding the length of Africa and had had a ball doing it. It was a great adventure and as a novice biker I'd learned that riding is a great way to travel, not least because of the fact that you don't have to carry a rucksack! The bike had placed me out in the world, with no physical barriers between me and the people whose lands I was travelling through. The bike had always been a good topic to start a conversation with strangers; it had been the best icebreaker ever. And it gave me flexibility. The only forced guiding restraints were length of a visa, the weather, the availability of fuel and water, and of course my budget. It was great not to have to worry about buying tickets for busses and trains. I enjoyed being able to go where I wanted to when I wanted to go. I enjoyed the added control the bike gave me over my travels and revelled in the adventures she seemed to quite naturally get me into. Not all were quite so fun though: I'd been arrested three times in Africa, shot at and fallen off hard enough to earn seventeen bone fractures. But during all the harsher adventures I'd had a guardian angel flying alongside, and as a result none of the dramas got completely out of hand.

I managed to book myself onto a container ship for the passage to Australia. I was absolutely delighted at this opportunity, as being on a big merchant vessel on the high seas had been an ambition from childhood. It also meant I'd be arriving in Australia with the bike, which made things simpler. And as the bike went on the manifest as hand luggage, I didn't have to pay for her passage, making it cheaper than shipping the bike, and me flying across.

For my money I had a cabin to myself on the MSC Sabrina, and the shipping company even provided me with a hand towel with my name embroidered on it. I could go anywhere on the ship and was to mess with the officers and the five other passengers. Most of the officers were Italian, which meant large quantities of a food I love and a never-ending supply of quality red wine. The other passengers were a South African family of four who had sold up and were emigrating to Australia. Val and Michael feared how South Africa was going to go when a white government was no longer in power, and they wanted to bring their two boys up in a secure environment. South Africa would struggle with the effects of the brain drain but who could blame people for seeking a more certain life elsewhere? The other passenger was an elderly lady who simply enjoyed travelling around the world on cargo ships. Jane said that they were much more interesting than cruise ships. She was a very interesting character who had worked all over the world and I suspected that as a result of that, she wasn't very comfortable in her homeland of the UK. We were all quite different, but it was very easy to rub along for the eleven-day passage.

I had a ball exploring the ship and even made it down as far as the engine room where I was allowed to polish the brass work, satisfying another childhood ambition. The crew were great fun and I suspect that the ship owners took passengers on board not as a profitable income, but as entertainment value for the men!

At first, the Indian Ocean was kind, rolling a gentle swell under cool overcast skies. But on day seven, this enormous ship turned into a heaving, wave smashing beast. We'd sailed into a force eight storm! For me it was fun. I'd well and truly got my sea legs by then and the motion was rather like being on a never-ending roller coaster ride. My stomach would frequently stay floating around the ceiling, while the rest of me dropped into another massive trough between the towering waves. At one moment, looking out of the spray-splattered windows, I realised that a small yacht was off our starboard side. The waves were maybe ten times taller than it was and, sails reefed in, it rode the waves as if hurtling up and down on a massive high-speed lift. I suspected that out there sea legs didn't matter a jot. Up on the bridge of the container ship, life went on as normal. Everyone was calm, lights on control panels blinked green or orange, and the radar swept back and forth. Other than the heaving of the deck, the only sign that there was a storm was the fact that the windscreen wipers were fighting a losing battle against the rain and the spray. The storm lasted a couple of days.

We were bound for Sydney, a city I knew a little about, but I'd never been anywhere near the docks. We'd left Durban in the hazy silver shades of dawn and arrived against the dock in Sydney in a twin light. The whole day stretched before us and that, I knew, couldn't have been more perfect. I wasn't expecting any real hassles – after all this was a First World port – but Australia does have some quirky self-protective rules. The first time I'd flown there, the other passengers and I had been sprayed with some sort of bug killer by the airhostess. With that in mind, I'd paid careful attention to the rules attached to bringing a bike into the country, and from Africa at that. Being on a massive island meant that Australians had a chance of keeping a certain number of diseases and bugs out of the country, which was vital if its unique flora and fauna were to remain unchanged. Modern travel means that the country is at ever increasing risk, so I spent a couple of days going over the bike, centimetre by centimetre, with a toothbrush and disinfectant before I had taken it to the docks in Durban. In a way it had been a rather sad exercise, as I'd been washing off a little of every country I'd travelled through. But it also gave me the chance to make sure that nothing was cracked or broken, and I knew for sure that the Australians would quarantine the bike if she wasn't immaculate. That would be a time consuming exercise, and I only had a six-month visa and a lot of adventuring planned. As for the expense, I'd never originally planned to come to Australia at all, but I'd had such an amazing time riding through Africa I'd decided to keep going. If I had to pay for the bike to be in quarantine, there were going to be days when I'd be broke.

The ships derrick swung the BMW over the side and down onto the dock. A bunch of the lads from the crew helped carry my kit down, and then I waited for the customs guys to turn up. While waiting, I checked her over.

In spite of having been swaddled in five layers of plastic sheet, the fact that she had been strapped up on the deck meant that she had

been open to the effects of the sea air. She was covered in a crusty layer of white salt, and the alloy had started to grow little mushrooms. I had hoped that the three-in-one oil I'd painted on before leaving would stop this happening, but perhaps I should have used engine oil instead!

The customs officer arrived before too long, and did a cursory check of the papers and my carnet de passage, which would allow me to import the bike on a temporary basis. No problems, but I had a longer wait for the quarantine office to arrive. I had to pay for his inspection and in relative terms it cost a fortune – it took just three minutes! But we passed, and then it was just a matter for the customs officer to do the final sign off and I'd be out of there. He came back with another man in tow. Documents signed and rubber-stamped, and I was ready. But then before I could climb on, the other man asked for the keys, stating that he was going to ride the bike the 300 metres to the gates. I don't know what it was that made me react the way I did next. I'm not sure I'm proud of myself for it, but what happened over the next hours was a perfect example of bureaucracy gone mad and my own pure stubbornness.

Perhaps the tone in his voice got to me, and perhaps I was still feeling budget burnt over the cost of that three-minute check, but I was darned if I was going to let someone else ride my bike, especially someone I didn't know. I told him that would not be possible unless he had his bike licence with him and a copy of his insurance document. If he didn't have them, I'd ride. I'm not normally this bolshie, but something made me stand my ground. The men went away, to return an hour later with a 'no'. I dug in, so they went away again to return yet another hour later. I think they were trying to wear me down, but they weren't used to African border crossings, and so far this was a pussycat operation by comparison. The man still had no papers, but now explained that it was a safety issue. I understood that to a certain extent, but was still not going to give way. No insurance, no licence, no ride.

I told them that if they didn't get their act together, then I'd set up camp on the dockside until they did. I had plenty of food in my panniers, and water too. I'd also no doubt that I'd get a bottle of wine dropped down to me as payment for the entertainment I was giving the crew. Another hour eased by, and I enjoyed sitting in the warm sunshine watching the busy life of the harbour buzz on around me. Then a port manager turned up with the customs officer to see what was happening.

He explained that not only was it a safety point but a union issue too, and that he said almost under his breath, was the real problem. That was enough for me, and before I realised what I was saying, I suggested that I should ride the bike and so that union and safety issues were satisfied, a man with a red flag should walk in front of me to the gates. I think the unions had been giving the manager a hard time about this and other things, and to my amazement, he thought this was a brilliant idea. So, my bike and I had an escorted red flag welcome to Australia. Strangely perfect.

Part of the reason that I'd plenty of time was that I knew where I was going to stay for the next few days. Rob and Fiona, travelling friends I'd made in Cape Town, had invited me to stay with their family when I got to Sydney. I was made very welcome and over the next few days I managed to get out and visit my old haunts in the city and to wash all the salt off the bike. I also had the chance to get rid of the rolling sailor's gait that I'd developed on board ship!

But I had a whole continent to explore, and I also had to find some work. I didn't have a work permit and I don't like breaking the law when I am a guest in a country, but needs must. I had enough money to get back to the UK, but not enough to allow for adventures and any set backs, which was potentially dangerous.

From almost the first day I'd arrived in Australia I'd been hearing people talk about the number of unemployed on the dole, and how rich it was that they were not being bussed out into the farms to pick crops instead of sitting around at home. I was also hearing stories of farmers who had to plough whole crops back into the ground because they couldn't find enough people to pick them. That seemed a travesty after all the hunger I'd seen in Africa. Armed with these thoughts I didn't feel too guilty at what I was setting out to do. The real problem was not going to be finding work, but finding work without papers.

I'd met quite a few Australians in Africa and had had a letter from one who was picking fruit in NW Victoria. 'Loads of work', Brian said, adding that I should get there as quickly as possible. The boss was a great bloke who was gutted at the crops he was losing; we could free camp on the farm and eat us much of the fruit and vegetables we were picking as we liked. This sounded perfect, though I knew that it was going to be very hard work. Professional Australian pickers have a real competitive pride in their skills, and the speed at which they work. It's a macho thing, though just as many of the pickers are women as men. Such pickers are a particular breed of people. They rarely settle in one place, and many are loners who work with a mate or keep themselves to themselves. They spend their year going from one picking season and one crop to another. Because Australia is so big there's always fruit or veg ready for harvest in one state or another. Some pickers are fussy though and will only pick one type of crop, the classic being the grape pickers.

I started off on a farm growing cherry tomatoes and capsicums. Brian and his friends were camping in the overgrown garden of the old farmhouse, which had become semi derelict when a new house had been built. There was shade, a standpipe, it was right next to the fields and in the old house the guys had dragged seats from the wrecked cars that stood on blocks next to the building. They had placed these around

18

the fireplace and though no one dared light a fire for fear of setting the tinder dry wreck of a structure ablaze, it still provided a natural

focal point to sit around each evening. The evenings were cold too, as this was late autumn, so it was a good feeling to get in out of the wind and occasional rain.

Neither Brian nor his friends came under the category of professional pickers. Swelling the ranks of the professionals are a couple of other groups of people. Some are travellers who are on gap years, and are working quite legally with permits. Most don't have to earn, but are there for the experience and the adventure, though the funds come in useful. In the main they were a nice bunch of people, but not particularly quick pickers and usually the first to stop for the day. Most suffered with hangovers in the morning, and who could blame them, they were on holiday doing a once in a lifetime thing.

The other group of people I called 'The lost'. Men and women who were mostly young, drifted from place to place with no real aim other than to eat, drink beer, buy dope and be able to really drop out for a week or two every so often. Quite a few had problem backgrounds and with that in common, seemed to gravitate towards each other. Living alongside them, I kept a close eye on my belongings. Most seemed harmless, but I was always conscious that they were unpredictable. That made them interesting.

I'd met Brian in Kenya, and he was one of the lost. He was far more adventurous than the others though, as from time to time he got his act together enough to venture far away from Australia. If his stories could be believed he'd had some amazing adventures, but I sometimes wondered if he had a death wish. Some of Brian's adventures had seemed totally mad to do, and he'd actually planned his way into them. He'd walked barefoot across Angola at the height of the war there, and had sneaked across the border into Somalia just as their war was kicking off. He looked like a hippy, and a joint was never far from his fingers. He had long, wavy, light brown hair and a small buccaneer beard and moustache. He dressed in caftan tops and jeans that he had adapted into flares, and had decorated with embroidery and small sewn-on mirrors. Girls seemed to love him, and I was never quite sure whether it was the rather dangerous air that hung about him, the fact that he was good looking and very different, or that when he talked to girls he seemed to focus on them so intensely that they must have felt like they were the only important person in the world. Perhaps this combination was so powerful that few could resist him.

I thought Brian was interesting and enjoyed being a fly on the wall watching his effect on other people. I was never quite sure what he would get up to next, as he had no fear of the outrageous and didn't seem to have the same boundaries that most of us are brought up with. He wasn't exactly a free spirit – he was too troubled for that – but there was side to him that seemed determined to ignore what was supposed to be. Without him though, I wouldn't have had an opening into work, and in spite of his image he did have respect from the professional pickers.

The working days were long and hot. Picking started at 7.00am. I'll never be able to face a cherry tomato again without remembering how hard they are to pick. They grow on great bushy vines which are planted in 100 metre long rows, and the tomatoes hang in bunches, rather like grapes. Red tomatoes got picked and discarded into the walkway between the rows, too red to make it to market before they started to turn. It felt an awful waste. We were looking for almost red and dark orange fruit - anything yellow or green stayed on the plant to be picked another day. You had to battle your way in under the vines to find the best fruit and before long your hands, arms and shirts turned green with the sap from the stems. Once a T-shirt was stained with this stuff, you could never really get it out, especially if hand washing clothes in cold water.

Towards the middle of the day we would stop minding being under the vines because at least there we were out of the sun. We all slapped sun cream on our faces and arms and kept topping it up during the day. It was rather like applying guacamole to your skin, as the suntan lotion mixed with the sap stain. The two-gallon tomato buckets take an age to fill, and as we were paid by the bucketful this is a key issue. After just half an hour break in the middle of the day for the traditional 'smoko', we dragged aching backs into the field, engaged autopilot and set off again. It was tough, but with a hard working mate to partner with, you could strip the two sides of a row like a couple of locusts. Completing a row was a really satisfying thing, and the better teams would race each other to complete their rows first. No one cheated as the loss of face would follow you around for the whole of your picking career.

The pickers worked very hard and played very hard. Some would eat, smoke and booze their earnings away, living for each day. Some of them had an amazing ability to put away vast quantities of booze in an evening, and show no after effects whatsoever. Not me, if I drank to keep up with them I'd always have a brain-splitting headache the next day. What was already exhausting work would become body numbing, and I'd be letting the pickers down by working too slowly.

Pickers always tried to get to town on a Friday night. They were like a bunch of sailors on leave for the first time in months, and it could be a very mad night. Other weekends, in prime season though, the fact that it was a Friday or a Saturday didn't register at all. The crops had to be picked and it was just like any other day. I didn't care. I just wanted to earn money, and lots of it at that. The boss still hadn't asked for my papers and I mostly managed to keep out of his way, not wanting

to have to lie to him. He seemed a nice bloke. I had suggested to him though that he was losing money by binning all the red tomatoes. I suggested that he should set up a mini bottling plant and make chutney or sauce out of those tomatoes, rather than let them go to waste. Months later, I was chuffed to hear that he had done just that. Marco was of Italian decent and I suppose that making a good tomato sauce was both in the genes, and that his family has some sort of secret and very tasty recipe. I was pleased to have made a difference, however small.

The immigration authorities simply did not have enough people power to track down all the illegal workers in Australia, and there were many of us. Western Europeans, Canadians, Americans, South Africans and many more from across S.E. Asia and China. There were even a few from Eastern Europe. The way to get work without papers was to go to the more remote areas where there was a limited local labour force for the farmers to tap into. You'd then supply a fake identity number, after 'forgetting' to bring it in with you for a few days. The wise farmers would get you straight to work and because they were incredibly busy at that time of year, they would then 'forget' to send off your details for a few days. It would take a fair few more days for your number to be processed, and for the farmer to be advised that it either didn't exist or the name didn't match the number in their records. By that time you'd been working for a few weeks and earned enough money to move on, or the crop had been fully picked. The risk came from immigration department raids. Every so often they would target an area or a particular farm that they had suspicions about. Immigration officials would combine with the local police to circle a farm with a human fence. This fence would work its way towards the centre of the farm and this sort of dragnet would collect up all those working. If you were caught, you were deported. There were no ifs and buts; you were out of the country on the first available flight. Many were not even given the chance to collect their belongings. Most would never get a visa for Australia again. It was harsh but fair. After all, we were all breaking the law, but it was a good feeling to have money in your pocket and to see smiles come across stressed farmers' faces, so the risk was worthwhile.

I'd worked hard and Marco offered me more work once the tomatoes were finished. So I worked capsicums for a few tense days and then decided that I had stretched things as far as I safely ought. It was time to load up the bike and get on the road again. I wanted to see some of Tasmania and I knew that I had family down there somewhere. I was also glad to leave pepper picking behind me; it's back breaking work and another vegetable I can only look at now with awe for the effort that has gone into getting them to table.

The dry Victoria countryside and the open, almost traffic-free roads eased me southwards through Robinvale and Swan Hill. The great Murray River flowed its muddy waters just to the east of me. I revelled in the sudden freedom, and the vibrations from the bumpy asphalt eased the kinks from my back. I rode gently, enjoying the greening landscape and the small towns.

I wasn't in the mood to deal with a big city so scooted straight through Melbourne and on down to the docks. I'd timed it just right to catch the morning sailing of the catamaran ferry, the 'Devil Cat'. The cat takes just 6 hours to make the crossing across the Bass Strait to George Town, and fortunately for me the weather was calm. This wasn't an issue as far as seasickness was concerned, but more because the cat doesn't sail if the waters are too choppy. The only alternative was to cross on the 'Spirit of Tasmania', a giant car ferry that takes 14 hours to plough back and forth. I was on a roll – quick was good!

Chapter 2

"Southern Winter"

'Each new moment is a memory waiting to be etched into my mind.'

Flores

Tasmania in winter is grey, can be very cold, and up in the mountains there's the threat of snow. It wasn't the ideal time to be this far south, but the breaks sometimes fall that way. I'd also planned to head even further south at the opportunity, aiming for New Zealand, which I knew would be even chillier than Tasmania. But at least the roads should be a lot quieter out of season and the chill of Tasmania would help get my Africa-acclimatised body used to harsher temperatures.

I'd met a girl called Gill on the Devil Cat, and she'd agreed to keep me company on the bike for a while. It was a great feeling to be back on the road again and this time, having someone to share the sights with made a lot of sense, though the bike felt strange two-up. I'd got so used to how it handled with just me and my gear aboard, that the weight of a passenger and her kit transformed the bike from a cruising roadrunner into a waddling hippo. For the first few miles I wondered if I had made a horrible mistake by inviting Gill to come with me. The riding was hard work, and it felt as if somehow I'd surrendered my freedom by sharing with someone else. This started me thinking. After a year on the road, mostly on my own, was I becoming some sort of two-wheeled hermit? It was very nice to be able to do whatever I wanted, when I wanted to do it, without having to consider anyone else. On the other hand perhaps I had become incredibly selfish, and perhaps meeting Gill had actually been fortuitous. Perhaps this review of the way I was beginning to see life was a timely reminder that we are not alone, wherever we are, and that we all have to get along somehow. But that thought didn't sit well as we rolled further away from civilisation. We rode on through forests, dark with wet and dripping trees, and covered in deep green moss, where almost prehistoric fern trees stood as evidence to the fact that there are still places in this world where man has made no mark.

But as the miles rolled by I became more used to Gill, and she became more used to the bike. The three of us started to move together as a unit and my heavy mood lifted. The next day the sun split the sky wide open and we rode past small wooden hamlets, through forests, round bays and past fishing villages that perched on the coastline like cormorants waiting for a catch, their wings spread out in the sunshine to dry. We rode over slow-flowing rivers, their

 waters so full of tannin that had seeped down from the forests that the water looked black and almost oily. Other streams rushed with clean clear water, past tall trees that stood naked in the world, their leaves, twigs and bark all gone, leaving them to stand rather like ghostly sentinels, staring at the mountains in the distance.

We were heading for Cradle Mountain and Lake St Clair. This is a world heritage area that includes Mt Ossa, Tasmania's highest mountain at 1617 metres, and is home to Australia's deepest fresh water lake. The landscape has been gouged by glaciers and tempered by time into a world of peaks, deep gorges and moorlands. We couldn't miss it but Gill and I knew that we were tempting fate by riding so high in mid-winter. Wintry conditions were going to be a real risk and there was no way I wanted to ride Libby two-up, with luggage, on snow. In the event the winter was kind to us, and we managed to hike through stunning scenery for a full day before snowflakes the size of bottle tops started to float down, almost in slow motion towards us. We hurriedly loaded Libby, paid for our bunks in the log cabin, and headed down the mountain as fast as we could go in the ever-heavier snow. That night the radio said that six inches had fallen.

Then Libby rebelled. My bike earned the name of Libby when I was roughly two thirds of the way through Africa. She had changed over the kilometres from being, 'the bike' and 'it', to 'her'. And then as I began to understand her more and what she had given me, she became Libby - short for Liberty. We were riding across an open plain, with clear blue skies above us and the mustards and sages of moorland to the sides, when she started to vibrate gently. A nasty clunk developed when opening the throttle and gear changing. I had no idea what the problem was, but it felt serious, though we weren't far from the central Tasmanian town of Launceston. My cousins lived there and as luck would have it, Launceston is also home to a BMW motorcycle dealer.

Somehow, after just 37,000 kilometres, I'd managed to break the drive shaft on the bike. On bikes, shafts are supposed to be reliable and to be far less work than a chain – both of those points had appealed to me when I was buying the bike. But I hadn't expected to break a shaft, and sod's law decreed that it happened two months after the warranty had expired. The part was ordered, I paid for it, and in due course it was fitted with no nasty side effects to deal with. All in all, I was lucky that the shaft had failed gradually and within riding distance of a BMW garage, but the money I had earmarked to get the bike down to New Zealand had suddenly disappeared. I was gutted, as I'd read that New Zealand is one of the best biking countries in the world, and this had been a major factor in my decision to come this way, rather than head for South America from Africa.

The upside of the delay was that I had more time to spend with my newfound cousins, but Gill moved on to see more of Tasmania, by bicycle. I'd enjoyed her company, but as with many friendships that are struck up along the travellers' way, they end at some time. They either survive long distance with letters and emails, or they remain a memory and a happy entry in your journal.

My cousins were on my mother's side of the family and though I'd known that they were there, I'd never been able to meet them before, but they made me very welcome. In Beth's ancestral photo albums I could see the influence of the gene pool on many faces and could even see parts of myself looking back out at me from the fading black and white and sepia photos. The family had headed out in the early days of colonialism and though the island was famous mostly for its prison in Port Arthur, it also has quality farming land. I suspect that many emigrated there because of the similarity to the British climate. Tasmania has four definite seasons, and the extremes of weather that we would expect in Northern Europe.

Port Arthur was founded in 1830 as the prison where those deported from the UK, who offended again in Australia, were sent as an Alcatraz of Australia. The big stone and red brick prison was set onto the Tasman Peninsula, joined to the mainland by just a strip of land, which could easily be patrolled by vicious guard dogs. To stop prisoners from escaping by sea, they were told that the water was shark infested! For many, this prison must have been a living hell, but for some the records show that perversely it gave them a better quality of life than they'd had at home. They had a roof overhead, fresh food every day (the prison had its own farm) and they had employment. No liberty though, but how many of them had any sense of liberty in the England of those times anyway? Many of the convicts had been sent there on charges for such things as stealing a loaf of bread. Even children were sent to Port Arthur, and the youngest was a nine-year-old lad who'd stolen a couple of boxes of toys. The convicts worked the farms, cut wood and if they had misbehaved then they ended up working in the coal mine. If they refused to comply then more years were added to their sentences, and some would serve forty years. The site looks quite picturesque now, but I could still imagine how grim a place it would have been for the prisoners.

Time to move on again – I'd decided to go to New Zealand anyway, and to leave Libby with my friends in Sydney. I'd lodged an appeal over the shaft being just outside warranty, but realised that a decision from BMW would take some time. In any case, once I'd made the decision to go without her, it all felt right. The bike was never supposed to be the reason for the adventure, more of a tool that would get me from one adventure to the next. I wasn't a purist and as I was deciding to go south and to hitchhike my way around, I knew that this was a useful addition to my growing list of transport methods used. I'd been on a massive car ferry between Greece and Egypt, on an ancient, rickety train in the Sudanese desert, on a truck in Kenya, a light plane in Uganda and Namibia, on a cargo ship and more recently on the ferry cat. I'd also used buses, taxis and a bicycle. I'd walked a lot too, but had never hitchhiked anywhere.

Three happy months followed. I liked the feeling New Zealand gave me from the moment I landed there, and the flight had given me another form of transport to add to my list. Auckland was a vastly overgrown town with pretensions of modern grandeur and even though I again wasn't in the mood for a big city, I liked it.

It's a mash of old and new, and though new concrete predominates in the centre, the suburbs are full of one-storey buildings with verandas and ornate wrought-iron balconies. I liked the people too. Later on, Kiwis would tell me that Aucklanders are  standoffish but I didn't notice that sensation at all. I liked the fact that New Zealanders didn't seem to place so much emphasis on how you dressed, and I saw people clad in everything from business suits to shorts and thongs (flip-flops), with everyone treating each other with respect, until they proved otherwise. I'd never been somewhere where first impressions could be so positive and not laced with assumptions based on one's appearance.

New Zealand sits in the Pacific Ocean and is 1,600 kilometres east of Australia. It's thought to have been first settled by Polynesians in around the tenth century. They must, initially, have been flummoxed by the difference between their original tropical home and this new land of mountains and seasonal climate. Abel Tasman was the first European to see New Zealand but it was Captain Cook who was the first to set foot here in 1769. It wasn't until the 1830s that the first settlers arrived, and it didn't take them long to draft out a treaty with the Maoris. This signed over vast tracts of land to the settlers, but there was considerable trickery involved which, when combined with cultural misunderstanding, had disastrous effects for the Maori people. When they realised the reality of the treaty, the Maoris rose up and rebelled. I'd read that the relationship between the European colonialists and the Maoris had been very tense for a long time and that even today there are groups who still dispute the treaty and the loss of both land and way of life. I wondered how much evidence of this I would see.

Hitchhiking was a dream. In three months of travel, the longest I had to wait for a lift was ten minutes. On many occasions I'd not even got my pack out of a car before another one had pulled up, the driver asking if I needed a lift. I was invited for meals and if a family was on a picnic outing, I was asked to join them. Way down in the south a family had even driven an hour inland, and back again, just so I could visit a site that my guidebook had said was worth a look. This type of generosity was amazing and put the one fear I had of hitchhiking to one side, that after the freedom to go anywhere by bike, I'd feel too restricted to enjoy myself. But not at all, and if anything it enhanced the visit, for no other reason than it allowed me to spend real time with people who lived and breathed the country. The upset between the Maoris and the European settlers didn't seem to be much in evidence, though I could see the difference that still remains in lifestyle. The Maoris I met seemed to have less in life, but many seemed to want less. I hitched with one large family in a beaten-up old car. They couldn't have been friendlier, and were some of the most relaxed people I'd ever met. Mum seemed to have no problem at all that her two-year old decided to use me as a climbing wall, and that the chocolate milkshake the child had was ending up more on me than down the inside of him!

I visited hot volcanic pools where I boiled eggs dangled on a bit of string into the sulphurous waters, worked briefly on a deer farm and visited a town that lived architecturally in the 1920s and 30s. Art deco was king, and to see the better part of a whole town designed and decorated in such style, was a hundred times better than seeing photos of the period or the set of a movie. I hitched through seaside towns, across rolling hillsides, and on southwards until I came to the city of Wellington, the kick off point for the ferry across to South Island.

Heading south, I'd become conscious of how much colder it was getting. Part of New Zealand's charm is that it's a tall, thin chain of islands that covers a lot of latitude. This means that the northernmost tip is quite dramatically different from the southernmost point. In the north you find almost tropical forests, a warm turquoise sea and weather hot enough even in winter to enjoy being able to wear shorts and a T-shirt.

In the south there are craggy snow-topped mountains, mile upon mile of open moorland, glaciers and great icy lakes. Mount Cook is New Zealand's tallest mountain at 3,754m and it sits astride the vast mountain chain of the Southern Alps, which are larger than the French, Austrian and Swiss Alps combined. One quarter of New Zealand is protected wilderness.

It was wonderful but I was running short of money again. I didn't know what the outcome of the BMW decision was and though I'd been living frugally, still had to be careful. The deer farm work had been for board and lodging, the next best thing to earning money. I didn't have a work permit and didn't want the hassle of getting snagged by immigration. If I could save money then that would be fine, so long as I was still exploring and having an adventure while I was doing so.

I found myself a job in a backpackers' hostel on the edge of the South Island town of Nelson. If I was on hand to change bedding, clean the rooms and the kitchen, to check guests out in the morning and to check them in over the late afternoon and evening, I could have free board and lodging. This seemed to be a perfect arrangement, and I could work overtime to accrue several days off at a time – I had plans for those.

The hostel was small and well run with a family atmosphere and travellers seemed to enjoy staying there, but in recent months the owner had come up against a problem. Other hostels had opened up in the centre of the town and he was losing trade. He met the buses coming into the town each day, and operated a minibus service to and from the town centre. He also rented out bicycles, and had kitted the hostel out

30

with everything travellers would reasonably need, but it wasn't enough. There wasn't a shop close by, and even worse, no pub within easy walking distance. The boss would even allow those on the financial edge to camp in the back garden, but he was running out of ideas.

I suggested that he should play on the welcoming nature of the hostel and find a way to get people talking about the place to other travellers. He already had a rule that when people arrived they should be offered a cup of tea or coffee, but we decided to go one step further, and offer free wedges of homemade bread and butter pudding, with lashings of fresh cream. It was a quirky idea that cost little to do, and it did the trick. Within a few days we started to fill up again. People were arriving and asking if this was the pudding place!

The Abel Tasman National Park is a hop, skip and jump away from Nelson and I wanted to walk it. Not only did it have a reputation for being a stunning, almost unique, section of coastline, but even at this time of year it was safely accessible. It lived up to its reputation and having done it, I knew that I would be able to recommend the hike to guests at the backpackers, with a clear conscience.

Late one evening a petite girl arrived at the hostel on a bicycle. She had large red-rimmed glasses and a shock of auburn hair. Birgit was German, travelling on her own and she was tired after a long day's ride over the ups and downs of the landscape. I was drawn to her instantly, and playing my role as 'mine host', managed to surprise her with the welcome. She was a bit stunned when I asked if she had any bags that I could help bring in – it was our standard practice.

I admired the few cyclists I'd seen furiously pedalling their way up and down some of the steepest roads in the world. I could see that it would be rather wonderful to be on two wheels and to have the freedom of one's own transport, but I much preferred the thought of my 'bicycle' with an engine. Those hills and mountains would have been eaten up by Libby's power, though for sure I wasn't anything like as fit as Birgit was.

For many reasons I wasn't looking for a relationship, and for equally many reasons neither was she, but we became friends. The friendship was decidedly hesitant to begin with, and when Birgit headed off to walk the Abel Tasman on her own, I suspected that our friendship would fizzle out and we would go our separate ways. She was certainly keeping me at arm's length and under the circumstances she was wise to do so, but we were still drawn to each other. To my delight when she returned to the hostel she agreed to head off up to the very north of South Island with me in a borrowed car. We'd heard that the Kennepura Sounds were a stunning but rarely visited area, due to the lack of transport in and out. The bright apple green Datsun was ours for a long weekend, and that was the perfect amount of time to explore some of the area. We loaded a few boxes of vegetables, meat and cereals, plus a few candles in case of power cuts wherever we managed to stay, and piled in a few bottles of wine for good measure.

I enjoyed not being on the bike. Sitting next to each other, we were able to guide whoever was doing the driving and to chat about what we were seeing along the way. The hillsides were covered in a blanket of bright yellow and green gorse. When we were skirting one of the sounds, this vibrant flash of contrasting colour was framed on two blue sides by the water and the very clear sky. The sun shone on us and the car behaved itself perfectly. The roads soon turned to graded dirt and gravel, and we could see that with snow or heavy rain this area would more than likely be cut off. Occasional houses nestled on the hillsides, showing that there were people around somewhere, but the only other creatures we saw were birds and sheep.

Hidden away on the edge of the Kenepura Sound is a Youth Hostel. Neither of us wanted to camp so this seemed like a good objective. When we got there we found that we were the only guests and at that time of year the manager didn't live on site. We had the overgrown, slightly ramshackle cottage with a magic view, all to ourselves. At one time it must have belonged to a crofter or a local farmer and was laid out as a family home. The front door was locked but the back door led straight into a small kitchen that was dominated by a free-standing iron stove. A small folding leaf table, two chairs, an electric cooker and a sink made up the rest of the furnishings; basic, but all we needed. The other main rooms were filled with iron bunk beds, and to one side were a couple of small bathrooms with basins, toilets and showers. The water in the latter was freezing. The cottage smelt musty and damp, as if no one had been in it for months, but everywhere looked dry.

In the yard outside the kitchen was a log shed full of blocks of wood, with a rusty, blunt-looking axe sitting outside on a tree stump. Assuming that they were there for our use I set to smashing the blocks into pieces that would be small enough to get into the stove – we were in for a very cold night if we couldn't get it going. The axe was so blunt that it didn't manage to split the blocks but rather mangled them into smaller pieces by brute force. The work at least warmed me up, though Birgit later told me I looked so frenzied that she began to wonder where the nearest doctor was, as I was sure to put the axe through my legs sooner or later!

Wood down to the right size, I spent twenty minutes trying to light the stove with no success. All this time Birgit had patiently buzzed around doing other things behind me. She then politely eased me to one side and within seconds, had a blazing fire on the go. So much for being a macho man – I could only laugh as she pulled my still attached leg.

By the time we'd prepared pasta with a bolognaise sauce, and opened a bottle of red long enough for it to breathe in the warming air; the two of us were absolutely ready to eat. Birgit placed a candle in the centre of the folding table, which we had opened out to its full size of about four feet square. Then she served up. It was all very romantic until just before she sat down, when I put my elbow on the table. The metal supports holding up the leaf collapsed on my side and my dinner ended up splattered all over my lap in a lumpy, dribbling red mess. Any sense of romance disappeared at that moment as we looked at each other, and laughed hard enough for tears to roll down our cheeks.

It was just what we needed, taking away the slight nervousness and the edginess that remained between us, in spite of the fact that we were enjoying each other's company so much.

It was a sad moment when Birgit set off to carry on with her tour. She was also due to head back to Germany to start a job, and that meant that neither of us could seriously entertain any thoughts of somehow travelling on together. Besides that, neither of us was ready for any such commitment at that time. We agreed to remain in contact by letter, and I knew that we would – this was a friendship that would not end up just as an entry fading in a journal with the passing of time.

After Birgit had gone I felt strangely empty and the backpackers no longer held enough of an attraction for me to stay. I headed south, aiming for Mt Cook, the Fox and Franz Joseph glaciers, and for new adventures. Hitching was a little slower in the south and it rained more, but I'd hit a freak weather year – despite the rain it was warmer and dryer than it had been for years. Eventually I swung back north and made it to Wellington just in time to see the British Lions play the All Blacks. The atmosphere in the city was a combination of electric

and good humour. All Black rugby stars are like royalty in New Zealand, and in the cities and towns close to Wellington I'd been surprised to see banners of the players hanging from the lampposts. They were treated like heroes. For 'fly on the wall' purposes I bought a ticket for the local section of the stadium, rather than join the Brits, though quite frankly the fans from both sides divided themselves, instead of being separated by the authorities. I stood in amongst a bunch of All Black fans that seemed to accept me quite readily and pulled my leg with good-natured humour every time I shouted out "Come on the Lions!" Beer had been flowing and in spite of that there was no violence at all. The alcohol only seemed to enhance the good-natured atmosphere.

Meanwhile, the clock was ticking. After three months on the islands I knew it was time to get a move on. I had to find out about my bike – I was missing her anyway – and I had to earn some more money before getting into SE Asia, as the chances of earning anything significant there were slim.

I headed back to Sydney, where I made a momentous decision. I decided that the only way I was going to make it safely back to Europe, to have fun along the way and to have enough loot to deal with problems, was to split the costs with a passenger. The drive shaft episode had brought it home to me how things can go expensively wrong when you are on a bike, and I simply had to allow for that now. I'd been lucky this time. Happily, BMW had agreed to pay for the new shaft, but even so, I'd had to stump up for the cost of the labour and that had hurt my budget. I'd no idea what sort of damage had been done to Libby by African roads but knew that she'd had a very hard life there. My plan seemed prudent, and I liked the idea of company, but I was also nervous of the idea because of the commitments that were attached.

In Africa I'd met an Australian girl called Jan. Out of all the people I knew who were in Australia at the time, she was the only one who seemed to be the right person to share the trip with. She had learned about travelling the hard way, and that was a great thing. I didn't want to have a travel novice on the bike as that would have meant too much of a difference between us, nor did I want someone I didn't know on the bike. It also helped that Jan was a slim, light person and I knew that Libby would like that! The final factor for me was that Jan had been talking about wanting to travel from Oz to the UK. So I wrote, asking if she was interested.

At roughly that moment, it turned out, she was sitting down to write to me to ask if I ever fancied having a passenger. Perfect. It was obviously meant to be, and we arranged to meet further up the coast in Queensland. We'd be able to discuss the trip and get her kitted out with all the right gear. Jan was a bit of a hippy and I suspected that the only thing we were going to come to verbal blows over was the fact that as far as I was concerned, she had to wear a decent helmet, a good leather jacket, boots and gloves. Without decent kit when I'd had my major prang in Namibia, I would have died and I was not going to be responsible for that with another person. But I knew persuading Jan would involve an argument! Bike kit is a hot and at times, an uncomfortable restriction.

35

I headed north again, this time on two wheels and it was a good feeling to be back on the bike. Sydney traffic is easy to deal with and the roads are well sign posted. Sydney Harbour Bridge is one of the key landmarks for the city and as I rode over the 20,000 tons of steel towards the north shore I began to feel strangely free. As soon as I hit the edge of the suburbs, the traffic died away leaving the road to me to enjoy. I felt like singing and we cruised northwards along the east coast so I could meet up with the South African family who had been on the ship from Durban. Val and Michael had bought themselves a unit in their new town and kitted it out as a second-hand furniture shop. It was going to be great to see them, and to find out how their fresh start in Australia was going.

I hadn't expected to have to deal with Peter hitting me with his van, but being rescued by Hells Angels was a nice twist and there were advantages to being forced to wait for the bike to be repaired. The first up side of the situation was that I had the chance to explore the area with Michael as he went out into the countryside to pick up furniture. Australia does have country lanes, but they don't look quite like the UK's. Their country cottages have the same purpose but look very different, many are up on low stilts, most are wooden and nearly all of them seemed to have verandas – all key issues to help deal with the heat. The best ones have views out over farmland or the blues and greens of the bush, and often you'll see a cottage nestling under the sweeping arms of an old eucalyptus tree. I liked them, and where they were clustered together I was reminded of English country villages of days gone by. There was a particular type of atmosphere that gave the feeling that people had time to talk, and an inclination to gossip.

Val and Michael also introduced me to the joys of car boot sales. As an ex-retailer, I don't like shopping much. I'd rather decide what I want, check out the options, buy the best I can and move on to the next thing in life. But car boot sales were an adventure for a foreigner. What do Australians keep in their homes? What do they discard? And just as interesting, what will they buy? I could easily tell if an area was a farming region by the types of things on sale. There would be pots, barrels, solid old furniture, hoses, farm machinery and the like. You'd often find small-scale livestock such as chickens and geese or the odd goat. Around towns, there'd be the usual household bric-a-brac – vases, cutlery, battered flatpack chests of drawers, lawn mowers and bicycles. I really enjoyed the fact that car boot sales seemed to be places to meet old friends and talk to neighbours. Better still, they enabled me to earn some money.

In South Africa, while recovering from my accident, I'd painted African designs on the front of white T-shirts and sold them to tourists. It had been very profitable and on the ship over to Australia I'd kept myself busy by painting more shirts; that's when I wasn't eating fine food, talking with the crew and passengers or exploring the ship. I'd hoped to be able to sell them but until now hadn't really had anywhere suitable to do it. Street vendors, as in most cities in the world, need permits and I'd not had the time for that sort of malarkey. The T-shirts had been handy as thank you gifts to people who'd helped me along the way, but I'd not made any money out of them. And just as important, I was getting fed up with having to strap the kit bag full of them on and off the bike all the time. So I set up shop at car boot sales – the weight reduced in the kit bag and the weight increased in the wallet. It was a fun thing to do too.

Two weeks later, Libby was repaired and ready. I said big thanks to Val and Michael, climbed back on board and carried on north. As I rode, I dipped in to places such as Coffs Harbour, where I stayed with a friend, John, and into Byron Bay. On a backpacking trip fifteen years earlier I'd explored the east coast of Australia pretty thoroughly, so didn't intend to spend much time revisiting old haunts, but I did want to take a quick squint. I feared that they would have changed dramatically, and so they had. Coffs had simply grown in size, but Byron Bay had changed significantly. Once it had been a sleepy seaside town with a tiny population of inhabitants and a slightly larger, ever-changing population of travellers and hippies. Now it was full of hostels and upmarket hotels. The lazy peace of the village and beaches had gone. The bay was now a magnet for travellers out to party their way around Australia. It was still pretty though and I was glad I'd been to look.

Brian – my tomato picking mate – had a grandfather who lived in Surfers Paradise, and I had an open invitation to drop in for a few days. At first glance, Surfers Paradise is the sort of place that repels me. I get an instant feeling of horror when I see several miles of tower block hotels, nightclubs and bars spread out along a white sand coast. Surfers is brash and garish – not my cup of tea at all, but it had never been built with the likes of me in mind. It was originally developed for Australians who spent most of their time in isolation, in the bush or in remote areas. The people it was built for must have revelled in the noise and the bright hustle and bustle of the town's party life.

With Brian being such a drop out hippy, I'd a preconceived idea of what his grandfather would be like, and I couldn't have been more wrong. He was a retired engineering millionaire. Once I would have been in awe of being with a millionaire, I probably would have felt inadequate, but not in Australia. Millionaires and ordinary workers meet on equal terms. When I'd seen the wealthy mingling with the striving, I could see that frequently they didn't like each other, but there was never an air of condescension from one side, and never an air of servility from the other. From both there would be a sort of superficial laid back atmosphere that almost hid the fact that all of them were joined together by being part of a hard working entrepreneurial society. Both sides gave the impression that they could handle anything, and could make anything work.

Brian's grandfather owned a very nice house in an old part of Surfers Paradise that was a long way away from the tower blocks and bright light glitz of the resort. He was a tall slim man with sunspots, thinning grey hair, and an angular face. He had a loose limbed but thoughtful gait that made me think of a stork. Jim and his wife couldn't have been more different from Brian, but I couldn't help but be impressed at the welcome they gave me. Cold beer, a great shower and an Australian-sized feed off the 'barbie'. He also had a fascination with my trip and asked if there was any way he could help "But, not with money", he said with a stern look straight into my eyes. I guessed that Brian had tried that on occasion and as I was his friend… But no, I didn't need anything, I thought. Not so Jim. He homed in on my panniers and said, "Bit of a mess these, think we should do something about that?"

He was right – the blue van had just about finished them off. I had to do something about them sooner or later, and I was already thinking about how I was going to cope with Jan's kit on the bike as well as my own. I didn't have the money to buy new panniers and I'd not seen any until this time that would have done the job anyway. Over a couple of VB beers we listed all the things the panniers needed to do. They needed to be much bigger, and I preferred the idea of them opening from the top rather than the 'suitcase', side-opening style of the current ones. One had to be smaller than the other to take into account the space taken up by Libby's high-level exhaust. They had to be tough enough to cope with being fallen off on, and they had to have good locks. They also had to be easy for me to put on and take off, and one final thought was that they shouldn't be wider than the bikes widest point – the handlebars. We doodled rough designs and I decided on the measurements.

"Yeah, no worries", Jim said. "We can cut these out of aluminium in my workshop, and I've a mate who will weld them up for you for a beer or two." I rather liked the idea of having luggage boxes made to my design by an eighty-year-old Australian millionaire!

Two days later I was running for the north again and the new boxes meant that I'd even been able to pack away the last of the painted T-shirts, with space to spare. Libby handled even better with more weight being down low, and though I'd decided at the last minute to make each box four centimetres wider than the handlebars I wasn't worried. The bike looked big and bulky, but safe, solid and secure. The boxes even looked as if they belonged on the bike, far more so than the plastic ones had.

I stopped off briefly with another friend, Dominique, and her family in Brisbane, before heading north with no further delay. Brian had sent me a note saying that the mango-picking season was on and that if I got a scoot on I'd have no worries getting work, with 'great pay', an issue that had gained in importance. I'd decided that as Jan was coming with me and would be sharing the costs of the ride back to Europe, if I earned enough then I would be able to learn to scuba dive, and what better place to learn to do it than the Barrier Reef? Jan was living in Townsville, a port which is only an hour and three quarters away from the reef, and scuba schools are not hard to find. It seemed too good an opportunity to miss.

Chapter 3

Outback

'Take time to dream, it is what the future is made of.'

Desiderata

Queensland is my kind of country, with my kind of climate. I like it warm, and humidity doesn't bother me at all. I'd discovered that I feel more alive when it's hot. Part of me seems to go into mental hibernation in the cold, but when it's warm I seem to fire on all cylinders.

In the Outback the vegetation changes quite dramatically at the same time as the weather, but from the main highway the only real changes you see are the variety of crops. As the temperature rose, I cruised past kilometre after kilometre of sugar cane. The plants are tall, and wave silkily in any slight breeze. From a distance this waving looks just like a gentle rolling swell on the open sea. Cane grows closely packed together and to harvest the crop the farmers burn off the leafy parts first, which works on the same principle as the scorched earth system farmers use in Africa. The burnt leaves fall to the earth and rain rapidly passes the nutrients back into the soil. With cane, a burning also clears the way sufficiently that the harvesters can get at the base of the plants with their machetes. Two additional advantages are that the flames get rid of the snakes and the horned toads, both of which are poisonous. I'm told that cane cutting is the hardest crop to work for labourers, and even looking at the job from a distance, I could see why; it would certainly be blister-making and bicep-building, and you'd spend your day breathing in soot. The money is supposed to be the best, but it's not a job for wimps, and I decided that I fell perfectly into that category.

Brian and some of the others from the tomato picking crew had found work on a mango plantation just outside the town of Ayr. They were all living on a campsite a few miles away from the plantation, and Brian was up for giving everyone a lift to work each day. Since I'd seen him last he'd bought himself an old Toyota panel van, which he'd kitted out with a bed, a table and a couple of benches. He'd decorated the inside with mirrors and bright colours, and had beads swinging from hooks along the sides. He'd painted flowers on the walls and the van smelt of joss sticks, which barely covered the richer scent of dope. He'd also found himself a small black and white cat, that seemed to be quite happy to travel along with him. But the cat could be a right pain, as it frequently decided to go off exploring when Brian wanted to get on the move.

I was happy to snag a lift to work with Brian, in spite of the fact that as a cautious driver he drove very gently, and had been pulled over one day for driving too slowly on an open road! The flashing lights had us all hoping that Brian didn't have any of his dope stash in the van! He didn't, but the policeman was decidedly dubious of us all once he had a look inside the van; it looked more as if it belonged on the hippy trail to Kathmandu than it did on a country road in Queensland.

Brian had a cushy job working in the sorting shed where he made up the boxes that the mangos would be packed into. He worked on his own in a room to the back of the shed, and kept himself entertained by listening to a most un-hippy like 'ghetto blaster', and by puffing weed all day.

I had a stroke of luck too. The person who was supposed to be working the conveyor belts and stacking the filled boxes before taking them to be stored in giant fridges, had just dropped out. The job was mine and I was delighted. It meant working out of the direct sun and with little risk of sap burns – mango sap is vicious stuff and the pickers were at constant risk of being burnt. You could tell someone who was new to picking by the dribble-shaped burn streaks across their hands, lower arms and legs.

Most of the people in the shed were women and girls, and they worked hard in small teams, washing the mangoes and then sorting them by size into the boxes. The conveyor belts were relentless, and there was no time for a break except at the official smokos. The pace of work didn't stop the chat though, and every so often the sound of laughter would peal out above the noise of the machinery. They were a good-natured bunch and I enjoyed working alongside them. Of

42

course my pommie accent had the mickey taken out of it mercilessly, but that was ok. They never did it when the boss was around, and so far I'd not been asked for any papers at all, just put to work. I was still being very cautious about the fact that I didn't have a work permit, but the women seemed to react to that as if it was quite the norm. They made fun of just about everyone and everything, but the only person no one made fun of was Brian, and I began to see why.

Conversation would stop when he came out of his room to stack up new piles of freshly made boxes. The women's eyes would go down and everyone would quietly focus on what they were doing. I watched this happen for several days, and started to worry. What had Brian done to earn this treatment? The looks he got were almost fearful. Brian seemed to notice that the treatment was getting worse too. As the conversations stopped ever more abruptly and he was studiously ignored, he seemed to become increasingly bad tempered. But he did nothing to find out why this was happening. I tried to find out what the problem was from him, but he simply blanked me.

One day, when Brian had been almost aggressive with one of the women, the most senior of them pulled me to one side. As she did so, her teammate racked up the speed she was working at to cover her, and the others watched us intently. Polly took me into the quiet hum of one of the fridges and said, "You're his mate. Yer gotta do something about this. The girls are afraid that he is going to hit one of 'em. He's bloody paranoid. If you don't friggin' well do something then I'm bloody well gunna!" Polly told me that before I'd arrived there'd been a day when Brian had let off an almost volcanic amount of temper, and that everyone had seen him do it. "He was bloody well out of control," Polly said.

This was weird. Brian always had a sort of dangerous air about him, but to many this edge seemed to be an attraction. When I'd been around him I'd never noticed any lack of control; if anything, it was exactly the opposite. He'd been, as you would expect a hippy to be, laid back and quite gentle. The only thing I had noticed was that now he seemed to be permanently stoned. Perhaps something big had gone wrong for him and he was trying to hide in the smoke, but whatever, it wasn't good news, and as his mate I had to try to do something. With one of the girls covering for me, I grabbed the bag of sweets that was always circulating round the sorting shed, and headed for Brian's room, but I'd no idea what I was going to say to him.

He had his music on so loud that the aluminium walls of his space were vibrating with the bass notes. He was furiously smacking boxes together and zapping them with the hot glue gun before slinging them to one side. The last time I'd gone in, he'd been carefully stacking the boxes along one of the walls. "Hey Brian!" I called out, trying to make myself heard over the music, which was some sort of psychedelic rock of a type I'd never heard him listen to before. He didn't see or hear me, so wrapped up in his anger as he was. "HEY BRIAN!" I yelled. "I'VE GOT SOMETHING TO TELL YOU!" He heard me that time, abruptly looked up, scowled and yelled, "FUCKIN' WHAT?" I tried to tell him that I'd brought him the sweets and that I was going to give him a break for a while, but he didn't hear me. The next thing I knew was that he, in pure unstoppable rage, was using his fist to pound his way through the ghetto blaster to make it stop – it obviously hadn't occurred to him to turn it down. With that, he grabbed his shirt and stormed out of the room. We didn't see him for the rest of the day.

That night he acted as if nothing at all had happened. I didn't push the issue, but worried at this new side of my friend, and decided to keep a close eye on him. At least if he did decide to talk, then I'd be there to listen.

Since getting back to Australia I'd been getting regular letters from Birgit and I'd been writing to her. Despite the distance between us, our relationship was growing, so much so that I began to regret having asked Jan to come with me on the trip and rather wished that I'd asked Birgit. Perhaps I might have been able to persuade her to come, but it was too late for that – Jan had made her plans and bought all of her kit. After the months apart, I also wasn't sure if our few weeks together in New Zealand really meant something, and I needed to see Birgit to make sure, one way or the other. I decided not to dive the reef but to use that money to fly to Germany instead. If I were to ship the bike to Indonesia from Darwin, then I could use the shipping time to fly to see her for a couple of weeks, and be back in Bali in time to link up with Jan. It seemed like a rather mad idea, but the right thing to do. I bought the tickets before I could change my mind and though I'd given myself a deadline to meet, I wasn't worried. I had to be out of the country sooner or later anyway, and Asia was calling. I was beginning to itch to get into lands that had less connection with my own culture, and knew that the longer I spent drifting in Australia the harder it would be to get out of that life.

The mango season was over and in spite of the ticket costs, my travel fund was full again. With Jan's share of the costs I knew that I was set to have a magic trip across Asia. But first there was a boat trip out to the Barrier Reef, and then Christmas and New Year to enjoy. The reef was simply spectacular and the waters enticing, but I'd no doubt that going to see Birgit was the right thing to do. Scuba diving would have to wait, and I reasoned with myself that the experience of learning to dive and then exploring the reef would be a good excuse to come back to Australia again at some time in the future.

The picking crew headed for Mission beach. We set up a gypsy camp on white sand by an azure sea, under the palm trees and scrubby bushes, and made ourselves at home. Everyone had

the glow of a good job well done, wallets were full again and the buzz of conversation was of who was doing what next. The only down side was that the sea at this time of year was full of jellyfish. Most just gave you a tingling sensation but some were quite dangerous – swimming was an eyes-open adventure that had an air of tempting fate about it. At the time I relied on the locals knowing what they were doing, but subsequently discovered that box jellyfish are lethal!

I then came into contact with Queensland's famous police, twice, and at the first meeting they lived up to their reputation of being the hardest-nosed police in the whole of Australia. I was on the bike, riding behind Brian, who was driving a friend's car in his usual very civilised fashion. I had a friend on the back of my bike and Brian had another girl with him. We were heading for the shops and the road was a winding narrow two-lane strip of asphalt that skirted the side of a hill looking down over the coast. As we rode past a parked up police car, I nervously checked our speed. No problem. I knew everything was working well on the bike, so relaxed. But the police didn't and within seconds they were behind us, siren on and blue lights flashing. I pulled over as quickly as I could but the police car blasted on past us and sat on Brian's tail. He cruised on gently, looking for a safe place to pull over, which took a while, and the police were obviously getting agitated as they tried to pull past him, but couldn't find the space to do so. By the time Brian had found a spot, the policemen were decidedly put out. I stopped a good fifty metres behind them and to my amazement the policemen leapt out, drawing their guns. One knelt behind the car's open door and pointed his gun directly at Brian's car. The other policeman, with arms stretched together in front of him, gun in hand and knees slightly bent, cautiously moved forward. Brian stayed sitting where he was, keeping his hands on the steering wheel until ordered out. Then the second policeman rushed over, and spinning Brian round, thrust him against the car, arms and legs splayed. He was searched without any attempt to be respectful or gentle, the car was searched too, with the gun still on him. Nothing suspicious was found. The policemen stomped back to their car and with a Starsky and Hutch wheel-spin on the gravel, disappeared over the brow of the road. No traffic has passed us, and none did so for the few minutes that we all stood recovering from this zealous stop and search. I had an odd feeling that it was all some sort of joke, and looked around for a hidden camera. Brian's only comment was, "Happened before, they don't like blokes with long hair!"

Later that evening I was out for a ride on my own, and coming out of a town on a sharp curve I realised that I had misjudged how tight the corner was. Concentrating on keeping the bike upright on the potholed road, I didn't watch my speed and didn't see the officer with the speed gun until it was too late. 'Uh oh', I thought to myself. I'd already heard that Queensland police are picky about speed limits and I knew that I'd almost certainly been going too fast. Just a little, but still too fast. The policeman indicated that I should pull over, in such a way that I suspected I'd be shot if I didn't. The events of earlier in the day were very much in my mind, though he wouldn't have been able to tell what length my hair was under the helmet! I stopped the bike, turned off the engine, took off my gloves, removed my lid and took a deep breath. By the time I had done that the policeman was next to me, notepad in one hand and pen in the other. "You do realise that you were doing 54 in a 50 kilometre zone do you, Sir?" he asked. "Um, I didn't at the time but when I saw you, I looked and saw that I was." There was no point in trying to talk my way out of it. The last time I'd tried to do that was in Uganda - I'd ended up being arrested, with a very angry policeman letting me know that they weren't stupid!

The policeman walked around to the back of the bike to take the registration number, and did a double take when he saw my Channel Island number plate. "Where the hell is that from mate?" he asked, his manner changing instantly. I explained that I'd started my trip in Jersey, that I'd ridden through Africa and was soon on my way up into S.E. Asia. "Hmmm, how soon would that be?" he asked. I told him just a few weeks. "Well", he said with a sideways look that was as good as a nod and a wink, "You'll be out of the country before you get the chance to pay this then, won't you?" With that he closed his book and strode away, without even giving me a copy of the ticket. Perhaps Queensland police weren't so bad after all.

New Year passed in the moonlight on the beach. With a van pulled down to the sand so we could listen to the stereo, people drank beer and danced a little, or sat on the cool sand and told tales in the glow of the fire. One of the guys was a juggler and he spent a couple of hours out on the sand in the darkness beyond the firelight. He had fire clubs, and kept us entranced as the flames hurtled skywards to fall back into his hands and away again. The only sounds were the stereo in the background, the gentle waves rolling onto the beach, the occasional hiss or pop from the fire, the murmur of quiet conversation and the whoosh of the flames as the fire sticks whirled round.

I bought a fresh set of tyres for the bike in a New Year sale, fixed a date to meet Jan in Indonesia, and set off for the vastness of the Australian Outback. I'd never been to Ayers Rock before and was keen to see the Katherine Gorge. After working around so many people I was also keen to get out on my own again. Brian was in a far better mood, and I put that in part down to the fact that he had a new girlfriend. It was hard to say goodbye to everyone, as I knew that I'd probably never see any of them again. We'd become an almost family-like unit, and it had been a good experience.

The Great Dividing Range, which splits the east coast from the Outback, comes really close to the coast in Queensland. It acts as a dividing line between the populated and much visited coastal areas, and the mostly barren inland regions. The Outback gets little of the coastal rains, but when it does the dry scrublands briefly come alive with vibrant greens and the startling colours of flowers. I should have been cruising through a giant garden, but this year the rains were late, so no such luck. This land looks barren but it only really lacks a regular supply of water. In the '60s and '70s there was a great ambition to build enough nuclear power stations to be able to produce sufficient fresh water to bring these areas to life permanently. The task was phenomenal and is ongoing, but with less emphasis on nuclear power. The two main hold-ups to the development of the outback are water, and enough people to work the land.

I dropped out of the range along the Flinders Highway into a land of dusty sidetracks, one-horse towns and vegetation that never really seemed to change. The scrubby trees, where there were any, were all the same height. Sometimes these sporadic trees would suddenly become the temporary resting places for flocks of brightly coloured parakeets or galahs. The flocks of cockatoos were my favourites though. These birds, who seemed to be either black or white, were all comedians. Sometimes I saw them settle on electric or telephone wires, and when they did so it was rather like watching a bunch of circus clowns attempting to walk the high wire. They'd fall off, wings fluttering madly to great shrieks of pretend dismay until they had almost reached the ground, when they would miraculously recover and shoot up for another session of Charlie Chaplin-style walking the line. The equally scrubby spindly bushes all seemed to be the same height too, and shade was at a premium. Their thin leaves didn't offer much protection at all, and the soil only changed in shade of red where a slight amount of moisture remained in the early hours. I saw small birds sitting on the power lines, but only where they could sit in the shade of the isolators. The road ran straight and hot, as the asphalt collected heat from a sun that hung in a cloudless sky. This sky is amazing. It's an everlasting transparent electric blue and it hangs above desert lands that seem to have been stunned by the silence.

Libby seemed to be enjoying the open road and the tread on my new tyres hummed beneath us. Everything seemed totally in sync, my luggage was nicely balanced and we settled into a cruising speed of about 90 kilometres per hour. With very few bends, the road seemed to disappear over the horizon, with an occasional pothole and truck tyre 'tramlines'  providing just about the only element of adventure. Monster trucks drive helter-skelter along these roads and their sheer weight is enough to form gullies in the heat-softened asphalt. The grit-covered tar was so hot in the middle of the day that my feet felt like they were cooking in my bike boots, when there was no choice but to take a break. The dry soil to the sides of the road was hot but far cooler to stand on, but mostly it felt a better option just to keep on the move.

As the midday heat grew I flipped my visor closed. Riding these temperatures was like sitting in front of an enormous air dryer at max temperature setting, going full blast. The asphalt-stored heat hammered up at me in shimmering waves and mirages jigged deceptive dances on the road. I was sweating like I hadn't since Northern Africa, my mouth struggled to keep moist, so drink breaks were vital, but the water in my bottles was decidedly unappetising. It was almost hot enough to make tea with, and the chemicals of Ayr's water system made it  almost undrinkable. I then remembered a tip I'd read about when getting ready for Africa. My water bottles were in canvas bags, strapped over the petrol tank. I carefully punched a hole in the tops of two of the bottles and as I rode a little water escaped onto the canvas of the bags. That moisture would then whip away in my slipstream and this form of sweating meant that the water in the bottles was almost cool; a delight after my attempts to drink hot swimming pool!

Even so, the dream of an ice-cold coke stayed with me across the gently undulating bush land for so long, that I just had to have one. It became an obsession. The trouble was, there were no shops and pubs were few and far between. I needed to stock up on water anyway. One of the advantages of long open roads like this is that there are plenty of places to pull off the highway, to free camp. That was good for my budget, and I found that camping in the middle of nowhere, with only the stars for company, was a spectacular thing to do. But water was always an issue.

So were bush fires. The land is as dry as a tinderbox and it doesn't take much to start a bush fire. It could be a carelessly discarded cigarette, a match dropped out of the window of a passing vehicle or simply a piece of broken glass. The results are horrific. I'd ridden past hundreds of kilometres of bush land that had been stripped of all colours except black. The world was a soft sooty black carpet that was only broken by the stark shape of occasional trees, whose twisted limbs had been big enough to remain standing as lonely silhouettes in a plain of devastation. I'd survived a bush fire in Africa and had no wish for a repeat performance.

My other fear of bush camping was the issue of snakes. I don't like them. As a child in Africa I'd seen what they could do. In Australia there are plenty of poisonous snakes but I'd read that only two were a real danger to the unwary. The Death Adder's bite is lethal and

Queensland's Taipan snake is to be feared; it's the only poisonous snake that will attack man unprovoked. Before I set up camp I'd always stamp around, when I could see where my feet were going – the vibrations from doing this should have been enough to encourage any snakes to slither away and my size 10 bike boots were apparently scary enough for the task.

The pub was a trucker's stop. Weathered board with peeling paint clad the walls; the roof was tin and the parking area was a great spread of oily dirt that had still managed to keep a few ruts that must have been made with the last rains. Everything was dust covered, tired, and shimmered with listless heat. Three four-trailer road-train trucks were parked up alongside a couple of beaten-up Toyota Landcruiser pickup trucks – 'Utes' as they are usually known, it's short for utility trucks. Next to them was a battered Land Rover of 1960s' vintage, and a white Holden estate car that had, in the dim and distant past, probably been someone's pride and joy. Each vehicle had a giant set of tubular bars attached to its front, and one of the pickup truck's bars was decidedly bent. A sheep dog lay in the shade of the veranda, but even with my unusual arrival it made no effort to do anything other than twitch an ear. I parked in the shade of one of the trucks, and immediately took my jacket off – then my helmet. The jacket came off first because if I didn't I'd instantly feel like I was boiling over.

There were three bars: saloon, lounge and ladies' bar. I was chuffed to see the latter as I knew that they were an important part of Outback history. In days gone by, it was considered improper for women to drink in the same bar as men, and with the language that was in full flow in the saloon bar, I could see why. Ladies' bars are supposed to be a thing of the past though. I stepped into the bar, and let my eyes get used to the gloom and my body used to the surprising cool. As I did so, all conversation stopped dead, and all eyes turned towards me, but the loud chat quickly resumed as I moved across the bare wooden boards towards the bar.

The sight of a Pommie wimp ordering a coke in this environment was sufficient for everyone to lose any interest in me at

51

all. That was fine as it gave me a chance to discreetly watch the men in the room. In front of each was an amber-coloured beer; the glasses were small and where hot fingers hadn't recently touched them, they had dew on the sides. All the men were clad in stained shorts, and singlets or T-shirts. Boots that probably hadn't seen any polish since they'd been new were the norm and yes, there were more than a few wide-brimmed sweat-stained hats on heads. Conversation was pure bloke – trucks, women, beer, the next load, a bastard copper, the footie and farming. It seemed that for every five words, there'd be a swear word thrown in for good measure, in case the listeners hadn't got the point. Suddenly, all conversation stopped again.

Into the bar had stepped an academic looking youngish man who, heaven forbid, was accompanied by a very pretty girl in a beige skirt and a yellow T-shirt. Like me they had tourist stamped all over them, but where I'd been accepted as being totally unimportant, these two were not. After all, this was the blokes' bar. All the men turned round in their seats, or on their stools, and blatantly looked her up and down – they must have made the girl feel like she was naked. They stared in silence so intensely that the two caught the message, and rapidly retreated. Not a word had been spoken – looks had done it. Once they'd gone the groups of men in the pub joined together to make a series of incredibly obscene remarks. Horribly unfair though it all had been, I felt privileged in a perverse sort of way to have been able to sit in a room full of dinosaurs, who didn't seem to realise that they ought soon to be extinct.

My two iced cokes had gone too quickly, and with water bottles filled almost begrudgingly by the barman, I stepped out into the heat again. At two o'clock in the afternoon it was almost a wall of heat out there, and even the dog's ear didn't twitch this time. Riding in the cool of the south and along the coast had made me lazy, and I knew that it was time for me to change my riding habits. It made a lot of sense to set off in the cool of the dawn, and ride only until midday. Or, find somewhere to hole up in the shade during the main heat of the day, then ride on in the cooling hours until dark. The risk out here was that dawn and dusk are the play times for kangaroos, and I'd already seen how much damage they could do to a pickup – they would be lethal to me on the bike. I'd not seen any live kangaroos at all, but there  had been plenty of fly-infested, stinking furry bundles by the roadsides. Some had been no bigger than a large dog but others had been big enough, I suspected, to have been able to damage even a big truck.

There were very few road signs along the way, but those that punctuated the roadsides with their vivid yellow frequently warned of kangaroos. Obliquely, since they were almost always shot up, they also warned of bored drivers with guns.

The next day, I set off in the peach and blueberry shades of dawn. I'd slept well and if there had been traffic passing my camping spot during the night, I'd not heard a thing. I'd been just a hundred metres off the road, but that had been far enough to wrestle the bike and there'd been enough bushes for me to tuck in behind. In daylight, I'd have been visible, but was well out of sight in the dark.

The air was gently warm and though I could still feel the remainder of the previous day's heat coming off the asphalt at me, the riding was good. The 'roos stayed away from me, and I settled into the saddle for another day's cruising on a road with enough dips for me to feel as if I were riding along a gently-graded roller coaster. By mid-morning the heat was intense again, and I started to look for some shade to rest and have a drink in. My eyelids began to droop, and a bead of sweat found its way into my left eye. The sting of the salt was enough to wake me up – I'd been dozing at 90kph! I had to stop and have a sleep, but it had to be in shade, so I rode on searching the scrubby horizon for a stand of trees. Then I woke up again! The bike was heading straight for the bush – another second's sleep and I'd have been flung off the bike, with potentially disastrous consequences.

Whilst coming up the east coast I'd heard all sorts of scare stories about bikers who had been totally unprepared for the Outback – they had either come a cropper or had disappeared, never to be seen again. One chap had obviously fallen asleep on his bike, as he'd been crossing the Nullabor desert. The road is quiet and he'd fallen far enough off the road for him to have remained hidden for days. The story went that he'd knocked himself unconscious and 'boiled' to death in his black bike gear. I'd met a Japanese guy in Sydney who'd told me that his plan was to ride across the centre of the continent. He'd equipped himself with a tourist map, which was probably more use as toilet paper on such a trip – it didn't even show where the cattle stations were along the way. He had just 250 miles fuel range and had 6 litres of water capacity, plus complete confidence that he was going to make it. I'd passed on the little experience I had, with the key being that if he really was serious, then he should make sure that he took every opportunity to let someone know where he was going and when he expected to get there.

There are simple keys to travelling in the Outback and to my mind it is no more dangerous than sailing a boat, if the rules are followed. Your transport has to be in top rate condition and you have to know how to use it properly – being able to fix problems is a major bonus. Repair stations are few and far between, though when you find one the guys can fix just about anything. You should stay on the beaten track, as if you break down, sooner or later someone will come along. If you do have trouble then you should stay with your vehicle. There are loads of stories about people who died because they didn't follow that rule. If you are planning to go off the beaten track, then you should tell someone responsible that you are doing so before you set off, and then you should report in when you reach your destination. Police stations, pubs, and bush stores are the perfect places to do this. You should also carry enough food, fuel and water to reach your destination, and to cover several days of being broken down in the bush. By staying in the shade and doing nothing, 10 litres of water will last you about 5 days. Find out how to make a solar still to augment your water supply. If the worst happens, then don't be afraid to set fire to your oil supply, with which you've covered anything that will burn. Something slightly green will help the oil to make a good smoke cloud. Take a mirror off your bike so you can use it to flash at any aeroplanes. You are going to be a dot in the middle of nowhere, so you must do everything you can to be seen. If the worst comes, set fire to a tyre – that'll give you a great smoke cloud! If that all fails then, when the day is at its coolest, collect rocks, bushes, wood and so on. Use them to make an enormous straight line or a circle. The bush is always filled with irregular shapes so if you make a regular shape it's highly likely to be noticed from above. Australia is a great land for the novice traveller to visit but it's very easy to be lulled into a false sense of security.

And now I had almost come a cropper. It was a big time wake up call, and the knowledge that I'd had such a narrow escape was a very well timed reminder that the Australian Outback demands respect.

The Flinders Highway turns into the Barkly Highway and in the middle of nowhere is a junction, aptly called 'Threeways'. I was in the Northern Territory, which I'd read was the most barren section of Australia, and with just one percent of the nation's population, the most deserted as well. At this junction you make a choice, north to Darwin, or south towards Alice Springs and Ayers Rock, or Uluru which is the Aboriginal name for the rocks. I took the Stuart Highway southwards, skirting the Tanami Desert as I did so. Small settlements such as Tennant Creek, Wauchope and Borrow Creek sit astride the highway as it dips and bobs its way southwards across a desert that looks like a brown sea.

Riding roads like this can be monotonous, but great thinking time. The challenges come not from the heat, which is intense, or the never-changing landscape, but from the road trains. These beasts are kings of the road and their drivers blast their way up the highway at such speed you'd think that the next pub had the last beers left in Australia. Their trailers swing from side to side, and the pure bulk of the train makes a sucking slipstream. It's enough to make eyeballs pop and knuckles go white in the attempt to stay upright and away from those hurtling wheels. There are so many, that if you did get sucked in, you'd be mincemeat in seconds and the truck driver would never even notice. I decided that discretion is the better part of valour and I pulled over whenever I saw a road-train coming. The long open road meant I could see the trains coming from kilometres away, but regular use of my mirrors was vital – often the trucks would be going faster than I wanted to. I was worried about tyre wear on the hot road, and was already glad to have the comfort blanket of a new set strapped to the back of the bike. At higher speeds, the hot asphalt seemed to strip off rubber at an amazing rate. I estimated that I was getting about half the usual kilometres out of them and decided that the only way to reduce the rate of wear was to ride slower in the cooler parts of the day. It was tempting to go fast to cover miles, but for me the additional niggle was the rate at which Libby drank fuel at speed. She would turn into a mechanical lush, and my beer allowance would end up being spent on yet more fuel!

Alice Springs held little interest for me, though on the way down I'd eased off the highway to do a little scrub riding. It's so deserted in this area that I felt total confidence in off-loading all my kit from the bike, leaving it behind a bush, and then playing on the tracks. They were an adventure, but not only was the exercise good for the body, the mental challenge was good for the grey cells. 'Bull dust' just confused them though. It's a very fine powdery dust that collects on the tracks and to me looked just like ordinary sand, so I never had any warning. A couple of times I hit great pans of the stuff at speed, and instantly felt as if I'd run into the middle of an enormous red blancmange. My wheels would slop around in the deep slippery dust and the air would be so full of the fine particles, that in larger pans I'd almost get disoriented! The dust gave my face a sort of red monster look, and would instantly turn into glue when mixed with sweat, my tears running in streaks down my cheeks to form knotty clusters in my beard. But whatever size the dustpans were, they always got my heart beating a bit faster, some of that came from the effort of picking the bike up after I'd taken a tumble. After a day on the dirt I felt invigorated, a good antidote to the slightly stodgy feeling I was getting from the cruising.

I also headed off to explore towns like Gem Tree or take a look at The Devil's Marbles. These are bizarre-looking rounded boulders that sit across the landscape. The Aborigines say that they are eggs that were laid by the great rainbow serpent. Geologists say that they are chunks of granite that were left after volcanic eruptions, and that they have been eroded into their current shapes by millions of years of weather. I liked the Aborigines' legend more.

One day on a dirt track adventure, I came across an aboriginal man, sitting in the thin shade of a bush. He was dressed in shorts, but had no shirt and to my surprise he had almost blond hair. Beside him lay a small well-worn bag and a staff. I stopped and said hello, and he looked up at me and simply replied "G'day." I'd not had a chance to speak to an original local before, though I'd seen plenty around the towns in Queensland. Some had looked drunk, but most had looked blank, almost as if in their heads they were somewhere else completely. I'd heard lots of derogatory stories about them, and those conversations had often ended with, 'Bloody Abos'. The culture clash made me sad, and having read some of the history, and about some of the dire things that had been done to the Aborigines, it was easy for me to be critical of white Australians – I had to remind myself that looking in from the outside gave me a different perspective.

I'd read that aboriginal life is very much ruled by their relationship with the land. Though they viewed the land as theirs, they didn't relate to the concept that they possessed it. Certain regions would be wandered and hunted by different clans, but that was as far as it went. This nomadic people respected the land as it gave them everything they needed to survive, and getting food would be one of the main tasks of any day. The men would concentrate on keeping and passing on the traditions, and would do the hunting. Their traditional values were often called 'dreamtime', and stored in dreamtime stories. Quite often songs and dances, based on the stories, would be the way that the traditions would be passed on, but rock and bark paintings are also key to continuing the heritage. In the north the people had a particular type of style that is called 'X-ray' painting. Animals are drawn with their outlines, but instead of those outlines being filled in, the animals organs are carefully painted into place. To me they looked stunning, but to the

57

artists perhaps they were a sort of a biology lesson. The women would 'farm' the land of fruits and the parts of plants that could be used as food. They would also be responsible for catching small animals such as birds and lizards, as well as making clothes and cooking.

This open form of life had been dramatically affected by colonialists who simply didn't understand it. I've no doubt that the aborigines were as baffled by the immigrants as the immigrants were by them. Historically, their culture said, what is the point of working monster hours to obtain material things that they did not need, and in fact would hamper a proven and happy way of life? The fact that there are over a hundred different aboriginal languages can't have helped either.

Reservations were built in a way that ignored the lifestyle of the aborigines. The aborigines didn't care about having houses, money or jobs and this rankled with the Europeans. They forcefully set about wrecking the social system and for a long period, shooting aborigines was considered to be good sport. By 1911 the continuity of the race was at great risk and in 1918 a very cruel law was passed that mixed race children had to be taken away from their parents. They were placed in special orphanages, or were given to foster parents, many of whom used the children as slaves. Many more reservations were formed in the 1950s to try to increase control over the people, and this just about finished off the way of life. The people were not allowed to choose the jobs they were forced to do and frequently would be made to work on farms where they would be forced to use their skills and understanding of the land to help the incomers take over the land that was in fact theirs.

By 1967 there were 300-plus reservations, but that year the people got full civil rights. Since then, aborigines have been free to either live on the reservations or to live in traditional style in the bush, though some have attempted to integrate themselves into modern Australian life. In spite of this, most still can only get underpaid work and their social structure has been so devastated, with all the related problems, that their death rate is two times higher than immigrants to

Australia. Whole books have been written about this section of Australian history and I apologise for merely skimming over just some of the issues, but it is an aspect of Australia that affected my journey, so I had to write about it.

I introduced myself to the man under the bush, and asked if I could rest a while with him. "No worries mate", he said and then told me his name was Bobbo. We sat together for quite some time with me making most of the conversation, not quite sure if I should push off. Perhaps I was a real bother to him, but Bobbo didn't treat me that way at all – the thought was in my own mind only. After a while he started to open up a little, telling me that usually he worked on cattle stations as a general hand. He could fix fences, repair anything wooden and he could cook. "It's an OK life", he told me. It seemed to me that the life of a stockman was very similar to that of a nomad – always on the move, knowledge of the land and so on. "I gotta good boss", he said. Apparently his boss was quite happy for him to come and go, and Bobbo was now on his way to link up with his family, but having their aboriginal workers 'go walkabout' must have been a great frustration to early immigrants.

I wished I could go with him to spend some time with his family but at that moment didn't feel like I could ask. I camped with him that night and he showed me how to find a root which, cooked in the coals of the fire, tasted very much like a sweet potato. We shared my water and my muesli bars, and then stretched out on the sand to sleep. It wasn't cold at all and the faint breeze had just a hint of warm to it still. Bobbo snored like a logger's saw rasping a tree trunk. He might have slept well, but I didn't.

It was a small price to pay, as the next morning we sat talking again. Bobbo had three sisters and four brothers; he didn't know for sure where his brothers were but said that they'd probably turn up for the meet. His sisters were still with his parents, as were two of his grandparents. He had a niece and a nephew to complete the family. He told me the name of the place they all lived but I never did find it on any map.

Just as abruptly as I had appeared, Bobbo stood up and said, "Gotta go now mate, go well ay". With that he turned and within seconds he had melted into the bush. I was really pleased that I had been lucky enough to meet him, though I did wonder if we'd have got on as well if there'd been other people around – our first hours together had been a real sussing out time.

The one thing I did want to see in Alice Springs was the railway station – I'd read about what should be one of the great train rides in the world. The Ghan set off from Adelaide, and across lines that were incredibly badly laid; the train would head right up into the interior. The train had an average speed of 30 kilometres an hour, and because much of the track was laid across and through gullies, passengers would frequently be stranded after heavy rain had washed the track away, until repairs could be made. I'd heard stories that the passengers would get stuck in such remote places that the only way to get supplies to them was to parachute them in. The train has the name of 'The Ghan' because for much of its life the track didn't make it all the way to Alice Springs – passengers were carried the last kilometres by Afghan camels and their drivers. Wild descendents of these camels still roam the interior and the main grass of the interior comes from seeds that were dropped from the grass that was used to stuff the saddles. Now, a new line has been laid all the way through. I suspect that the journey is a lot easier and a darned sight more reliable, but as romantic and such a source of tall tales? I doubt it.

When most people think of Australia, I suspect that an image of either the Sydney Opera House or Ayers Rock comes into mind. For me the rock is the more special of the two. It's natural, beautiful and  surrounded by myths and legends. The rock is 3.6 kilometres long and at its highest point reaches 348 metres, rising straight out of the surrounding desert, and at first sight doesn't look as if it belongs there at all, more as if it was dumped there by some greater being. At dawn and dusk the stone changes colour through multiple shades of reds, pinks and purples. It's a religious site for the Aboriginal people and a Mecca for tourists. I knew that I wasn't going to enjoy the inevitable hoards of visitors but wasn't going to be put off seeing this magical place for myself.

I thought that if I got to the site early enough, I'd at least get a few moments' peace – I should have known better. With just the first couple of rays popping over the horizon, visitors were there too. Some climbed the rock, but I chose not to. I'd read that the Aborigines aren't too happy with people climbing on their special place and had decided I'd respect their thoughts. In any case, the best of the colours would be seen from below.

Roughly thirty kilometres away from Ayers Rock are a set of monoliths called the Olgas, or Kata Tjuta. Here I found my peace and quiet, and quite frankly the beauty of these rocks elicited a greater strength of feeling from me than Uluru had. I also enjoyed the fact that I was standing at the start of the route across the centre of the continent to Kalgoorlie and Perth. Not a trip I was going to make this time, but at least I'd find the kick off point on another occasion. Visitors are well organised at both sites. There are parking areas, picnic tables, toilets and well-marked walks through the bush, though this amount of traffic and this amount of organisation makes the cost of staying anywhere in the area a very expensive thing to do. Finding somewhere to free camp isn't easy as there are fences everywhere. But I was blowed if I was going to give away a week's food money for one night, so I persevered. It's nice only having a bike to hide, and some of the gaps in the fence were just wide enough to get Libby through! Perfect.

The Stuart Highway running north seemed like an old friend, and I enjoyed the opportunity to see things from a different direction. The change in the angle of the light seemed to make a massive difference to how the road and its surroundings looked, and the kilometres passed quickly. Libby was into full cruise mode, and everything was as close to perfect as it could be. As I got further north, I called in at Katherine Gorge. It's another well-visited site, but with good reason. There are thirteen gorges in the National Park, each separated from the other by rapids. They aren't particularly deep but the swimming is good, there's shade and the flowing water seems to cool the surrounding land quite pleasantly. People canoe the gorge and there's even a riverboat cruise, which I took and thought good value. It was an excellent way to see the gorge.

That night I even paid to stay on a camping site. Having just swum in the gorge I didn't need a shower, but I'd heard that wallabies were regular visitors to the site. Though by now I'd seen plenty of kangaroos, I still hadn't seen a wallaby. These are smaller versions of a kangaroo and were supposedly rather cute – I wasn't disappointed. I never saw anyone feeding them but they simply seemed to like a little human contact. The following morning I woke to a fine sunny day. The raucous maniacal laughter of a Kookaburra shocked me awake. One of the things I liked about my tent was that it had a yellow inner and when the day was good outside, this would seem to attract sunshine in under the flysheet. If it was damp, it still gave me the illusion that the day wasn't too bad out there. But this particular morning, something rather strange had happened to it. The inner seemed to have somehow collapsed in the middle. I carefully moved to the front and eased the doorway zip up to look. The inner hadn't collapsed at all but there, fast asleep, was a wallaby who had decided to use the inner as a hammock!

I was heading for the Kakadu National Park, but as I rode further north with the vegetation becoming greener around me all the time, I knew that I had to go to Darwin first. I had a ship to

arrange and I knew that doing this could quite possibly take weeks. With just a day's ride to go, I eased over for a rest under the shade of some ghost gum trees. These eucalyptus trees have stark white trunks, fluffy pale green leaves, and a warm sharp medicinal scent. I was enjoying the sight of a flock of black cockatoos that had screeched in from nowhere, when I heard another sound. It was very loud, but seemed to fade in and out of hearing. The cockatoos took off again and once their awesome level of noise had gone, I recognised the sound. It was a bike. Probably a big one, and it sounded as if it didn't have a silencer. Then it appeared over the brow of the hill as a black and tan blob, which changed from blobby silhouette to man on bike. The rider pulled over when he saw me, parked the 1,000cc Kawasaki, which brought peace back to the world, and leaned over to say, "G'day mate, noice one ay". The biker was wearing a pair of black shorts, some black rubber thongs on his feet, and he had a tiny black pudding bowl helmet on his head; that was all. He was heavily tanned and needed a shave. His bike had been roughly spray-painted matt black from tyres to handlebar grips.

"Wherea yer from mate?" he asked. I told him my tale and where I was off to next. But I wanted to know what had happened with him. "You've got no jacket, no jeans and no boots, and, um, nice black bike you've got there." "Ahh well," he said laconically. "I got in a bit of bother with the law, so 'ad to skip town. Ah reckoned that I was a bit recognisable in me gear and me boike, well, she was red before and ah reckoned she were a tad obvious n'all. So, I zapped her with a bit of paint. Nice job ay", he said, grinning. With that, he pressed the starter, the world lost its peace and he blasted off up the highway towards Darwin. My ears rang for at least two minutes after he'd disappeared over the next hill.

Chapter 4

Disaster and a Surfer's Paradise

*'What you've done becomes the judge of what you're going to do -
especially in other people's minds. When you're traveling, you are what you
are right there and then. People don't have your past to hold against you.
No yesterdays on the road.'*

William Least Heat Moon, Blue Highways

Darwin is the capital of the Northern Territory and for me
it was to be an exclamation mark at the end of Australia. The city,
which has only really been such since WW2, still has an air of frontier
town about it, and it had a series of nasty surprises in store for me.
The happy months cruising through Australia and New Zealand were
about to end with a painful crunch.

I'd been looking forward to Darwin, as it has a reputation
that sounded as if it would fit with my mood – the perfect place to
mentally wind up for Asia. The city stands at the edge of Asia but
has a pure Australian atmosphere. The streets have palm and gum
trees, and bougainvillea hangs over fences and climbs up walls. The
lifestyle is easygoing in a steamy heat that holds scents of warm sea,
mangroves, tropical forest and the usual mix of smells that humans
create. But it's surprisingly modern when bearing in mind how far
it is from everything else that's modern in Oz. Modern was good as
far as I was concerned, because I had a fair bit or organising to do. I
needed to find a ship to take me across the Timor Sea and critically, I
was also waiting to find out if I was going to get my permit for Libby
to get into Indonesia. There was also just a chance that I was going to
get permission to ride through China.

I'd been in contact with the Chinese Embassy for about nine
months by this time and I was trying to do something that not a lot of
people had managed. If I could get my bike into China I would be set
up for a massive adventure. The whole thing was a bit of a punt, but I'd
been working on the premise that those who don't ask don't get. I was
already pretty sure that I wasn't going to be able to get through Burma,

as all my approaches to them had been met with a series of negatives, followed by silence. Far from being a consolation prize, China would be a real gem in my journey. At this stage I hadn't even talked about the prospect with Jan though. I was sure the application would be unsuccessful and I didn't want to muddy the waters – nor did I want to start off our journey together with a negative event. I'd done my best though, and ever the optimist I'd put together a sort of business plan to go with my application. The research I'd done had made it clear that the Chinese officials didn't like westerners floating around their country, with their own transport.

My business plan included my planned route, the condition of my bike, the amount of experience I had, my proposed budget, my CV, my aim for the visit and how long I'd need. I'd put down four months, working on the old rule of asking for more than you hope you'll get. In reality, a couple of months would be very nice. I'd supported everything with whatever evidence I could pull together, and I felt that I'd done a good job □ in fact it was rather like putting together an application for a job! After I'd submitted it I'd only gone as far as phoning once a month to see how it was progressing. I didn't want to make such a nuisance of myself that I'd get turned down, but I hadn't wanted them to forget about me. I also hoped that if I was polite and respectful every time I called, then perhaps this would stand me in good stead. I was due to find out in Darwin.

Getting the bike into Indonesia had been the same sort of hassle, but on a much lesser scale. The authorities didn't like the thought of a big tourist bike in the country, and there was considerable political unease at the time which wasn't going to help. I'd spent hours writing letters, faxes, telexes, and on the telephone, and the exercise was one of the most frustrating things I'd ever had to do. This person wasn't available, that number was wrong and I'd run around the houses only to find myself back with the original number, and so it went on. Finally, in Townsville I'd had a breakthrough. If I could prove that I had a booking for the bike to ship into the country, a confirmed ticket for the bike out again and if I could get myself sponsored by a motorcycling organisation in the country, then my application would be seriously considered.

My research had thrown up a small shipping company called Perkins Shipping. Perkins, based in Darwin, had started up just after the Second World War using redundant front-loading landing craft to carry cargo across the Timor Sea. The company sailed a sort of bus route from Darwin to Singapore and back again, calling at various ports along the way. Sadly, their ships weren't landing craft any more. In the early stages of planning, I'd read between the lines that I might have been able to ship across on the same vessel as the bike, but that was no longer an issue, with me about to fly to Germany. Now I hoped to be able to ship the bike with Perkins into Kupang on the island of East Timor. That in itself was a bit of an issue as rebels, who wanted independence from the central government, had been more visibly active, but for me it was the logical starting point. Indonesia is made up of a long string of islands and, rather perfectly from a biker's point of view, most are joined together by small roll-on-roll-off ferries. They would allow me to start in the east and island-hop my way across to Sumatra. From there I could get another ferry across to Penang in Malaysia. It would be no problem for Jan to fly across to Kupang from Darwin either, though due to the uncertainty of it all, we still had plan number one as being to meet up in Bali.

Pieces of the Indonesia jigsaw puzzle began to fall into place. Yes, Perkins would take the bike, but only when I had confirmation from the authorities that they would be able to land it. Perkins wrote a letter to the Indonesians stating just that. Then the Harley-Davidson club in Jakarta sent me a fax confirming that they would be delighted to sponsor me. But I just could not get anyone in the Sumatran port of Medan to confirm that passage was manageable for the bike to get to Penang. I spent three weeks food budget on telephone calls and yet more faxes. I knew that ferries ran the route, I had the contact details for the ferry companies and I knew that it was possible to get bikes on board. But could I get a ticket? Emphatically, no! Without that, the whole plan was completely scuppered.

I was sad to have failed after all that effort, but the exercise had been an interesting experience. I'd dealt with a lot of people to get even as far as I had, and without the bike I wouldn't have had any reason to do so. I called Jan to let her know that Bali was on and booked with Perkins for the bike to be shipped to Singapore. In the meantime, we'd see some of Indonesia with a rucksack and local transport. Perkins helpfully agreed to store Libby at no charge for six weeks so that we would have time to do that. When the time came, they also dealt with customs so that the bike could be 'bonded', allowing me to leave without the bike being shipped at the same time. Singapore docks intended to charge arms and legs for the storage, so this was good news.

I was staying with relations of my friends in Sydney. I've rarely visited a country where as a stranger I was made so welcome or helped on my way by so many. Complete strangers had invited me to stay on the slimmest of connections and I'd almost always been treated as a member of the family.

Australians seemed genuinely interested in what I as a visitor thought about their country, and they had a hunger to know about other countries. Many seemed to feel a little isolated, which I felt was a small price to pay for the ability to keep the more ridiculous aspects of the rest of the world at bay. As a very large island, Australia has the ability to control undesirable influences. As a relatively new country they have the chance to learn by other countries' mistakes and they seemed to have learned a lot about how to handle immigration. If you are going be an immigrant in Australia, you have to have something important to bring with you, you have to be tough and you have to be keen to help build.

Immigrants bring fresh ideas but the trick seemed to be that not so many were allowed in that the original essence of Australian culture was diluted. It was almost as if anyone who wasn't going to sit like an indigestible lump in society was going to be welcome. Integration seemed to be the key. If you were going to call Australia your home then you were going to be an Australian; you were not going to be a British Australian or a Greek Australian. For many years immigration had been a 'white only' thing, but in recent years Australians seemed driven to make stronger connections with the countries on their own doorstep, rather than those thousands of miles away in Europe. The Asian immigrant population has grown dramatically as a result. Darwin was a point involved in this issue. It's only a couple of hundred kilometres away from several Asian countries, but over a thousand away from other main Australian cities.

Brit immigrants often had the reputation for being 'whingeing poms' – the 'pom' coming from 'prisoners of her Majesty'. It's derogatory and from the sounds of it, sometimes well deserved. British immigrants after WW2 came from a country where the welfare state was in full flow. It wasn't in Australia. In this country, if you needed something, you made it happen for yourself and this was a considerable culture shock. I wondered if the cultures of Asia were closer to the Australian way of life and values, and if the new immigrants would settle down very quickly indeed. Perhaps that aspect alone would ensure that there would never be Asian Australians.

My new friends had a really pleasant bungalow set in flower gardens on the edge of this remote city and, as with everyone in the family I'd met, they made me very welcome. The two of them ran a small filming business and invited me to come along for a bit of work, an opportunity too good to be missed, so when I wasn't chasing embassies and organisations, I was with the crew. They had been commissioned to film government road safety adverts for television. When they told me that, I'd thought that it would all be a bit tame, certainly no Hollywood experience, but that thought soon changed.

Australians like to roll their 'utes', or at least so it seemed, and the death rate was significant. Some deaths came because wearing a seat belt didn't seem to be a priority, but most came from passengers being thrown out of the open pickup beds. There seemed to be a never-ending list of reasons why the utes would roll, but top of the list were drunk driving, the grim state of many Outback roads and the fact that a lot of utes are tall. They have good ground clearance, but that added height makes them more inclined to topple, if not always handled exactly right. The adverts were filmed in true Australian style – no holds barred! Graphic is far too soft a word to describe the way they were put together. Out filming segments, it's not easy to visualise what the finished product will look like, but one final edit actually made me feel ill. I thought about the road safety adverts at home and wondered if they had any effect at all – they were far too soft in a world of mega movies in which extreme bloody violence is the norm.

Chasing the Indonesians, the Chinese and working on the gory road safety films meant that I ran out of time to do much exploring around Darwin. I did get out and about with the crew and frequently locations were well out in the bush, which was a consolation prize, but I wasn't going to get into the Kakadu. The National Park is just 230 kilometres away from Darwin, and home to superb landscape, a high concentration of really diverse wildlife, and some of the best Aboriginal rock paintings in Australia. With all that to see I'd decided that it needed a couple of weeks, unless I was going to take a tour, and my budget wasn't going to run to that option. Or at least, my budget-conscious brain wouldn't let me spend the money on something such as a tour. There is something of a travel snob in a long distance traveller, and sometimes that gets in the way. The longer you are on the road, the more you itch to be out there having experiences, but they cost money. The trick is to remain within running cost budget, but to have a separate budget for jollies. A tour to Kakadu should have come out of my non-existent jollies budget and it was a lesson learned. In a way I also felt a little stupid for leaving the chance to get into really rugged northern country until last. But I understood that there simply isn't enough time to 'do' everything when on the road; it's more a case of thoroughly enjoying what you can get involved with. I had no complaints about my Australian activities but, once again, it had simply underlined that this is a big island and there's a phenomenal amount to see.

The Chinese embassy finally got back to me and to my amazement they said yes! They were actually going to give me a permit for both the bike and I to ride in China. I was stunned, but there it was, in my hand, confirmation.

Then I read the small print, which hid the bad news. It would cost me $100 US, per day, to be there with the bike. This would cover the costs of administration, a guide's wages, his vehicle, accommodation and his food – it took a millisecond to work out that I wasn't going to China. With the costs involved with getting the bike there in the first place, it just wasn't going to happen. My budget simply wasn't big enough, and in fact, $100 was roughly my budget for 2-3 weeks on the road. But it was very nice to have been granted a yes.

The last day with the film crew turned into a disaster. Though I didn't understand what had happened to me at the time, I slipped a disc in my lower back. I've always been an active, energetic, maker of things to happen, and over my various travels I'd pushed my body to its limits, perhaps a few times too often. At school and in my late teens I'd played rugby, and that had probably started to weaken my back. I'd done loads of travel type jobs over the years, and all had worked their own bit of damage: digging sewers in the stony ground of Greece is hard work; waiting on tables in restaurants, sometimes on fifteen-hour days, is hard going on your back; working on building sites can be punishing and the months of picking tomatoes, capsicums, and grapes in Australia must have also done their own damage. The 17-bone fracture accident in Namibia can't have helped and quite frankly, I don't suppose the number of times I'd fallen off the bike on dirt roads could have helped much either.

The disc slipped in an almost Buster Keaton-ish way. I was bending down to pick up a heavy bit of film kit in a storeroom, when one of the crew walked in. He didn't know I was there but the door hit me when I was half way up with the kit, just enough for my back to kink with a nasty click. It was sore, but I'd taken knocks before so didn't fret. In any case I was due to fly to Bali and then on to Germany the next day, so I'd not have to be on the bike or working. That meant any thoughts of fitness pressure just weren't there. All that remained was for the bike to be taken by trailer to the docks. That night though, I caused the real problem.

Libby weighs 250 kilos and her centre stand had been badly damaged in Namibia. It had been repaired, but I'd not spent the money on a new stand, so it didn't line up properly. So much was the stand out of line that she could be a bit of a pig to get up onto it. That night, with a warm breeze filling the flower garden with a hundred scents, I went to put the bike on the stand. As I did so I had shooting pain, which was accompanied by a sort of ripping gristle sound from my back. I broke into an instant sweat and as my whole body seemed to flush with pain I felt violently sick. I hardly slept that night.

On the plane to Bali, the pain wasn't too bad, but my couple of days stopover wasn't paradise, but the flight onwards to Frankfurt was good, with my back only giving me twinges. Birgit met me at the airport in her Volkswagen camper van, and she could instantly see that something was really wrong. After being stuck on aeroplanes for the bulk of 11 hours, walking was hard, but the true state of affairs didn't strike for some days. Being the sort of person who doesn't like to be ill, I decided to ease into some of my old rugby exercises. I was certain that I'd just got unfit and that gentle exercise would soon bring me back up to speed.

Big mistake! Half a dozen trunk curls did for me and Birgit came home to find me stuck on the floor; I'd been there unable to move for hours. She had to pull me up and it didn't help that I couldn't stop laughing through the agony. How perverse; the work I was doing to get rid of the pain had dramatically increased it. I should have just been a slob. My laugh was an almost out of control, slightly hysterical and very disappointed giggle that only just stopped me breaking into tears of pain and deep, shocked, despondency.

I had three thoughts in my mind. The first thought being, 'So much for a romantic couple of weeks with Birgit'. And the second, 'Riding a bike like this is going to suck.' And the third, 'At least my medical travel insurance will cover me for Germany'. To add to my feeling of gloom, it was bitterly cold and I couldn't shake off the feeling of jet lag. All in all, I can't have been much fun to be around.

I couldn't stand comfortably, or sit and even lying down was painful. Birgit spent the next weeks taking me back and forth to doctors, the hospital and to work with physiotherapists. One of the upsides to all of this was that I finally got the chance to sit and read 'Zen and the Art of Motorcycle Maintenance'. I'd tried to read it on two other occasions, but had finally decided that it was a book that had to be read when forced to!

Fortunately my insurance company came up trumps, and once again I was incredibly thankful that I had not allowed the thought of additional days on the road to outweigh the cost of a decent insurance policy. I'd met a couple of bikers who had no insurance whatsoever, and after the last couple of years of adventures, that seemed the wrong end to be saving money. It had cost my insurance company thousands of pounds to get me put back together after the accident, and they had also paid out for 'lurgie' checks in South Africa. They had even paid for me to be tested for Aids, after I feared I might have caught it in hospital up on the Namibian border with Angola.

We were lucky enough to find a sports physio who was also a biker and therefore understood exactly what was needed. My couple of weeks in Germany turned into six weeks, and the doctors said that it would be at least six months before I'd be able to ride a bike again, at best! "I think perhaps that you should never ride a bike again." He said. The diagnosis was that I had two badly prolapsed discs.

But I had a bike in South East Asia, somewhere, and a trip to do – a dream to live. I didn't believe that I wouldn't be fit for six months, so set to work on my physio exercises with painful enthusiasm. I only considered the thought of not riding at all for a few seconds. Birgit was a star and gave every encouragement possible. I really liked her for the caring but matter of fact, determined and efficient way she dealt with the whole situation. The only other up side to the situation was that Jan was able to delay her departure to Bali, but this was exactly what I hadn't wanted to happen. The trip together was now going to start on the downer of major uncertainty.

My travel insurance – such a boon – was now a worry as well. If the doctor stated that I shouldn't travel, or that I mustn't ride the bike, then I wouldn't be covered. The only option was to go to the doctor and beg with great enthusiasm and as much confidence as I could muster. Either I must have been convincing, or Birgit's translation work had been spiced up, because it worked. The doctor wasn't happy but could see the issues at hand. He was a good sport and wasn't going to kill the trip.

Birgit took me back to Frankfurt, with me laying flat on my back in her camper van. Neither of us knew how I'd fare on the flight, but both of us suspected that it wasn't going to be easy. Thankfully, this time I was going to be doing a bit of individual flying on the painkillers and anti-inflammatory tablets the doctor had given me. As for Birgit and I, we decided to stay in touch and see how things developed between us. We'd also decided that Birgit was going to try to link up with me for a month in Asia somewhere, if she could get that long off work. Nepal seemed like a good option.

The flight was manageable, but I didn't dare uncurl myself from the seat, even to go to the loo. Normally when I'm on a plane, especially when I'm on a travel budget, I ask for second and third helpings of every meal. It's not greed, just a way to stock up on calories. I always pay good attention to the food I'm eating when on the road, but it's inevitable that on a traveller's budget, you get a little thin. This time I couldn't even face eating the first helping. I drank little and stayed wedged in place until the plane hit the runway at Bali's airport in Denpasar. Birgit, knowing that I wasn't going to feel much like hunting for food when I got there, had sent me off armed with supplies for a day, including a loaf of good solid dark German bread. I'd grown to love this stuff, though it's as different from English bread as cornflakes are to porridge. But the customs officials were highly suspicious of why someone would bring bread to Bali, especially as it looked unlike any bread that they had ever seen before. My wonderful loaf was duly hacked to pieces by an official who wielded a 12-inch bladed knife with almost maniacal enthusiasm. He had an equal level of disappointment when he found that the loaf of bread was yes, just a loaf of weird-looking bread.

It's only a few miles to Bali's main resort of Kuta from the airport, so I elected to walk. Striding out would loosen me up, and I'd already been finding that walking was the best form of pain relief. Over my months in Australia I'd done a lot of bare-footing around and the soles of my feet had developed a thick hard layer of skin. As an attempt at getting myself back into the freedom of travel, I eased my boots off, hung them on my backpack and started walking.

This was not a sensible thing to do. At some time I must have walked on something very sharp and sliced a layer of skin off the bottom of my left foot. There was no pain, but I had the sensation that something was sticking to the bottom of my foot. I wondered what I had trodden in, perhaps chewing gum. I looked, and found a three by five-centimetre strip of skin flapping loose. Not a good start to Bali, but my skin was so thick that no blood had been drawn, and there was just another layer of pink skin underneath.

Kuta is a magnet for travellers of all budgets, and it's busy. The main advantage is that there are numerous places to stay, from real budget accommodation to pure luxury. I headed for the hostel I'd stayed in on my first visit, and thankfully they had room for me. By the time I got there I'd just about had it, and a hard bed to lie on was a moment of major bliss.

Hostels in Bali have a unique form of hospitality. Each room is supplied daily with large metal thermos flasks of tea, and these battered, cork-topped flasks are topped up whenever you ask. Breakfast is included in the price of the room, usually fresh local fruits such as pineapples or bananas, and if you hit the right hostel then you will also get the option of such delights as banana pancakes. The rooms in the sorts of hostels I could afford were basic, but had everything I needed – a bed with clean sheets, a shower, a basin and a toilet. If you were lucky then you also had a mosquito net, which was vital, as mosquitoes were almost as hungry as Australian Outback flies. My room also had an overhead fan that worked, and kept the mossies off me at night – when I had the fan turned on full blast. It must have been like flying a Cessna in a hurricane! If you didn't have a fan, then you had to rely on

74

burning green mosquito coils through the night. They worked well, but I often wondered what that smoke was doing to my lungs as I breathed it in all night.

Bali is a seal head-shaped island that's mostly covered in lush vegetation, be it natural or cultivated. The coast is dotted with idyllic beaches, it's dominated by active volcanoes, and is said to have been inhabited for 3000 years. It's one of the 18,000 equatorial islands  that make up the Indonesian archipelago, the largest and most varied on earth, covering nearly two million square kilometres. The population of Bali is mostly Hindu and this is a major difference from Indonesia's other islands, which tend to be mostly Muslim. Every village and town is dotted with temples and shrines, all of which are worth stopping to look at, though if you did that it would take you a very long time to get anywhere! It's well worth taking time to explore, and I really wanted to get up to the town of Ubud, described as the cultural centre of Bali. I just wanted to see the woodcarvings too, even if I was to see little else of the island.

I arrived a couple of days before Jan and that gave me the chance to get over the inevitable stiffness from the journey. I liked Kuta's brash, over the top, backpackers' world. Condensed down into the alleyways running from the beach, was a whole network of suppliers of backpackers' needs. The streets and alleyways were crooked and many didn't have name signs. It was like a maze and getting lost was the easiest thing to do, but each time I did, I'd see something new, bizarre or simply useful. Tiny food stalls stood next to clothes shops, souvenir shops, travel agents, moneychangers, car and bike hire shops, and restaurants. There were bars everywhere and most advertised showings of the latest movies. The bars were open-sided and rough and ready, but fully formed with partying in mind. And people would party, long into the night, every night. You could surf from Kuta, you could sail, dive, go fishing or even set up rafting trips. Kuta buzzed. I got the feeling that many backpackers never saw any of the rest of Bali.

None of those things were for me though, as I had to save money. I bargained for everything, and I bought my meals from the men and women who would set up charcoal braziers in the side streets. They produced staple meals of nasi-goreng – slightly flavoured rice with a few vegetables either mixed in or laid on top. I'd gone into full 'budget mode' while I was on my own because I suspected that Jan would have more money than me, and I didn't want to hold her adventures back by being skint at the time of an opportunity. But I did enjoy seeing how little I could live on each day – I got my daily budget for food down to $1.50 US and still ate well, though perhaps not particularly healthily. Bali portions are small, so I began to lose weight, but that wasn't a problem as I found that in the heat I simply didn't need to eat so much.

I particularly liked one of the food stalls, because of the owners. They were two of the warmest people I'd ever met, both with round jolly faces that seemed to glow somehow. The two of them were just five foot two or three tall. Their stall looked as if it had been put together on a framework of salvaged wooden pallets, and saplings from the forest, and brightly coloured batiks stretched over the top, with which the owners' sarongs and shirts always clashed perfectly. The whole scene was almost eye-aching from the bright colours, but what made it so special was the smile of welcome, and if you went there more than once you were always remembered, which I found fascinating bearing in mind the number of tourists that must have passed through each week. They had a speciality dish of rice, vegetables, garlic and chilli sauce with a fried egg on top. This was cooked to perfection, and a larger portion than usual. The couple obviously liked each other and enjoyed what they did, and that always set the mood for the rest of an evening.

One evening though, they offered me magic mushrooms. These hallucinogens are illegal in Bali, but not a lot of notice was ever taken of that. The mushrooms were on sale in quite a few places, and if it was an eatery then you had a choice of having them made into an omelette, or into a tea. I seemed to have passed some sort of test.

Money changing was an experience too. I counted thirty-two moneychangers in Kuta, and each had a different rate. It wasn't a case of there being good deal moneychangers, or bad. Their rates seemed to change at random each day, so to get the best deal, I had to go round all and hope that by the time I'd found the cheapest one, and got back to them, they hadn't amended their rate. But the hunt was still worthwhile. Not only could I save myself the price of a meal or two, but my money change tour was also a great excuse to catch up on what was going on.

I walked out to the airport to meet Jan, and when she appeared through the arrivals area I almost didn't recognise her. She was wearing Dr Marten boots, black flared jeans, and a baby blue smock top, but the real change from her usual visible self was her hair. She had it dyed bright orange and it was in three-inch long dreadlocks. As she walked through the airport towards me, the ends of the dreads bobbed along with the motion. My first thought (after 'good grief!') was how on earth is she going to get her crash helmet on over that lot?

My next thought was that having a travel partner was going to change things more than I'd estimated. Usually I liked to ease into places without making too much of a stir. I liked to be able to check out the lie of the land before I got involved in things, and I didn't like to draw attention to myself, more than the bike did already. One of the things I liked about Libby was that she was quiet – at low speed she would almost purr along. Drawing attention to myself before I'd found my feet made me feel vulnerable. I'd always felt that we travel with a percentage of 'vulnerability allowance' which we shouldn't exceed or bad things will happen. It's a nutty superstition, but so far it had worked well for me and I'd certainly not had any shortage of adventures. I'd still had plenty of scrapes, and had got away with most of them, perhaps because I'd not used up my vulnerability quota! Either that or I really did have a biker's guardian angel.

Jan and I got into an in-depth conversation that night. How was my back going to affect things? I told her that I was sure I'd be able to ride in a couple of months. We decided to extend our planned stay in

Indonesia and to spend the time travelling by bus across the islands of Bali, Lombok, Java and Sumatra. We'd then catch the ferry to Penang, and travel on to Singapore to pick up the bike. I'd have to pay storage, but so be it. There wasn't much of a choice and we both knew that it would be a close thing. The thought that I might not ride again hung heavy between us, but Jan had obviously decided to simply get on with life, and see what happened, which was a relief for me.

Jan was a firm believer in the Tarot cards and one day she told me that the cards kept saying she was going to fall madly in love in South East Asia. This came as a warning, but I was too busy coping with my back and exploring, to take real notice. Besides, I thought that Tarot cards were a load of rubbish, though I tried very hard not to show that to Jan! She was so convinced, she read her cards everyday and sometimes I felt that she wouldn't do much unless the cards said she could. This was a side of her that I'd not seen before – in Africa she'd been happy-go-lucky and up for just about anything, loving adventures. I'd thought that we had so many things in common that, where we differed, it would be no problem, so I was a bit stunned at the first signs that she wasn't perhaps the person I thought I knew. Whatever happened, I suspected that travelling with Jan was going to be an adventure in itself. I hoped that she would add a different level to my travels and looked forward to that, but had a couple of concerns attached. Was she going to be a limit to adventure if she stuck to the cards advice, or even a risk as a result of them? Also, without her splitting the costs I'd have problems making it back to the UK if anything went wrong.

Jan showed a side of herself that I liked when she was down on the beach at Kuta one day. Sunbathing wasn't really a very peaceful thing to do as there was always someone trying to sell you something, be it clothes, an ice cream, jewellery or a massage. This wasn't a hassle though – the vendors would always gracefully accept a 'no' with a smile and would move on. A massage lady approached us. I wasn't going to let a stranger loose on my back but Jan was up for the idea. She didn't want to pay the full fee though, and struck a deal with the lady that she would pay for her massage part in cash and part by giving the woman a massage in return! To my surprise, and laughter from the other massage ladies, she agreed, and afterwards both looked happy that they'd got a good deal.

One night I let Jan read my palm. I'd been resisting this as I think it's a load of tosh, but she'd been so patient with me over my back and was now being so insistent about reading my palm, I gave in. As she believed in it so firmly, I wondered if she was doing it to reassure herself that there were no more disasters in store. She took a long calm look at my hand and after some stroking of the lines on my palm, she told me what she'd seen there. "Sam," she said, "You are going to have a long life, you'll have major health problems when you are 50, you are going to continue to travel all your life, your heart balances your head and you aren't selfish." With that she looked at me seemingly satisfied, and maybe, somewhat relieved.

We linked up with a bunch of other backpackers to travel on with. The way this happens when you are on the road is one of the great things about travel. People don't ask much about you other than perhaps, which country you come from, though you can tell that from accent anyway. I've travelled with people for days, sometimes weeks, with no idea what they did back in 'real life'. In some instances, I never even knew their names, but there were other priorities: does being with this other person feel good? Do they want to do similar things? Do they have similar attitudes to life? Can you have a laugh with them?

You do get a few questions about where you've been and with some travellers, this seems to be really important. It's almost as if they are counting the number of notches on your belt and comparing them to theirs, but I can't be doing with that and don't tend to hang around people like that for long. However, sometimes the questions are a genuine quest for information, a sort of travellers' jungle drum. Who better to ask about countries or areas you are planning to go to than someone who has just been there, especially if you like them. And liking them is an issue – it's an instinct, and this sense becomes quite enhanced as you settle into travel. It warns you that you shouldn't take some people at face value. If there's an absence of warning bells, you can relax and get on with the business of enjoying life, people and the world. It's uncomplicated, and for most travellers I'm convinced that when they are tuned into it, it rarely fails.

There have been times when I've ignored the instinct and have had an adventure that has seen me walking a situation tightrope. I've had my fingers burnt a few times too, but I've always come through safely, and always had an adventure. Ignoring the instinct has been a good wake up call sometimes; at others it has allowed me to do something quite daft, just to see what would happen. Sometimes it really is fun to do something that you know could end in tears.

For example, when in Australia, I bought some shares in a gold mine, of all things, in full knowledge that this was thinly disguised theft. I didn't mind one bit as the whole exchange was pure theatre.

Another time, a really dodgy looking character told me that he could find me a place to stay, with off-road parking for the bike. I'd been looking for hours, was tired at the end of a day's riding, and it was getting dark. He looked so dodgy that I double took, but instinct kicked in and off we went anyway – it would work or it wouldn't. In those situations, what was the worst that could happen? I could get robbed – things can be replaced. I could die – highly unlikely and if I did, well I wouldn't be around to worry about it. On this occasion, my dodgy character turned out to be a gem. The place he took me to was off the beaten track, but clean, safe, cheap, with good people, and yes it had off-road parking for Libby. He also turned out to be the perfect guide and for the next few days, I had a tour that holidaymakers of the fatter wallet type would have had to pay hundreds of dollars for.

Between us we hired a small mini bus to get us to the east coast ferry port of Padangbai, which was cheaper and far less hassle than catching the local bus. The ferry was, as I'd read, a roll-on roll-off type, and I sat envying the locals as they bumped aboard on their 125 and 90cc bikes. Some of the riders were dressed in slightly dusty but very smart business clothes, and the other end of the scale saw bikers dressed as if they had come straight out of the paddy fields.

Sometimes it was nice to be without Libby, but not this time. The roads looked great to ride and I missed the freedom the bike gave me to go where I wanted, when I wanted to. I wasn't enjoying being bikeless, though perhaps that feeling came more from the fact that I still hurt and was nervous about how my dodgy back would cope with travelling local style. If any of the roads turned 'African' then I was going to be in trouble in a bus. I'd been keeping quiet about the pain I was in, as I didn't want to put a stop on anyone else's plans. It was my problem to sort and I was determined not to become a whinger about it. On the few occasions I did have to say something, I felt quite embarrassed and rather a wimp. It was hard to be suddenly disabled like this. Coping with a permanent injury was not one of life's experiences for me to date, and the uncertainty niggled in the back of my mind a lot of the time.

At the end of its five-hour crossing, the Pelini ferry eased past a fishing village that stood on bamboo stilts out over the bay, and on past a graveyard of obsolete shipping that lay blistering and rotting in the salt air sunshine. The first thing that struck me about the island of Lombok was the clothes that the women were wearing. On Bali, you can tell that the women are curvy and their deep tanned skin can be seen quite naturally. On Muslim Lombok, the women were dressed in long robes and headscarves.

Jan and our new friends were in holiday mood. They wanted a beach, and that suited me fine. The driver of the mini bus, or bemo as they are known, set off through the crowds with a skill that said this man knew exactly how long and how wide his bus was. He could even judge how many passengers made what difference to the weight of the bus, and therefore, how much time he needed to squeeze it through gaps. Chickens ran in front of us, necks craned and wings flapping – the driver didn't seem bothered about them at all. Another obvious difference between Bali and Lombok was that we hardly passed a hotel, but it was touristy enough for the driver to insist that we stop at his brother's for a break. This consisted of banana soup, which was rather revolting, and palm wine, which was very nice but sadly without enough flavour to nullify the taste of the soup.

We'd elected to head for Gili Trawangan, which is one of a group of three islands just off the north west coast. Open, diesel-powered boats trundle a ferry service back and forth, which they do all day but never leave until a boat is full. This laid back but sensible system sets the mood for the islands – there are no cars or bikes, just miles of sand, bamboo cabins, a few tiny bars, basic restaurants, and some excellent diving.

Once our boat was full enough, of both backpackers and locals, we set off out onto the turquoise waters. The crew had been happily fishing over the side while we'd been waiting, and had left lines out as we chugged along with the outrigger leaving a double wake behind us. To cheers from the passengers half way into the ride, the youngest crewmember, a lad of about fourteen, pulled up a two-foot long Barracuda that shimmered silver, rose and turquoise as it was gaffed aboard.

Our cabin on Trawangan was up on stilts to catch the breeze, and to lift us out of the worst of the mosquitoes, which tend to buzz around closer to the ground. We were set to enjoy a taste of tropical paradise. The snorkelling was superb; a coral reef ran just off the beach, the sea was slightly cooler than bath temperature, waves almost non-existent and the weather fine. I felt like I'd been given a consolation prize for having missed out on the Barrier Reef. A current

swept past the island and just ten metres off the shore it was strong enough to take hold of me and pass me over hundreds of metres of reef without having to do so much as flop a flipper. I spent blissful hours doing this, getting my exercise wandering back up the creamy yellow sand of the beach.

Food in the little restaurants was good but basic, though I discovered that I didn't like gado gado very much. This is a dish that's found all over Indonesia, one of the staple meals and is made up of whatever vegetables are available that day, smothered with a very sweet, spicy peanut sauce. But other than gado gado, the days drifted by gently in this paradise, and life started to feel good again.

Life on the island introduced me to one of the characters of the road. A petite French girl, with a pin through her nose, blonde hair and an excellent tan, tagged on to us. Gwen was travelling by herself, and had quite a story. She'd been brought up in a sexually abusive family and had run away from home when she was just thirteen. She'd been on the road ever since, and made her way by odd jobbing as she went. She was a pretty girl and that must have helped her – the plum earning travel jobs seem to go to those who look good. With no home and no family behind her, she needed everything else to be going for her, and I wondered how long Gwen would have survived on the road had she not been such a vivacious and attractive girl. She was also a nutty and quite flamboyant creature who had a very fatalistic attitude to life, and no shame of her body. But underneath this enthusiastic exterior I learned that she was a vulnerable, insecure person who was really rather lost in life. She told me that she had just finished a stint working in Japan where she had been a waitress in a Karaoke bar. She told me that Japanese love having foreign girls working in such places and if you are a blonde, so much the better! She also told me that she had become expert at smacking exploring hands away, and that her first Japanese words had been, 'Don't do that!' But the money had been excellent and she estimated that she had enough cash saved for her to be able to travel and not work in Asia for almost a year. "But I will work," she said "If the opportunity is there, why not?"

Suddenly it was time to get on the move again. It was almost as if the group had come to this decision at the same moment without a word being spoken. Back to Bali, and then on to the capital island of Java, stopping to see the wood carvings in Ubud on the way. In the old days, woodcarvers would work almost exclusively to decorate temples and palaces, but now they are a perfect example of how old skills have moved with the times. Carvers use the same techniques to carve the animals that are their speciality, but they now concentrate on highly stylised creations that appeal to modern tastes. One major change from days gone by is that the carvers no longer paint their completed work, but leave the wood quite natural, which simply adds to the feeling that though forever still, the creatures actually live.

I also needed to be postman for a friend. Katya had lived in Ubud for three months whilst learning to play Gamelan music, a unique sound based on instruments that reminded me of kettledrums, with a thin layer of bronze instead of having a skin top. Katya had lived with a local family and had given me a package of photos and cassettes of her music to give to them. They lived about three kilometres outside of the town and, with what turned out to be excellent directions, I set off to find them. Danga was a painter of batiks and he and his family lived in a stunningly beautiful spot. Their house looked out over kilometres of patchwork, lush green paddy fields and coconut groves. The family all came out to meet me and were delighted to hear news of Katya. It was the sort of place where it would be very easy to get stuck, and must have been a wonderful place to study.

To round off Ubud, I had a chance to see some traditional dancing. It's almost a fake situation as the dancing is put on just for tourists, and this sort of thing is a battle for me. When I'm on the road I simply don't like being herded along with the flow of time-limited two-week holidaymakers, but there are times when it's just not possible to search things out for myself. This time playing the tourist rather than the traveller worked very well. We were shown through into a small ruined amphitheatre and, in full masked costume, the dancers whirled to the gamelan. With all lights lowered, the climax was a barefoot dance on burning coconut husks. Sparks shot skywards in the darkness as the dancers stamped and scuffed their feet as they whirled in time to the music. They should have earned themselves third degree burns, but no, just sooty feet.

The way to move between island centres seemed to be by long distance bus. The fares included the cost of the ferry which was far less hassle. There was the choice of luxury buses, or those that were far cheaper, but decidedly not luxury, or mini buses – Bemos – which stop a lot along the way. The bigger buses power along as kings of the road, and some of the driving was so dreadful I could only wonder if the drivers had passed their tests at all, or had bought their way into jobs. Belligerence was the name of the game and to be a passenger, you had to have the mental ability to click off, or total confidence that this day is not the one where you are going to be called to another world.

The first time we caught a bus, I was impressed at the way everyone stood in a straight line, patiently waiting for whatever lopsided heap hauled itself up to the stop, smoke belching and leaf springs groaning. The panels of the buses always seemed to be bashed and dented, almost as if a demented, blind panel beater had done his erratic best! When the bus arrived, the queue dissolved into a mad dash of 'me first'. People threw packages through windows, as if that would bag them a seat, though maybe it was just easier to battle the way onto the bus for any seat, without the bulk of a bundle under an arm. Travelling at the weekend or in a holiday time, whole families would be on the move, all dressed in what looked like their version of 'Sunday best', and the ride to come is treated as a sort of celebration. For many it would have been and, even though by our standards the tickets were cheap, for many they were expensive and savings would have been hoarded to buy them. Soft drinks and sticky cakes were consumed at a rate of knots in the bus queue. Small children managed to produce amazingly loud burps from the quantity of fizz they'd consumed; the atmosphere was great as old friends greeted each other; wished each other safe journeys, and good holidays.

With everyone finally settled aboard, the bus waddled off. The driver doing his best to miss the potholes but inevitably one of the wheels would hit something and I soon learned that the prized seats were those between the fore and aft wheels. A seat right at the front of the bus was the very best option for me, as not only did I get an uninterrupted view, but I got vital extra legroom. It is the most dangerous seat in an accident though! But wherever I sat, the seats were uncomfortable, not just hard, but they are designed for people much smaller than me. The fixed headrests become shoulder rests for lanky people, so I had to either sit forward all the time, or where legroom allowed, slump until the neck rest was in the right place. By the time a bus was out of a town, male passengers had started a masochistic race to prove who could smoke the most cigarettes. The problem for travellers comes not from the fact that it's cigarette smoke or the quantity of it, but for the fact that the cigarettes are laced with cloves. This rich scent is quite nauseating to the innocent visitor's nostrils when sucked up in this quantity. Meanwhile, the bus raced past small villages that clustered by the roadside, past paddy fields and clumps of palm trees. It did battle with cars, trucks, motorbikes, children with no road sense, lumbering water buffalo, dogs, goats and chickens. As the road curved, the bus rocked horribly.

On one journey across Java, the narrow asphalt took us rocking up into the hills. Our bus took its load of already green-gilled passengers swooping down into valleys. It would heave itself over the brow of a hill, and then gut-wrenchingly on down the next slope. A child had the first accident, and the rancid acidic stink of sweet vomit eased through the clove-saturated air inside the bus. Within minutes, just about every other child aboard had joined in, and we adults were concentrating hard on hanging on to our breakfasts. Vomit ran in rivulets up and down the floor of the bus like a growing tide as the bus continued to blast its way up and down and round the hills. Then adults started to vomit too, but the driver, window open, seemed quite oblivious. He was on a time schedule and anyway, it probably wasn't going to be his job to clean up when we finally got to the terminus. He just battled on, concentrating on keeping his eyes open by swilling litres of very black coffee.

The driver's mate is in the best place to catch fresh air, as it's his job to lean out of the door of the bus, yelling at other traffic to get out of the way. He also has to shout out the name of the bus's destination as it comes into a stop, so people know which bus to get on. These lads are raucous characters who get paid a percentage of the total take, so they work hard.

As the stench of the vomit grew, I had to get some fresh air, so stood up to put my face out of the small sliding glass panel at the top of the window beside me, my head turned sideways so it would fit through. It was then that I made a big mistake. Looking towards the front of the bus, I took a big breath at exactly the same time as some poor passenger had put his head out of a similar window to be sick. With my mouth open and sucking in fresh air, head wedged through the window and eyes squinting against the slipstream, I was never going to get out of the way fast enough and moments later my face was covered in vomit. I even swallowed a mouthful of the stuff and that taste stayed with me for the whole of the rest of the journey.

The cheaper buses stop a lot to pick up or let off passengers, but they rarely stop to let anyone eat or rest. If you need the toilet, you can only cross your legs, which meant that I had no chance to wash my face. My moustache had soaked up its fair share of the results of my fellow passenger's enthusiastic and relieved throwing-up session, so I couldn't even breathe without the smell of fast crusting vomit coming up into my nostrils!

Roughly two hundred kilometres into Java from Bali is the active volcano Bromo. Indonesia has some 400 volcanos, and 90 of them are still active. I'd seen live volcanos from a fair distance before but I'd never been close to one. Bromo stands 2392 metres high and is part of the Tengger Massif range. The landscape looked as if it could have been chosen as a practice ground for astronauts. Bromo is one of three peaks which stand up from an ancient caldera, formed originally by the Tengger volcano itself. Bromo had erupted sixty times since records began in 1767 and in a way that added spice to the adventure. We'd been told that the best time to appreciate the volcano was at dawn, which meant getting under way at 4.30am. It was cold at this altitude, especially after the weeks we had been down on the coast playing in the sunshine, and I hadn't been as chilly as this since I was with Birgit, but at least it wasn't snowing as it had been in Southern Germany.

The walk began by meandering across the lava plain. It would have been easy to get lost in the dark were it not for the large white-painted boulders that marked the way. We had elected not to climb Bromo itself, but the peak next door. From there we could watch the sun come up on the volcano, and we would miss the rush of people trekking the main path. The crater was gently steaming a great column into the sky, and the sun hazed through the steam in mini-rainbows as it rose. Despite having every layer of clothes on, it was still cold, but that made the rays of the new day even more welcome. Across the moonscape, shadows shortened and colours changed. Above the moonscape, the rising sun reflected peaches, pinks and oranges against a thin layer of puffy cloud.

Just a few months after we had been there, Bromo erupted with no warning at all – those on the rim were killed.

One of my main reasons for visiting Indonesia was to see Bororbudur. At one time Buddhism was the key religion in Java and this amazing temple had been built at the peak. But with the eventual decline of Buddhism, the temple was allowed to fall into disrepair and was virtually forgotten by everyone – layers of volcanic ash pretty much buried it from sight. It wasn't until Sir T.S. Raffles was governing Java in 1815 that the temple was rediscovered and the site cleared. Later, the Dutch started restoring the temple and it was recognised as one of the greatest Buddhist sites in S.E. Asia.

However, there were problems. The land had become waterlogged and the great stones had subsided, deteriorating further as the years went by. Thankfully between 1973 and 1983 a massive multi-million dollar restoration project was undertaken, and the site restored as close to its former glory as possible. The temple is one hundred and eighteen metres square and made up of six square terraces, upon which sit three more circular terraces. You access these by one of four stairways, each of which is topped by an ornate carved gateway. It's thought that in the days it was built all this stone was painted, but to my mind the raw grey stone is still spectacular.

Much of the temple is covered in carvings, which are considered to be the story of the cosmos from the Buddhist point of view. They start with the normal world and wind on up all the way through to nirvana. The carvings deal with passion and desire, with reincarnation, and with punishment. They document in fine detail many aspects of Javanese life of the times, with carvings of elephants, ships, dancing girls, warriors and kings. On the upper levels, four hundred and thirty two Buddha images look out at you serene-faced, and higher still, another seventy-two Buddhas stare out from the latticed stupas. It's all decidedly magnificent.

One of the things I was battling with in Indonesia was the number of scare stories about theft. Of course, we in our western clothes on extended holiday must have looked like walking banks to a good percentage of the locals. Common sense was the key, and that meant, money belts, spreading funds through several 'safe' places and being generally wary of anything that sounded too good to be true. With all the scams that were going on, it paid to be suspicious, but I didn't like that – it felt as if I was tarring everyone with the same brush. Part of the problem was that we were still travelling in a group. This had its fun advantages but it did make us a target and I was increasingly aware that I would never really get the opportunity to spend time with locals who weren't sharks. Normally I enjoyed getting involved with local people – it's a wonderful way to learn and certainly easier on my own. A lone traveller does not come across as a threat, so genuine people are more open to you. I missed this, but could no longer decide just for myself. Jan was in full holiday mode, and she was enjoying the others. I was glad of the company they gave her, so came to the conclusion that for the moment group travel pros outweighed the cons.

We spent the next weeks meandering from one place of note to the next, from mainland Java, to Sumatra. The days blended into each other. Our buses took us through great rain forests, across kilometres of rice-growing paddy fields, and on through villages that reeked of dead and drying fish. We ate nasi goreng until it came out of our ears, though as we moved across Java and Sumatra there seemed to be more vegetables cooked in with the rice. Markets always had bunches of bananas and giant, very sweet pineapples. There was sweet creamy jackfruit and salaks too, the latter have a brown, almost snakeskin look to them and taste like a cross between strong dried walnut and apple. Thankfully it wasn't the season for durian so I wasn't going to make myself eat this fruit – its flesh has the reputation or smelling like baby's diarrhoea! We stayed in backpacker accommodation that varied from filthy dirty and generally grim, to clean, friendly and in stunning locations. The holiday rolled on, and slowly my back got stronger.

We arrived in the central Sumatran town of Bukkitingi at ten-thirty at night. Incredibly, our bus arrived nine hours early, but I really dislike arriving in a new town in the dark. It was another thing that made me feel vulnerable, and miss having the bike. On a bus, I just wasn't in control. We were due to meet up with a couple of friends I'd made while wandering around Borobadur, but as we were so late into the night we didn't disturb them. I was also concerned about Jan, who was ill. She had been suffering with an upset stomach for weeks and though stoic about it, long bus rides, unusual food and not enough to drink on a regular basis had been hard going for her.

That first night in Bukkitingi she started to feel really under the weather with muscle aches, a tinge of nausea, and fever. She was nothing like her usual energetic self and I got really worried about her, but as she became more ill she started to refuse any help. Justin, Lauren and I did what we could to keep her hydrated, thinking that she'd now picked up a pretty severe stomach upset, or that the one she had was peaking. She didn't want to eat and couldn't keep any food down when she tried. All she wanted was to be left alone. She could be quite stubborn and usually knew exactly what she wanted, so to begin with we tried to respect her wishes, but she just got worse. By the time we managed to persuade her to go to a doctor, she was in a mess. The local hospital looked clean and quite well organised, but Jan and I were in for a long wait. Above our heads large white bladed fans hung on two metre-long poles from the ceiling. The blades fluttered like giant moths on leashes and the poles that were acting as those leashes, wobbled and squeaked with the effort of slicing through the heavy air. The wait was OK though as we had a stroke of luck. There was a doctor who could speak English. I'd been getting worried that perhaps Jan had picked up malaria, the symptoms certainly seemed right and Jan had decided not to take prophylaxis. Dr Maun though, listened carefully, took blood tests and advised that it wasn't malaria. We never did discover what she had picked up but whatever it was, Dr Maun's medicine seemed to start to take the edge off.

Too soon, Jan decided that she wanted to be on the move. She was weak and tired very quickly, and it was then that I discovered how stubborn she really could be. Her tarot cards said to move on, but if we were going to go somewhere else, I thought it had to be to somewhere she could convalesce properly. If it had been me, I'd have stayed put for some more days, but Jan was insistent and sometimes downright grumpy in her insistence to get going. We decided that there could be no better place to get well than a small island off the south coast of Sumatra. Nias has a reputation for being a surfer's paradise, and we reckoned that if nothing else, the sight of all the surfer blokes would put a smile back on her face. Justin and Lauren had already left for the island by the time Jan was ready to travel, and said that they would look out for a good place for us to stay.

It was a good job they had. The journey was a mini-nightmare with Jan being ever more irrational and increasingly edgy. She snapped at us, grumped at the locals, didn't trust anyone we met, and on top of all that, the three buses we had to take were in grim condition and very overcrowded. The drivers though, all knew their stuff, and when we passed a major accident that involved a bus and a logging truck, we were thankful that we had struck lucky.

We arrived at the fishing port of Sibolga in dark humidity. There were no streetlights, the moon wasn't even able to force a faint glow through the heavy clouds overhead, and the place reeked of dead fish and open drains. With not a hotel in sight, and Jan too tired by now to do more than snarl at everyone, we were gently hassled by the local touts. One in particular spoke good English and at that moment I couldn't have wished for better. He was really informative about accommodation and gave us details of the ferry across to the island, but Jan didn't like him, didn't trust him and didn't want anything to do with him. Then it started to rain.

Faced with the choice of trusting the tout or stumbling around in the dark and rain, hoping that we might find somewhere to stay, we went with the tout. He took us to a small hotel just by the ferry jetty, and then told us that the next ferry left in a day's time. With Jan's current state, it was just the right thing to hear, as she was just about falling over with fatigue. But she didn't see that at all. As far as she was concerned the trip had gone bad and everything was wrong. She no longer wanted to eat Indonesian food, she was feeling nauseous all the time and she veered from being angry to simply wanting to cry. It was unlike her and I veered between total sympathy and annoyed frustration at how obtuse and cantankerous she was being.

Thankfully she slept well, but the next day we didn't manage to find any European food. I also couldn't find her any antihistamine tablets, which I hoped would help combat the nausea. That evening, as we forced our way through mosquitoes that flew so deep they were almost at plague level, Jan heard someone playing a guitar. She loved music, and an element of joy had suddenly disappeared when a freak wave on a Lombok beach drowned her walkman. The guitarist knew what he was doing and I cheered a little as I saw Jan begin to relax for the first time in days.

In the morning she was the brightest I'd seen her for nearly two weeks. I arranged tickets for the night ferry over to Nias, and bought two weeks' supply of mossie coils. Back at the hotel, Jan was hanging out for an ice cream. A positive sign, though I didn't like to think what water the ice cream had been made with or how well it had been kept frozen. At least she wanted to eat something.

I'd made friends with a lad called Pantu, who had been hanging around the hotel, obviously wanting to earn a little money. A skinny lad, he seemed all knees and elbows, had shaggy longish hair and a smile that almost split his thin face in two when he grinned, which he did often. He also had more energy than anyone had a right to have in the hot humidity of Sibolga. I told him that I was looking for antihistamine, and I explained what it was. "No problem Mr Sam," he said. Jan, Pantu and I piled aboard a bekak, a three-wheel scooter taxi, and set off into the town centre, with Pantu leaning out of the side yelling directions to the driver. He took us straight to a chemist that I wouldn't have had a hope of finding on my own, and then to the bus station so we could find out about buses for when we came back from the island. Pantu earned his wage that day.

That night, as we were preparing to catch the ferry, the wind rose, a storm rolled in and we knew that we were in for a very rough crossing. The thought of the twelve hour crossing in this weather put Jan into her determined, 'don't hassle me, I'm going to make it if it kills me' mode. This mood wasn't fun to be around, and I just hoped that Nias was going to give her what she needed.

Fortunately, the boat was clean even smelling clean, and our tiny cabin was well ventilated, which would be vital to keep seasickness at bay. The two of us crashed and I suspect that though the storm was still raging outside, the seasickness tablets we had both taken helped us sleep though the worst of it. There are moments in a day where you can feel no other emotion than gratitude.

By morning the storm had blown itself out and patchy sunshine lit the green low-lying island of Nias – it felt like the start of something good. We were aiming for the village of Lagundi, which has one of the best surfing waves in the southern hemisphere, but how to get there? There were two options, each of us on the back of mopeds, or share the back of a truck. We opted for the truck and bargained our price with the driver. It's vital to do this because even if you have an idea of roughly how much the fare should be, if you don't set the price at the start, then you could have a very nasty surprise and loads of hassle at the end of the ride.

As we climbed aboard, two lads hopped on too. "Are you Sam?" one of them asked. Robin and Marcus worked at the hostel where Justin and Lauren were staying and they'd asked the lads to come down to the port to look out for us. Nice.

We made it no more than a kilometre out of the port, when the truck suddenly stopped and the driver turned off his engine. The crafty sod wanted to double the fare! There were ten of us on the truck and seven didn't care. They were quite happy to pay extra, but for me it was the difference between eating three meals or not. I also didn't like the idea of being taken for an idiot, and that was how the truck driver made me feel. The other two passengers felt the same way, and we argued, they with all the arm waving, passion and enthusiasm of the French, while I put on my stubborn but terribly British face and voice. The combination worked, and we were soon underway, at the original fare.

Lagundi is a beautiful horseshoe-shaped bay with a great beach. On one side of the bay, gentle waves roll in, and on the other, a magnificently curling wave speeds in, with a dramatic white crested break. Accommodation is split along the same lines – a quieter area of wood and palm chalets where the waves roll in, and the brightly coloured and vibrant village of losmen (local 'hotels') above the main break. We chose to stay with Justin and Lauren, who were glad to see us, especially as we had brought sunshine with us. They had had days of rain, and the storm of the night before had made them wonder if it was worth staying any longer. It made sense for us to get a room on the quieter section of the beach so that Jan could get some real rest,

but also from my budget point of view – if we weren't living in a losmen in the middle of the party town further round, then I was sure that I'd spend less of my budget on beer!

How many versions of paradise can there be? Gili Trawangan had been paradise, but so was this, just very different. Over the following lazy days we ate fresh fruit, played cards, wandered the beach, body surfed in the warm sea, read books, watched the surfers hurtling in on the break, and enjoyed the magnificent greens and blues around us. We feasted on fresh tuna and for the first time I tried shark. It's very meaty but does taste of fish, though I wasn't sure why I thought it might not. Jan took the chance to have long lie-ins, and was soon ready to party again. I felt a bit of an old mother as I watched how quickly she flung herself into the life up in the surfer town, but she seemed far happier and that was brilliant to see.

One day I realised that my Swiss Army knife had gone missing from my room. This was a major blow as a good knife like this is a fantastic piece of kit when you are travelling. No one knew anything about it, so I offered a reward. I didn't hold out much hope of getting it back but knew that it would be a very long time before I was somewhere I could get a new one.

I woke in the morning feeling quite down. I was missing Birgit, the knife was still gone and I was also having doubts about my back being strong enough to ride the bike. On top of that, I'd hardly seen anything of Jan for days and I had a nasty feeling that she was going to come and tell me that she was going to travel on with someone else. Perhaps I'd been over protective of her when she was ill, and somehow I'd annoyed her. Travelling with someone else, or even other people, made life on the road so much more complicated, but perhaps it was still the right thing for both of us to be doing. Time would tell.

Suddenly, everyone felt that it was time to migrate again. We took last swims, and my knife mysteriously turned up through an intermediary. We ate last meals and bathed for the last time with the mandis. A mandi is a large container of water from which you scoop water to wash yourself – it helps conserve water and you still get perfectly clean. We might as well have not bothered though; the days of sunshine had dried the road to the port and as the truck clattered its way back, we all collected a thick layer of dust.

Then we were back into 'civilisation'! People, noise, dirt, market stalls, staring faces and flies but, happily, not a jot of hassle. While waiting for the ferry to get under way I sat on the jetty with a local man. He was a sign of the developing times. Until  very recently, Nias had been a well-kept surfers' secret, but the word was now out and tourism was on the up. My new friend was telling me that he worked for the Nias water board and that his task was to get fresh filtered water into all of the villages, including Lagundi. This was good news for the locals as it would increase both trade and health for them, but I was glad we had visited while the bay was still something of a sleepy backwater.

Chapter 5

The Bag Thief

"Twenty years from now you will be more disappointed by the things that you didn't do, than by the ones you did do. So throw off the bowlines. Sail away from the safe harbor. Catch the trade winds in your sails. Explore. Dream. Discover."

Mark Twain

I wanted to see orang-utangs in the wild, but that wasn't going to be an easy thing to do. They are solitary creatures who steer clear of humans as much as possible. Humans hunt and trap them, or they kill them by clearing away their natural habitat to plant crops, or to harvest the timber in Indonesia's forests. Young orang-utangs are captured and if they survive they are sold into a sort of slavery. This practice has been illegal for many years but it still goes on. The babies are amazingly cute and behave in a very child-like fashion, but the problem is that though they are manageable and cute when they are young, they grow tall and strong when they are older. At which point many are killed or just dumped.

I had a quirky personal connection to these apes, as a result of the Indonesian and Malay language. My surname means 'man of the wooded valley'. In Bahasia, orang-utang means 'person, or man of the forest'. They are also balding and hairy, which completes the connection. There are many myths and legends about them, including carrying off pretty girls into the forest. I wondered if this was where the idea for Tarzan originally came from.

The village of Bukit Lawang sits on the edge of the Gunung Leuser National Park in Sumatra, which is home to the largest population of wild orang-utangs in the world. But that doesn't make it any easier to see these superb creatures. The park is wild dense jungle, veined with fast flowing rivers. It's also home of a project that aims to rehabilitate rescued or dumped orphans, so they can be released back into the wild.

We arrived by bus and as usual, a score of helpers and accommodation touts leapt forward to meet us. It's instant hassle and we found that it paid to have a plan when arriving in a more popular tourist destination such as this. Usually, we would just ease our way firmly through the touts, walk a few hundred yards away, and then get our bearings. You are made to feel something like a politician must feel when surrounded by a score of the pushiest paparazzi in existence. I couldn't blame the locals for the strength of the hassle, as competition for the tourist buck is the name of the game, and even though quite a lot of tourists come to Bukit Lawang, the village itself gives the true picture of the financial state of the locals – they are poor.

This time though, I had a new plan. We got off the bus and I explained that we had come to stay with relations of mine. The touts looked totally confused for a moment, stared at me, took in the hairy and bald bits, then the red tint to my hair, and fits of laughter pealed out. They parted to let us through and we strode off, shouts of 'Orang-Utan' followed us up the rough dirt lane away from the bus station. For the rest of our stay people pointed at me, nudged each other and, giggling, muttered my new name. Indonesians were fascinated by my hairy arms and chest as their bodies are virtually hairless. And children would ask to stroke my arms, before running away shrieking with laughter.

Besides the chance to see orang-utangs, Gunung Leuser offered the chance to float down the river. Not by boat, but some enterprising local has taken up the idea of inflating truck inner tubes, which could be rented by the day. The plan is to set off from the village and float down through the forest, and at a certain point in the river you can paddle ashore to catch the bus back up again. The timing has to be good to do that or you face a long walk. The few minor rapids were easily manageable, though further down there were rapids that would be a major worry in a tube. It's hot and humid in the jungle and tubing the river as it wends its way along through the tangled wildness is a magical thing to do. Its cooler on the water and more peaceful than on dry land.

But we'd come for the orang-utangs, and to get to them we had to cross the river, and then trek right into the jungle along a tan-coloured beaten earth path that wound its way through great stands of trees. We were in a group, but the sounds of the jungle all around us had an eerie quality. Birds called, and somewhere in the distance we could hear a creature that sounded as if it was wailing over some tremendous loss. The air smelled with ever changing variations of dank, musty, rich scents. It was still hot under the trees but nothing like as much as it had been in the village. The air though was less humid, as if the trees were sucking moisture out of the air. Great shafts of light made their way through the canopy to form irregular, soft-edged pools of light on the sparse vegetation at ground level. Every so often one of these beams of light would angle across the path and temporarily illuminate, in a shimmering spotlight, whoever was moving along it. The trek wasn't for the faint-hearted and I was glad that I had my boots on, though a couple of wealthier Indonesians in our group were not dressed for a jungle trek at all. The man was simply immaculate, with black business shoes, black trousers and a pale pink, open neck shirt. He was slipping and sliding along, and it didn't take long before he started to look as travel-worn as we were, while his wife struggled in her pretty summer dress and two-inch heels!

The rehabilitation of the apes is quite a process. When a new orang-utang arrives at the centre, it's put into quarantine where its health is checked over. They pick up a lot of illnesses from their contact with humans, we were told. Many have forgotten how to climb trees, or were taken at such a young age that they never learned, so they even have to be taught this basic survival skill. Orang-utangs live in the trees for most of their lives and sleep in nests that they make, sometimes on a daily basis, as they move through the treetops. They feed on fruit, shoots, nuts and tree bark, or insects and eggs too, when they find them. Small mammals are also on the menu from time to time, if they are slow enough to get caught!

The centre teaches the primates to fend for themselves in as many ways as possible, with the emphasis on getting them back into the jungle for good. It can be a slow process in which it's hard to keep the balance between teaching them to survive, and keeping them alive while they are being taught. Once they are fit enough to be released, they are set free into the jungle, but each day they have a feeding time up on a platform in the trees. They are fed milk and bananas only, and apparently the monotony of this diet, though healthy, encourages them to find food for themselves. When they have become comfortable with feeding themselves, they rarely if ever, pay a visit to the feeding platform. I'd read that wild orang-utang would visit the reserve, and that it was thought that they interacted with the orphans, helping them to adapt to their return to the wild.

As we approached the platform, the surrounding jungle came alive with these, ginger-coloured, long-armed creatures crashing through the trees. They did so with such ease that it could have been in slow motion. There were about fifteen of them, and to my surprise, they all looked quite different. Age accounted for some of the difference, but just as telling were the facial features and their hair. Some had hair that was quite long and others even had beards! All seemed to have different characters too. There was a fool who was whizzing around showing off to us. One of them seemed sad; he sat on the edge of the platform looking at us and making E.T-like finger motions in our direction. There was a serious one who looked down at us with an expression of great disdain – he only needed a monocle to finish the effect. And there was a greedy one who stuffed ten bananas into his mouth until it was absolutely bulging and even then managed to cram in a couple more that hung from his mouth like a set of Dracula's fangs.

I could have sat watching for hours, but once they'd eaten their fill, most of the orang-utang reached up to grab an overhanging branch and used that to spring back into the trees again. Not all did though, and one must have been a highway robber in a past life.

We set off back along the path, only to find another group of people coming towards us. This time they were all Indonesians and totally inappropriately dressed for the jungle. We moved off the path to let them pass. One lady, who looked dressed for the Ascot races, was clearly struggling and with her handbag clasped in front of her was daintily picking her way around muddy puddles and over the roots that fanned out across sections of the path. Her handbag was the size and shape of a lever arch file, with two large brass clasps along the top edge which gleamed when she passed through a beam of light. She was about ten paces behind the rest of her group and, as we were waiting for her to go past, an adult orang-utang landed out of the trees onto the path in front of her. She started in surprise, and dropped her handbag onto the path. She seemed glued to the spot and though she looked like she wanted to scream, not a sound came out of her open mouth. The ape stood on his legs, and with one hand on his hip, looked her up and down. Then, with surprising speed, he grabbed the handbag and leapt to the top of a tree trunk, hooked the toes of his feet around the tree trunk, and waved the handbag at the lady, chattering as if he was saying, 'So, what are you going to do about it, eh?' He then used both his hands to open the clasps on the bag, as if he knew exactly what

he was doing, and he carefully took each item out, one by one, inspected it and discarded it. Once he had finished, he frizzbied the bag off into the bush, and with a parting glance that was decidedly triumphant, swung off through the trees chattering to himself. I swear that his chatter sounded more like laughter! The poor woman looked quite traumatised.

Finally, we were in the port of Medan and I wanted to find out for myself if it would have been possible to get the bike on a boat to Penang. No bike of course, but it was important for me to find out for my own sanity, so I went straight into the ferry office. "I have a foreign registered 800cc motorcycle that I want to get to Penang with me on the ferry. Is that possible?" The man behind the counter looked at me as if I was stupid and said, "Yes of course it's possible. When do you want to go – today or on the next sailing?" A couple of beers did their best to act as a consolation prize that night.

Once we'd made the ferry crossing across the Strait of Malacca to Penang, Jan and I were keen to get on to Singapore. The group split up in Penang as some elected to head north, some to the Cameron

Highlands, and some to catch the train straight on to Thailand, but we needed to get to the bike in Singapore. Perkins had already advised me that Libby was in storage in the docks and the longer she stayed there, the more it was costing. I was nervous, but keen to see if I could ride again. It was now over three months since I'd slipped my discs and in the circumstances I felt pretty good. Jan didn't put me under any pressure, but I could see that the uncertainty was affecting her too – this was now just as much her dream that was hanging in the balance as it was mine.

Singapore is a strange place. Even more so for those that have been living and travelling through a Third World of jungles and villages, plus ramshackle cities and towns that seemed to have been thrown together, rather than designed and planned. There are also some very particular Singaporean rules. These were quite amusing in a way, but also felt a bit Big Brother-ish. 'No Spitting' I could live with and after having experienced the morning ritual of the hawking and spitting of the Chinese in Penang, would be rather nice and certainly more peaceful. But, 'No Chewing Gum' was going to be a pain. Ever since I'd broken my jaw and four teeth in Africa, I'd been a habitual chewer of gum. I'd started with the thought that if I'd been chewing gum when I'd had the accident, the rubbery wedge would have been enough of a shock absorber that I might have got away with just bruises and a sore jaw. It had become an addictive habit, so I smuggled a couple of weeks' supply of gum in with me, hoping that this time when I went though customs, I wouldn't get checked! I wasn't, and spent the next days as a secret gum chewer.

Immigration gave me loads of hassle though. At every border crossing I'd had to date, the officials hadn't liked the look of my passport and this time the officials were really picky. The problem was quite simple. Whoever had issued my passport in the UK had such lousy handwriting that no one could really read my name. I'd been on such a short timetable to get on the road to Africa that my passport had only arrived a month before I was due to set off. There'd been no chance to try to get it sorted, because it had spent the remaining time doing the rounds of the Embassies of Egypt, Sudan and Ethiopia. The hassle I kept having just underlined what sort of trouble I'd have been in if I'd had a Third World passport with the same problem! Her Majesty's crest still meant a lot out on the road.

For a city in South East Asia, Singapore is clean. The streets are swept. There are very few potholes. The buildings range from pockets  of old and traditional, to gleaming towers of glass and concrete in the city centre. Traffic obeyed the rules, and even stopped when lights were on red. There were shopping malls, and high-priced hotels and restaurants. Vehicles never looked as if they were about to expire in a cloud of greasy black smoke, and none were held together with loops of galvanised wire stitching. The city hustled and bustled in an air that actually tasted clean after the sticky, smelly air in Medan and Kuala Lumpur. But after the last months of gentle freedom in a pretty green land, the city felt claustrophobic and I felt like a blot on the landscape in my aging traveller's clothes. I was always clean, and so were my clothes, but from the stares I got from the locals, I can't have looked it.

The only place I didn't feel like some sort of scab on civilisation was in Chinatown, where things were more rough and ready. This is a flamboyant renegade in comparison to the rest of the city and I had no difficulty in imagining that there would be rats on the streets at night-time. Jan had decided that she wanted to get her nose pierced and had found a place in Chinatown where the prices were good and the jeweller would do the piercing. What she hadn't expected was that she'd be shown into the jeweller's workshop to have it done. It was rather like stepping back into the Middle Ages. The grimy stone steps were worn down in the middle, from years of foot traffic. This jeweller made everything by hand, and the dingy, low-ceilinged workshop was full of amazing instruments that hung from ancient wooden racks. Some looked as if they would be perfect instruments of torture! The jeweller sat at a rough wooden bench, whose filthy surface was cluttered with tools, metal shavings, a magnifying glass on a stand, and a plate of half-eaten food. The jeweller's fat-fingered hands looked as if he'd washed them in boot polish and his fingernails had black grime caked under them. It was these hands that shoved a large needle, which hadn't been disinfected first, though Jan's nose. His thumb then went up the inside of her nostril, and the stud was pushed through. She winced in pain but not a tear came to her eyes. I think she was too stunned by the matter of fact, almost brutal way it was done, to say or do anything.

The agent for Perkins Shipping confirmed that my bike had arrived and told me what I needed to do to get her out of the harbour. I'd organised insurance in Kuala Lumpur – just £5 for 6 months' third party cover. This hadn't been an easy exercise as the size of the bike was not something that the local insurance companies seemed to be used to, but in the end, the South East Asia Insurance Company sorted me out. I also had to have a confirmation permit from the Singapore AA. I found that out from a surprise note left by Mike and Sally for me at the Poste Restante. The last time I had seen them was in Namibia, when they were about to set sail for South America with their BMW R80GS. I'd ridden through Egypt, Sudan and Ethiopia with them, and they'd been through the Americas in the time I'd been in Australasia. They were now in S.E. Asia, running about a month ahead of me. I was sad to have missed them, but it was typical of the duo that they'd left a helping note for me. I was chuffed that their trip was working so well, and wondered if I'd meet up with them anywhere in Thailand or Malaysia.

As Singapore is so organised, the hunt for the documents I needed was a pleasure. In fact, the documents were a good excuse to get out and explore. Tree-lined streets in the areas surrounding the city centre were a pleasure to be in; still clean, but they felt less hard-edged. Bougainvillea abounds and palm trees rustled their unique sound in the breeze. It was easy to find a shady side of the street to walk on, and the AA on the River Valley Road were incredibly helpful. Nothing was a problem and they gave me a giant Singapore AA sticker to be fixed to the bike. With the paperwork done, and a hostel found with just enough space in their back yard for me to get Libby off the road and we were set.

The docks were enormous. Singapore is a major hub for shipping, with cargoes heading off to just about every part of the world from its wharves. Like the city, the docks are neat, tidy and organised, so I was surprised when I was taken to Libby to find that she had been dumped uncovered in the corner of a yard. Around her were rusting, twenty-foot long bundles of concrete reinforcing rods. Wooden pallets were stacked right next to her, in a wobbling pile that made me glad I'd arrived before some distracted forklift driver could topple them over. But, though filthy, Libby was fine and my luggage boxes didn't look as if they had been broken into. My loose luggage was also safe, having been kindly taken care of by the agent.

The agent and his team took really good care of me too and, while I was completing their paperwork, they had kept me supplied with glasses of freshly squeezed mango, papaya and orange juice. But they had bad news for me – the storage fee for the bike came to one hundred and fourteen dollars, which was double what I'd been expecting. I couldn't complain though, at least the bike was safe.

Customs arrived, eventually, and with a bored air the officer rubber-stamped the inevitable reams of paperwork. Then all of a sudden, I was alone. It all felt a bit of an anti-climax after my other harbour adventures. But now was the moment of truth – could I ride? I had an image of my German physio's face looking at me with a 'tut tut' expression, and another of the doctor's with a 'You're an idiot' expression on his.

I poured a couple of litres of fuel from the bottle I'd been carrying into her tank, rolled Libby off the centre stand and with helmet on, gently swung my leg over. My back twinged as I went through this now unnatural action and I realised that I should have been practising the motion. I could have told everyone that I'd taken up tai chi! I pushed the starter button and Libby fired up at the first go. Black smoke belched out of her exhaust but she was running smoothly so I wasn't worried. I conducted my own version of a pre-flight check as I readied for the off. Each thing that I was doing, checking or getting the feel of, normally happened without me thinking about it. But now, after three months away from the bike, each thing became an individual item, and as each was checked off my mental list, the time to ride came closer. I had mixed feelings – part of me hungered for the chance to ride again and part of me was scared. I was determined that I could and would ride but a nasty niggle said 'You're doing it too soon!'

Gear in and throttle open, we moved hesitantly across the shiny train tracks in the yard, easing round multi-coloured stacks of containers and then through shallow puddles of water holding perfect reflections of the surrounding ships, sheds and offices. I passed a first red and white striped barrier where the uniformed guard just gave me a lazy wave.

At the second the barrier was down. Around me streamed dockworkers on foot or on bicycles. Vendors of food had stalls set up along the wall and a queue of people stood outside the gates looking in. A guard came towards me, obviously agitated and rattled at me in a language I didn't understand at all. He spoke fast and as he wasn't getting any reaction from me, except a tentative smile and a 'Hello' in greeting, he started to shout. By this time I was off the bike and the guard, who was shorter than me, spat as he shouted up at me. "Off, Off, Off!" he yelled, with an ever more red face. Then, "Out!" he shouted, pointing at the panniers as he did so. The penny dropped. I unlocked the boxes and lifted open the lids. "Out! Out! Out!" he shouted at me again, making it very clear that I had to empty the panniers. I wasn't happy at doing this, as it would mean that all my belongings would be spread on the pavement around me, and by now a crowd had collected. I worried that in the confusion some vital piece of kit would go missing, but I had no choice.

Out came my cooking pans, my plate, my cooker, some pasta, some soup mixes, a couple of tins of tuna, my mixed herbs and curry powder, and finally, plastic tubs of spare parts and inner tubes. The guard picked through my belongings as if he were shopping at a flea market. Each item was handled, turned around and shaken before being dumped back onto the ground. Then he got to my mixed herbs, and I thought he was going to blow a gasket. With the lid off the jar and a pinch of the contents between his fingers, he was shouting excitedly. I simply could not work out what the problem was. One moment he was waving the jar at me, shouting as he did so, and the next he was jabbing a finger into my chest, still shouting, and spittle flying as he did so.

The excitement had attracted an officer. He came hurrying over and listened to my guard jabbering at him. The guard's finger stabbed in my direction. The officer took the jar from him, took a pinch of the fading green vegetation inside, and lifted that to his nose. Then, looking at the guard he said in perfect but scornful English, "It's – just – mixed – herbs". Once said, he turned on his heel and went back the way he'd come. My guard looked totally deflated for a moment, ignored me, and then brashly pushed his way through the crowd, shouting at them this time. I'd obviously been 'fortunate' enough to get the guard who had no sense of smell.

The fuss and bother had been great – once I'd realised that I wasn't going to be in trouble. I'd been standing there with thoughts of someone swapping the contents of my jar to something dangerous, if I was arrested. There were stories on the travellers' grapevine of this happening and in some instances it had got very nasty for those who had been caught. I loaded up in a tense peace – an invisible line that no one could cross had apparently been drawn around the bike and I. Normally everything gets packed away as a sort of 3D jigsaw puzzle. Every space gets used and things that would rub against each other and cause damage from the vibrations of the road, would be carefully separated. Not this time, I just wanted to get under way, so crammed everything in as best I could. I was worried that if I lingered, something dire might kick off with my guard. He was obviously furious that I had caused him such loss of face.

Libby seemed horribly big as I eased out into the traffic. She felt heavy and for the first mile, I felt as if I was no longer born to be riding a bike, but by the time I got back to the hostel, I knew it was going to be worth the risk of riding on. We planned that for the next weeks we'd be riding short days, and I was glad we were going to be heading north through Malaysia. From what I'd seen of the roads so far, they weren't going to be too hard on the bones. As Jan and I talked about it that night, we could both see the advantages of shorter riding days; we would be encouraged to explore more wherever we stopped.

That night Jan gave me a hand to clean Libby, and we did so with an air of quiet teamwork. It was almost as if by doing this, Jan was taking part ownership of the bike and the trip on it. At that moment, it was exactly the right feeling.

After we'd explored Singapore, there was one final thing we wanted to do before we moved north. In our own scruffy, oily and battered way we were tourists, and a visit to the historic Raffles Hotel for a drink or an ice cream was a very touristy thing to do, but so what? That was until we saw the prices! After reading the menu, we just enjoyed being in the cool, green shuttered, starkly white building that down the decades, had seen so many adventuring characters strike deals, party or simply rest in its rattan chairs.

Chapter 6

Hi-Tec Mummy

'The soul of a journey is liberty, perfect liberty, to think, to feel, and do just as one pleases.'

William Hazlitt

Sometimes, one of the paradoxes attached to travelling by bike is that the very freedom of doing it can become a curse. I could set off when I wanted to and I could keep going until I wanted to stop, but if I was really enjoying the ride and there was still plenty of daylight left, I'd sometimes keep going. But that meant I didn't stop to look at all the things I should have. I'd be enjoying the ride, but missing things to the same extent as travelling by bus – in Indonesia and southern Malaysia it had been a major source of frustration as the bus swooped past sites and things of interest without the ability to get out for a look-see. With that thought in my mind, Jan, Libby and I headed north.

The Singaporean side of the border was decidedly civilised with a special channel for motorbikes, which speeded things up no end, and the Malaysian officials couldn't have been more courteous or friendly. It was almost as if the bike had given us a higher rank than the backpackers. We obviously had wealth and therefore, respect was apparently appropriate – it helped that Jan's dreadlocks were tucked away under her helmet!

Once we were through the Strait of Johore we got lost, were given directions by three blokes hanging out of the back of the truck in front of us and got on the right road only to find fifty kilometres of road works to deal with. Sandy or muddy diversions took us swinging off to the left of the road for stretches that challenged my back horribly. I didn't dare ask Jan how she was doing on this, her first taste of the road by bike. I had hoped that we would be able to ease her into it gently. But by the end of the day we both agreed that the worst thing about the one hundred and fifty-kilometre ride was that our backsides ached miserably. Both of us were skinny and neither of us had the sorts of muscles that regular biking builds up on the backside to protect it from hours of sitting in one place.

Once clear of the roadworks we cruised along perfect asphalt, through one rubber or palm nut oil plantation after another. Tall, regimented rows of trees stood right up to the roadsides, so close that we could easily see the sloping cuts that had been made in the rubber trees with a small bowl at the base of each cut to collect the latex sap as it bled from the trees.

That night we met Michael and his two daughters. Michael was a lanky, silver-blond Frenchman who had once been a high-level businessman. His wife had died giving birth to his youngest daughter who was now just two years old. His other daughter was twelve. He'd been so shocked by what had happened that suddenly realising that none of us can be certain what will happen to us next he'd sold his business, bought two bicycles and had headed to Asia with the girls. They had been cycling  around Malaysia and Thailand for months. They were kitted out on the cheap, and in fact their bicycle panniers were no more than wire supermarket baskets that had been strapped to racks. The youngest rode on a second seat on Michael's bike, but Emiline rode her own bicycle. They were one of the closest family units I'd ever met; they obviously loved and supported each other and this journey together was simply making that bond stronger. I felt privileged to have been able to spend some time with such happy and aware people.

That night was also planning time for us. Our Townsville discussions seemed like a lifetime away and with all the uncertainty of the past months it simply hadn't felt right to get down to the nitty gritty until this moment. To my delight, Jan got stuck straight in and for a second time, I felt sure that we were going to travel well together. She didn't blink an eye when the figures stacked up. My own budget was working out at ten pounds sterling per day for the next ten months. In the UK that would have bought me three pints of beer and a bag of fish and chips but here it had to cover fuel, food, accommodation, adventure costs, shipping the bike, visa costs, any insurances and taxes, and hopefully it would still run to a beer every now and again. It was going to be slim going but I was sure that it was manageable, if nothing went wrong.

There's a wide variety of accommodation for the budget traveller in Malaysia and we decided to try as many types as we could. We stayed at 'farm stays' which worked nicely, though none were more than smallholdings, and we kipped in hostels set up for backpackers. These were almost always noisy but they worked nicely too and some of them were attractive beach huts. The key issue for all was that they had to have off-road parking for the bike and Malaysia turned out to be well endowed with that.

My favourites were the Chinese hotels. They have a spectacularly distinctive character all of their own. They always had parking, as they seemed to cater for travelling businessmen on a budget, but frequently the dividing walls between the rooms stopped short of the ceiling by about twenty centimetres. This meant that enormous but decidedly ineffective ceiling fans could service all the rooms, which cut costs, but also meant that the rooms were worse to try to sleep in than a backpackers' dormitory. The walls gave the illusion of privacy, so guests did whatever they wanted. If a couple were making love, we could all hear it. If someone farted or belched, was grinding their teeth or having a nightmare, we shared the results. But in the first light of day it got worse.

Great lung-ripping, hacking coughs would echo over the tops of the walls. Rasping, gut-turning hawking would follow with an enthusiasm that would have won medals for effort at the Olympics. Then, seconds later, the sound of pressurised phlegm spurting through pursed lips at a rate of knots, would precede the sounds of these gloopy projectiles hitting the tin spittoons that are always strategically placed in Chinese hotel rooms. Next, great round farts would rip out, and these would finally be followed by blissful sighs of satisfaction. It was the Chinese dawn chorus and we certainly didn't need an alarm clock!

I liked the restaurants in these hotels. The staff always had their favourite customers, though we were never destined to become such. Our food was served with such ill grace that it could have been a fat Basil Fawlty in a stained vest smacking down the plates of chow mein, or whatever was on the menu that day. But I didn't mind because mealtimes were great for people-watching. The Chinese liked to shout at each other in shrill raucous voices and I liked to linger over my food to watch what was going on. I enjoyed trying to work out what the men around us did. Was this one a salesman for rubber plantation machinery? Was that one a buyer of fish from the many fishing villages that we'd seen dotting the coastline? Was this one a truck driver and was that one a door-to-door salesman? In a way it was frustrating not to know if our guesses were correct but we did get the door-to-door chappie right. His suitcase was full of plastic kitchen cleaning equipment and we caught a glimpse of him failing to sell any to the stubborn-faced hotel owner.

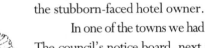

In one of the towns we had a wake up call. The council's notice board, next to their tourist map of the area, was covered in graphic photos of vehicle accidents and their victims. As with my friends in Darwin, no punches had been pulled.

A few days up the coast we realised that there was a definite pattern to the weather each day. The early hours were the coolest and driest; by midday, it was stinking hot and very humid, each time we had to slow down we'd be dripping inside our leather jackets; by mid afternoon it always rained hard. Visibility would be down to just a few metres. The few times that we'd got our day's planning wrong, or had stopped to look at too many things along the way, it was very edgy riding. Sometimes though, it was a simple toss up – see, experience and enjoy the sights, or make it to the destination in the dry.

There were times we'd arrive somewhere in the dark and heavy gloom of an imminent storm, thanking our lucky stars that we'd made it. Sometimes there'd not be a breath of wind, as if life had stood still or had taken cover before the skies could open. We'd hurry inside, eat, wash and settle down in safety for the night. The rain would then blast down and if we'd chosen a place with a corrugated iron roof, the thundering sound of rain on iron sheet would blank out the rest of the world in deafening waves as if it were not rain coming down but millions of tiny nails being poured on us by the bucket-load. If there was a bar to hand, Jan would scurry over to check it out, leaving me to get on with writing my journal, or writing letters, whilst conserving my budget in the dry. If the hostel was naturally gloomy in the morning then we'd plan to move on but too often the bright sunshine of the new day would show the newly washed place in such an attractive light that at the last minute we'd end up staying another night. The bike gave us this flexibility and I was chuffed to have some sort of control back again.

As we headed northwards along the coast, the vegetation became less cultivated. There weren't so many plantations and the villages, or kampongs, were more spaced out and ever more rag-tag, though the road was still good. Each bridge we crossed had a collection of fishing boats clustered underneath and as we passed through the kampongs we could have bought fish that was just plucked from the sea.

Jan woke me up one morning to say, "Sam, Happy Birthday!" I'd been lying half-asleep listening to the world waking up around our bamboo cabin. The breeze had been rustling the dried palm leaves on the roof, and below the cabin a goat was breakfasting. I could hear it ripping out chunks of whatever vegetation was surviving down there, then the rhythmic chomping of its teeth mangling the food. I'd just heard a coconut hit the ground outside with a thump, and was lazily thinking that the day felt like it was going to be a good one, but I'd forgotten that it was my birthday. Jan treated me to breakfast and had even made me a card. A great day was about to roll.

The odd thing was, except for the fact that it felt like a great day, no one spectacular thing happened. We'd both slept well and eaten well. Neither of us had colds or stomach upsets and my back felt like I had no problem at all. The bike felt good, sounded just right and she seemed to be floating along a road in almost perfect condition, without much help from me, almost as if she knew where she was going and that as it was my birthday, she was giving me the present of an easy ride. Jan was in a good mood too, and she even seemed to have mastered navigating, with her left and right hand problem not interfering – a few days into the trip she'd told me that she struggled with remembering which was which! Roadside flowers made a cheerful contrast to the usual dark greens, and no chickens or dogs ran out in front of us all day. We found petrol when we needed it and a roadside snack bar with great food at lunchtime. The rain stayed away and we cruised at a gentle, road-eating, scenery-watching, ninety kilometres an hour. Life felt absolutely marvellous.

To round the day off, we found a magic place to stay in a town called Kota Bharu. 'Mummy's Hi Tec Hostel' was a gem with a weird name. It had been run for decades by a woman called 'Mummy', and yes, she liked to be a surrogate mother to those on the road. But we were told that she'd been a mother with a wicked twinkle in her eye. She'd recently died and had left her wooden hostel to continue to provide a haven for travellers. Flowering shrubs burst out from just about every nook and cranny around the house, whose rambling lopsided wooden walls had been witness to many a party and a lot of laughter over the years. The walls in fact staggered out from Mummy's original four-roomed house in the form of extensions that had been almost casually tacked on each time more space had been needed. Inside, none of the rough wooden floors was level and even the steps seemed to be cut off at half height in some places. The lounge was filled with battered, over-stuffed sofas and ancient armchairs. But Mummy had been a real character and when she had been alive there should have been a sign hanging over the door that stated, 'Beware all young men that enter this place'. Mummy's sexual appetite was reputed to have been voracious. As a reminder of her conquests she had a special notice board, and each young chap that she had somehow enticed into her bed was recorded there with a passport photo. The memories must have kept her very much alive in her latter years, though Kumar who with a friend had taken over running the place, said to me one day, "Age? That never stopped her!"

I liked Kumar straight away. He was a tall, skinny man with a hooknose and a shock of jet-black hair that looked as if it had been styled on a 1970s pop star. He had a kind and gentle manner, treating all the guests with friendly respect and people warmed to him fast. In time I also saw that he was a very good judge of character and it was this ability that allowed him to be so open with people, without being taken advantage of more than he wanted to be. Some people tried to do just that and he treated them with amused tolerance. Kumar also had a phenomenal memory and was like a sponge for any news about life outside Malaysia. His ambition was to travel the world and I hoped if I were to meet him as a visitor to my own country, that I would be just as welcoming as he was to us.

Mummy's held additional spice in that the other person who had taken over running the hostel with Kumar was rumoured to be ex Thai mafia. Damrian certainly looked as if he could handle himself and had that same dangerous, quiet, confident air about him that Brian, my Australian friend, had had. He also had a dash of hard man arrogance which made him the sort of bloke you wouldn't want to cross. At first, I ignored the rumour as just another tale of the road, but then I noticed the heavily-built men in immaculate suits who turned up for meetings. They arrived in flash cars with darkened windows, and while the meetings went on, minders in dark glasses patrolled the compound. These 'businessmen' oozed power, and Damrian showed a subservient respect I'd never seen before. If he'd worn a hat it would have been off his head and being wrung in sweaty hands! I was told that the only reason Damrian had been allowed to leave the mafia in Thailand, was that he had agreed to work as a contact for them in Kota Bharu. Smuggling was probably the name of the game, though I steered well clear of meeting times at the hostel as soon as I realised what was going on, and certainly didn't ask any direct questions. It was better to be seen to be unaware, to be just another travel bum.

Kota Bharu is a key town for overlanders as it's right on the border and has a Thai Embassy. This means you can judge the usage of the time allowed on your visa to a max. Getting this visa was the easiest ever, and the six rubber stamps that made up the permission to enter took up a full page in my passport.

The town was also home to the most magnificent fruit and vegetable market I'd seen in Asia. The variety of stock on sale was superb and though I prided myself on knowing what things were, this market defeated me. Everything was displayed with precision, thought and artistic flair. Colours coordinated or clashed, depending on whatever method the stallholder thought would attract the most custom.

Kota Bharu had another gem tucked away within its repertoire – it's the kick-off point for the Perhentian Islands. The people, geography and history of mainland Malaysia had been interesting for

me but what we'd seen so far hadn't been anything that'd felt unique. On the other hand we'd heard that the islands were of the type that holiday brochures use to mesmerise potential punters with scenes of white sandy beaches and turquoise waters.

Kumar organised a lift to the port for us, with an Indian salesman called Guitmar. I liked Guitmar instantly, and soon found out why he liked to stay in places such as Mummy's. He was an ex-hippy and in his youth, along with his German wife, he had travelled the hippy trail across Asia. He treated us to Jimi Hendrix and Led Zeppelin that powered out of giant speakers from his van's stereo all the way to the port. "I really miss those days," he told us.

I'd thought that what we had seen in Indonesia had been touches of paradise, but they were nothing compared to these islands. The sand was almost pure white – enough to make 'snow' blindness an issue with the bright sun. The sand was also so incredibly fine that it was like walking on talcum powder, and actually squeaked as the pressure of each footstep sunk into it. The sea really was turquoise, a pale shade that I'd never seen before, the water so clear and calm that it acted as a giant magnifying glass, giving a perfect view of everything below us on the seabed. It was warm too – just a touch below bath water temperature and the breeze that eased gently across the island was enough to cool without chilling. Just a few kilometres away on the mainland the heat had been intense. Palm trees stood rustling along the shore and coconuts lay scattered underneath them. Bamboo and palm thatch cabins were ours to rent for almost nothing and a few enterprising souls had set up just enough local eateries to keep travellers fed. One day slipped into the next, though the feeling I had was that time had virtually stood still.

Back on the mainland, there'd been a disaster. The previous evening we'd sat on the island watching purple grey clouds unfold and roll across the mainland coast. They had done so at such speed they'd almost looked as if they were writhing and battling with each other. Great shafts of lightning powered down towards the earth and even where we were, we could hear the thunderclaps that seemed to be centred on the coast. When our boat back from the island arrived at what was left of the jetty, we were greeted by a scene of almost total devastation. Fishing boats had  been battered virtually out of recognition, buildings flattened and palm trees stripped of all their leaves; electrical cables hung torn and sparking from leaning posts, debris lined the streets and sombre silence lined the people's faces. Several buildings still smouldered; having been hit by lightning, adding a woody scent to the smell of death and decay that was already beginning to strengthen in the intense humid heat.

I felt depressed and helpless. Around us, people had lost family members, belongings and livestock, businesses and livelihoods. My mood, as we wandered through the ravaged village, combined with the realisation that we had in fact been very close to this horribly powerful storm. I started to think of my family at home. Families have a hard time when you are out on the road. When you are out there having adventures, they are stuck with their fears and the information you do give them when you get in touch. I always tried to keep in touch with my family on a bi-weekly rota, but that sometimes backfired on me. I once stayed on an island for a month; it was stunningly beautiful and I'd not been able to resist the temptation. But unbeknown to me, the island's postbag didn't go over to the mainland until it was full. My family didn't hear from me for six weeks, and started to worry. If you do die out on the road – the costs involved can be astronomical. A family member would have to travel out to get you and then there would be the costs of getting your body back for burial. The stress of having to do that must be grim. I always write a will saying that if I keel over for whatever reason, I want to be buried wherever I am, with only my belongings being packed up and sent home. Much easier for everyone all round and I like the idea of being out there in a strange land.

I was impressed with the stoic, calm way in which many of the villagers were already putting their lives back together, and I wondered how many times this had happened to them before. Amid this devastation the market was running almost as usual. Stalls had been cobbled together and trading was under way again. Second hand shirts hung next to baskets of chickens and ducklings, bolts of bright cloth, stacks of pots and pans, piles of vegetables and machinery parts. Seeing this bright, busy normality made me feel more positive, but the whole experience reminded me that my life on the road as a westerner was one of virtually carefree luxury. At home, my budget of ten pounds per day would be worth little, but here I was a wealthy man of leisure.

The storm had hit Mummy's too, and the bad news was that Libby had been damaged by falling timber. The rear luggage rack had been snapped off on one side and the bike was sounding like an asthmatic in a carbon monoxide fog. A local welder fixed the rack for next to nothing and while he was doing that I gave the bike a service. The shady peace of Mummy's was the perfect place to be doing this, and I wanted to make sure that there was no hidden damage to the bike after the storm. The rough engine was down to water in the carburettors. I couldn't be sure how it had got in there but suspected that it could only have been condensation after the hot ride in, or that there had been water in the petrol I'd bought from the rougher than usual petrol station where I'd last filled up.

I was also finally prompted to do something about the slow puncture the front tyre had had since Singapore, but I'd been too lazy to fix. The tyre valve was ok, so with effort the tyre came off. The tube showed no sign of a leak anywhere, so I was stumped. I was dripping sweat by the time I came to put the tyre and tube back on, but I just could not get the tyre to sit back on the rim properly. After an hour of trying, Kumar came across to me with a bottle of palm oil. The washing up liquid I'd been using seemed to evaporate as soon as it hit the rim. But the palm oil greasily did the trick and with a small pop, the tyre was finally on. We were ready for the road again.

On the roll again, Malaysia had one last smile in store. Loaded up and heading for the border, we realised that there was a police checkpoint in front of us. It hadn't been there the day before and it seemed to be stopping only mopeds and scooters. The smile came from the fact that the only two-wheelers they managed to stop, besides us, were those who had riders that weren't paying attention. Everyone else saw the checkpoint and shot off down the side road that was just a couple of hundred metres before it!

Chapter 7

Full Moon Fever

"The border means more than a customs house, a passport officer, a man with a gun. Over there everything is going to be different; life is never going to be quite the same again after your passport has been stamped."

Graham Greene

Getting out of Malaysia was the same pleasant, organised affair that entering had been, but getting into Thailand was a different ballgame altogether. The officials were disorganised, and not one of them knew what to do with the carnet. I ended up having to show them, and hoped that the exit docket would actually link up in the right place with my entry slip. This was the first time since Africa that this had happened, and after the organisation of Malaysia I wondered if this border crossing was going to see us travelling into a completely different type of country. Though neighbours,

 I wondered if again the line drawn on a map was going to be a man-made divider between Second and Third World. I wasn't sure how Thais would like to be referred to as being 'Third World', but if the officials at the crossing were anything to go by, then a new adventure was about to begin. It was almost as if the situation was a wake up call, that if I didn't shake myself into alertness, then I would get into trouble. Malaysia had been easy to travel in, and I wondered if that was one of the reasons that so little of it had inspired me. Not that I was complaining. The ease of travel had given me breathing space to get my back used to being on the bike, and it felt pretty darned good.

I'd allowed myself to have preconceived ideas of what Thailand would be like. The picture I had was that it was going to be exotic, and overrun with tourists, and I feared that I wasn't going to enjoy that. I was afraid that mass tourism was going to have taken away, or rounded off the country's uniqueness, and turned it into some sort of efficient but bland McDonald's of Asia. I'd also read that Thailand was virtually under siege from hoards of drunken tourists.

As we rode towards the border I'd even had thoughts about whether to go there or not. But a last minute turn around wasn't on the cards as Jan was full of enthusiasm for Thailand. I persuaded myself that I shouldn't have such strong ideas about a place before I'd been there – I had to have an open mind.

Trucks and buses were the instant challenge. These beasts rattled along at eighty kilometres an hour and most spewed great clouds of black smoke. Size mattered, and many a moped rider would have to leap his bike off the road to let one of these rumbling monsters heave their way past. Their overtaking techniques were those of muscular bullies on steroids. The roads away from the border were packed with these vehicles, and their pace sucked. Libby never felt comfortable cruising unless she was doing at least ninety kilometres an hour; below that she felt unbalanced, as if everything was an effort.

Headlight on full beam and with adrenaline pumping seemed to be the only way to deal with these adversaries. We were constantly flashed in return as if drivers were saying, 'Oy, you've left your light on.' That was OK though – it meant that at least we had been seen!

For the first time in the trip I didn't have a decent map for a new country before getting there, and the one we had was as much good as one drawn by a three-year old! It didn't help that Thailand doesn't put many of its signs in Roman lettering, but why should they? Perhaps the country wasn't going to be completely tourist-oriented after all. I was glad I had Jan navigating on the back of the bike, leaving me free to deal with the traffic, but even she was struggling to deal with the signs. I still had time to notice how much rubbish was strewn along the roadsides, something very different from the Malaysian side where people seemed to have a complete aversion to roadside dumping. I'd read that Thai people were incredibly clean and that they were scornful of sweaty 'pharang' (foreign) visitors, but their countryside didn't seem as important as their bodies!

A smartly clad policeman on a motorcycle was just what we needed and as luck would have it, just when we had decided that we were totally lost in a beaten-up town, we found one. He didn't speak any language Jan and I could manage, but after several attempts from the two of us to say Songkhla, he hopped on his bike and headed us in the right direction.

The next time we had to ask directions we were helped by four policemen, and I nearly made a complete prat of myself in front of them. If it hadn't been for Jan's quick wits and her ability to leap off the bike, I would have dropped Libby right in front of them. A combination of fatigue, manic traffic, sweaty heat, the desire not to run them over, and a line of loose gravel at just the wrong moment meant that the bike just didn't stop in the way it should have. I think that after they'd got over the fright of nearly having three hundred kilos of bike and two tourists dropped on them, they were quite glad to send us off in the right direction.

Jan and I ducked and dived our way up the east coast, through countryside that was either forested or given over to paddy fields. Small towns broke the ride, in that they and their immediate surroundings seemed like scars on the lush landscape. By the time we had reached the port of Surat Thani, Jan had made up her mind that we needed to escape. We'd been hearing tales of bizarre, anything goes, 'Full Moon' parties on the island of Pha Ngan. The parties were supposed to be unique and were a major attraction on the backpackers' trail. Jan was ready to party, and I thought 'why not?' If the tales were even close to the mark, then we had an experience in store for ourselves. I wondered if this was one of the places in Thailand that was under siege from drunken tourists, but from what we had heard, alcohol wasn't the drug of choice.

The first step was to get over to the island of Samui, or Kho Samui as everyone called it. No problem, we were just in time to take the car ferry across the eighty-kilometre passage which was supposed to be an event of its own as it wound through some of the eighty islands off the coast of Surat Thani.

We'd no intention of staying long on Kho Samui as the full moon was approaching fast and if we missed this party we might not be able to get back for one when the moon would actually be visible. The injury to my back had meant that we were now running late and the rainy season was due to start in Thailand. The real problem was shipping Libby over to Kho Pha Ngan, and after a day of fruitless chasing we had to give up. Then the tourist police offered to store her in their compound until we got back. I was uneasy about this, as I'd heard stories about corruption amongst Thai police. But I had plenty of witnesses and decided that I really should try to keep up with my theory that most people can be trusted until they prove otherwise.

Having made the crossing as foot passengers we learned that Hat Rin, the village where the Full Moon party happened, wasn't far away, so to save money Jan and I decided to walk. After four kilometres we were both exhausted – the weeks of lounging around on islands or sitting still on the bike, combined with the muggy, sweaty heat to finish us off. As luck would have it at that moment a songthaew (mini bus) belted over the sandy rise in the road, and it was going to Hat Rin.

Hat Rin was once just a fishing village. Now it's a backpackers' centre and almost anything they want could be got there. In daylight it was a gentle place that centred on a crossroads between its two beaches. Around the crossroads were chalets, mini-supermarkets, bars and restaurants. At night, bright lights came on, music turned up full volume and the streets filled with people and the scents of cooking food. Even more bars and open-sided restaurants dotted one sandy beach, where the party would be held. Jan wanted to stay right there, but I could imagine what it was going to be like trying to sleep. In the middle of the day the area was virtually deserted and to me that meant the revellers were inside sleeping hangovers off. I wanted to enjoy the day as well as the night, and not being the party animal Jan could be, I wanted to find somewhere a little out of the centre. We headed south with Jan tagging along only, I thought, because a room for two was far cheaper than a single.

Hat Rin is a great meeting place and at the full moon, hundreds of travellers converge there which made it the perfect spot to link up with people we'd met before. We found friends we'd made in Indonesia, Singapore and Malaysia. It was almost like a family reunion, with the feeling that for a change you didn't have to answer all the 'where are you from, where are you going?' types of questions. It was also a change not to be the person who is standing out from all the locals, as you do when you are on the road. That alone made the visit there into something of real value and it wasn't until this thought clicked that I realised I was tired of the road. Strangely, in spite of the stunning and peaceful islands we'd been visiting over the weeks, it felt as if it was time to sit in one place, to take stock and recharge my batteries. I realised that the reason I'd been thinking so many negative thoughts was that I was feeling tired. 'Travel blindness', I call it. When I got like this, getting somewhere was more important than what I could see and get involved in along the way. I had a little chuckle to myself when I realised that in spite of the fact I was on an extended holiday, I was worn out.

All places to stay had filled up over the final couple of days and there was an expectant air everywhere. As soon as night fell, the Full Moon Party kicked off with a bang. People were laughing and partying, the rich scent of ganja wafted through the village, and everywhere people walked hand in hand with bottles of Singha beer as they headed barefoot for the beach. Many had bought jars of fluorescent face paint with them and their lime green and pink faces almost floated in the bright lights. Spaced out along the beach, three discos on the sand were in full swing, with eardrum-shattering music that was grabbing and hypnotic. Mesmerised travellers danced with freedom and abandon. The moon hung glowing, bright and large above us. I could see the man in the moon and he seemed to have a grin on his face as he watched us all. Out on the headland, dancers leapt with arms waving

 to the music that they could hear as loudly as if they were in a disco at home. And as the sun rose gently behind them, their shapes were silhouetted against the deep orange glow.

Within a couple of recovery days, most people had left the island to find new adventures, and the village slipped back into its peaceful existence. As I strolled through the quiet streets I imagined that I could hear the locals counting the piles of money that must have

been spent over the past seven days. The party was no siege, but a far better source of income than fishing ever would be; and not just the fishermen, but all these people depended on the monthly riotous parties for their livings – the songthaew drivers, the ferrymen, the postman, the fishermen, the hut builders, the booze suppliers, and yes, the suppliers of dope that was so freely available.

Back on Kho Samui, though Libby was fine and my fears had been completely unfounded, it was hard to leave the island life. So, we persuaded ourselves that we should explore a little and found a place to stay in the resort of Chaweng. This beach town seemed to be wobbling on the edge of turning into a full-blown tourist destination, and backpackers, though still welcome, no longer really seemed to fit. Further along the beach, the first of the large hotels were going up and the shops stocked goodies that would appeal to those on two-week holidays rather than those travelling long term on tight budgets.

Mentally I felt completely refreshed but physically, something was wrong. For the first day there I had no energy and felt nauseous. Then I had a pounding head and was running a raging temperature – I'd obviously picked up a bug, perhaps a rough stomach upset. I could only wait it out. I stocked up on bottles of Seven Up, mineral water and biscuits, but within a day I'd become so weak that the walk from our cabin to the toilet, just ten metres away, took me an hour for the return journey. It would have taken longer, or perhaps I'd not have made it at all, if there hadn't been logs along the side of the path. Within a few steps I'd needed to sit down, shaking and quite exhausted. If I'd sat on the ground there's a good chance that I'd not have made it back up again.

Meantime Jan had lost all patience with me. She'd been reading her tarot cards and was unusually secretive about what they were telling her. I was feeling too ill to care much and for the next day or two she popped in only to shower and change her clothes. Then I didn't see her.

By now I wasn't thinking clearly. I still felt sick all the time but couldn't vomit. I didn't need to go to the toilet at all and wasn't in the least bit hungry. I wasn't even thirsty most of the time. I was still sweating though, but not much and where my sheets just days before had been permanently drenched, they were now just damp. I didn't care. At night I hardly slept and when I did, I had full-blown nightmares

In our first days at Chaweng, I got talking to the very pretty Thai girl living in the bamboo hut next to ours. She was quite petite and had black hair so shiny it seemed to glow. Kulap was very easy to look at and equally easy to talk to, and as we got to know each other better, she told me her story. She was a victim of poverty and tourism, but had a dream that was worth having. She was one of three daughters of a very poor farmer who lived on the mainland, and as such, her future was almost certainly to continue life living on the edge of poverty. But she'd been to school and knew that if she could get a degree then she could get her and her family a better life. The only way she could achieve that was

 to earn her uni fees by becoming a prostitute to pharang visitors. She told me that she had been doing this for a year, but seemed to have no real concept of the risk she was taking with Aids and other STDs. I had a lot of explaining to do and she seemed grateful, and she also seemed to enjoy talking to a tourist who didn't want sex with her.

Kulap knocked on our door. She'd seen that Libby was still there but hadn't seen me around, so had been worrying. I tried to call out to her but only a croak came out. She came straight in, took one look at me and disappeared. At that moment I felt deserted and incredibly lonely. The last time I'd felt this lonely was just after I'd been mugged in Namibia. I shouldn't have allowed myself to doubt her though. Within the hour she was back in the cabin, this time without knocking and her arms were full of bottles of drink. She had travelled twenty kilometres to another town to see a pharmacist. "I know this illness", she said. "This is dengue fever, you must drink and you must take these now." I suspect that if she hadn't come in at that time I would have simply dehydrated into nothing.

Within a day of taking the tablets I could feel the difference. The liquids that Kulap made me drink, with such tender care, seemed to flush through my body and it was almost as if I could feel myself coming alive

125

again. I must have looked like some raggedy old plant in a pot that was dying to be watered! I started sweating again, and needing a pee. Kulap helped me there and back, though my pride was still stubbornly strong enough to manage in the cubical myself! A day later I was up and about, and within three days I was able to walk again. Kulap was the perfect example of the kindness and genuine behaviour of the ordinary Thai person.

Whilst sick, I'd rolled over on my glasses and broken one of the arms off. To add to my debt to Kulap, she arranged for a very cute girlfriend (who I subsequently discovered wasn't a girl at all) to take me on her/his scooter to the opticians to get them fixed. I spent the next days pottering, drinking, and nibbling biscuits before falling onto my bed knackered, but as each day passed I got a little stronger.

Kulap and Jonng took me out to eat as soon as they felt I was ready; the first proper food I'd had and suddenly I was ravenous. During the meal, yet another disaster struck. I lost a big filling and was instantly in pain. I couldn't believe it. What else was going to go wrong?

The pain was so intense that I had no choice. I had to find a dentist. Stupidly I rode the bike, but being back on her was like a breath of fresh air and in spite of the pain, I knew that I was well and truly on the mend. The dentist was brilliant too, though I was nervous about using one I didn't know and in Thailand at that. I shouldn't have been prejudiced, for he decided that I needed a root filling and forty-five minutes later I walked out dribbling, but with no pain and a rather magnificent gold filling. It cost me next to nothing, so I didn't even bother to claim from my insurance.

I was glad that I'd managed to steer clear of the local hospital, but not all visitors were so lucky. I'd met Mich on Kho Pha Ngan, and even then I'd thought that he didn't look well. He'd told me that after the full moon party he was going to get himself checked out. Mich had been in Borneo where he'd picked up malaria. "It comes back every so often", he'd said. He wasn't worried; this had happened so often that he knew what to do. As I'd had malaria too, I kept an eye on him, and he seemed to be doing OK. Then suddenly his bout turned into a raging dose. A doctor had checked him straight into the hospital.

I went to visit him there and as I climbed the steps up, two gorgeous girls walked down towards me. Both were very tanned and had long hair, one was blonde and the other a brunette. The brunette was wearing baggy dark green Thai trousers and a tight white top, the blonde girl was wearing a yellow loose-fitting short skirt and a bikini top. As she turned to talk to her friend I saw that the left side of her face was completely covered in crusty and weeping purple brown scab. Before I could stop myself, I asked what had happened to her. They stopped and looked towards me on the step below them, and as they did so I could see that the girl had massive rashes, scrapes and scabs down one side of her body. She looked awful, but not surprised at the reaction she was getting from me. "Stupid huh," she said. "I was on my boyfriend's moped on a dirt road, and yes, I was only wearing my bikini. We came off on a corner – I've just been told by the doctor that I'm going to need plastic surgery."

For weeks I'd begrudged wearing bike gear in the heat of S.E. Asia. With thick padded jeans, a helmet and a leather jacket on, we sweated like mad every time we had to slow down. On the move the gear was fine, but when trawling through towns and villages or looking for somewhere to stay, it was grim. The humid heat was far worse than anything I'd encountered in either Africa or Australia, and it was very tempting to strap the jackets onto the bike so we could ride in freedom. Jan for one would have been delighted – she'd hated having to wear her kit. But now I was firmly reminded that the purgatory we'd been struggling with was the right thing to have done. If we had ended up as battered as the blonde girl, the trip would almost certainly have been over.

By the time I was fit enough to travel, it was time for the next full moon party, so yes, we went again. It was even better than the first one and I met Roland from Sweden, the first experienced travelling biker I'd met since Africa. We gelled instantly – it was like meeting a brother that I'd not seen in years. Roland had travelled across the Middle East and India to get to Thailand and we spent hours sitting swapping hints and tips, roads to ride, places to stay and things to watch out for. He was heading for Africa.

Roland's style of trip was different from my own though. I'd long since worked out that though travelling bikers have a lot of things in common, there's usually only one thing that's the same, and that is the dream to travel by motorcycle. Bikes are inevitably kitted out in completely different ways and there is no one bike that is the best for the job. What kit to take is an issue; again, everyone's is different, though the basics always consist of a decent tent, a quality sleeping bag, sleeping mat and a petrol cooker. I'd originally packed for every eventuality and had waddled off looking and feeling completely overloaded. For a long time I'd been down to the basics and was a lot happier as a result, and so was Libby! Now with two of us on board she was overloaded again, but it could have been worse as Jan knew how to travel light.

Roland had learnt to travel light too, but was hampered by what he couldn't get rid of. He'd been sponsored for everything he had, from his Yamaha Teneré right through to the fluid for his contact lenses. In a way I was envious. In some countries he even had free fuel. But there was a price to pay that I wasn't happy with. Not only could he not get his kit down to the bare minimum required, but he had constant deadlines to meet. He was writing for a Swedish bike magazine and a couple of newspapers there. He also had to phone back reports for a radio station, and every so often he would have to link up with a TV crew, even if it meant going well out of his way. When we were all heading for the beach or a bar, he inevitably had a deadline to meet and had to bail out. He didn't seem unhappy though and I suspected that he was rather enjoying the challenge of juggling the fun and hassles of travel, with the commitments he had made.

The night of the full moon party, Jan told me that her tarot cards prediction had come true; she'd fallen in love. Boong was a local guy and Jan was elated – it explained where she had been when I was ill, but this was a blow that I'd not wanted to think about. Because I was cynical of tarot cards I didn't believe that she was going to fall in love, in spite of the fact that she had been working at it at every opportunity. With the dalliances she'd had to date, she'd never told me that she was in love, just that she was having fun.

Roland and I had planned to ride up to the north of Thailand together. He had a girlfriend on the back of his bike and I still needed someone to share the costs of accommodation and fuel. Jan had decided that she wasn't going to come, and I could understand that, but a part of me also hoped that during the month or so I was away, perhaps the relationship would fizzle out and then we could be on our way again. A selfish thought, but I hung on to it.

Jan had a friend, Caroline, who wanted to come on the trip, but I was torn. I was faced with a choice: take someone I didn't know with me and share the costs, or go on my own and see far less of Thailand, with the complication that I'd be back earlier and that Jan's relationship might still be in full swing. I chose to take Caroline with me, and on the up side she also knew how to travel light. All of Jan's bike kit fitted her too so I didn't even have to worry about that. It wasn't a bad start and as we headed north I found that she was actually a good pillion passenger. She seemed to enjoy being on the bike and as long as she had dope to smoke, she seemed to enjoy the time off the bike too. Perhaps it was going to work.

It was fun to ride with another biker and it made a change to have someone else take the lead. Roland seemed to like being in front, so we quite naturally slipped into a routine. Libby felt quite strange for the first couple of days, almost as if she had to settle down into a new routine herself. It was either that or she was paying me back for having let her stand, hardly ridden, for so long!

By now the weather was overcast all day every day and we could feel that it was on the turn. The temperature in the early hours of the day wasn't too bad, but the heat intensified towards the late morning. Rain was the only thing that would break this cycle, but none of us wanted that, we'd rather struggle on in the ever-growing heat. Both Roland and I had seen tropical rainfall, so we knew what was on the way.

At a gas station I discovered that Libby had developed an oil leak from the drive shaft. There was nothing I could do about it but while I was checking it out, an enthusiastic spectator accidentally ripped off one of Libby's indicators. The expression on his face was a picture as he stood there looking down at the indicator that had somehow detached itself from the bike and magically appeared in his hand. That at least I could fix, and the gobsmacked expression on his face was payment enough for the hassle.

The raggedy-edged asphalt roads weren't too bad and even though we were still battling with the Thai road signs, we were making good progress, until Roland hit a dog. I'd already decided that Thai dogs had the least road sense of any canines I'd come across so far. They would meander out in front of traffic as if they had every right to be putting their own lives at risk. Sometimes they would sit quite patiently on the dusty verges, usually in the shade of a tree, and then at the most illogical moment they'd casually step out. It was almost as if the dogs were playing some sort of bizarre game of chicken, with the main rule being that you weren't allowed to run. This dog was a fully-grown tan coloured mutt who at the last minute got up and lazily stepped out straight under Roland's front wheel. He had no time whatsoever to react and hit the dog hard, throwing it screaming into the roadside undergrowth. Roland and Sophie did a massive wobble right across both lanes of the road before he managed to get the bike under control again. It said a lot for his riding ability that he had managed to keep them upright, but Sophie was devastated. This was the first time she had been on a bike and had been sitting stiff and nervous behind Roland. She battled to keep calm and was taking large gulps of air as she fought not to cry. Roland was shaking too as it began to dawn on him that they had just had a very lucky escape.

This was just the start of a long hard day. We set off again, this time with Caroline and I in front; the only real damage the suicidal dog had done to Roland's bike was that it had wrecked the speedo cable. We'd heard stories of how particular Thai police are about speed limits being broken, and were determined not to get caught out. But suddenly Roland and Sophie were no longer in my mirror. They had a flat; the first for Roland since leaving Sweden. Sophie was now looking very uncertain about being on the bike and if there had been a way to escape at that moment, I think she would have taken it. The puncture happened suddenly too, with a rapid loss of air that had the two of them hanging on for dear life again.

Then the first rains started, and hot rain is rather like riding through an earthily exotic scented sauna. Two kilometres further down a road that had become potholed and covered in heat heaves, Roland had yet another flat tyre. With the mix of rain, heat heaves and the puncture, any sense of riding romance disappeared. Heat heaves are where the asphalt has become deeply rippled from the combination of intense heat, whatever surface the road was laid on, and the weight of large vehicles. These unpredictable, meandering, snake-like gullies are very dangerous for an unwary biker – they try to forcibly dictate where you go. If you don't see them well enough in advance it can be like suddenly finding your wheels stuck in drunken tramlines! In spite of this collection of hazards, once again Roland managed to keep the bike upright, but by now Sophie looked rather stunned. This time, he'd blown the tyre right by a puncture repair stall at the roadside, so we were able to do the repair in the shelter and with good light, but the bad news was that the new puncture had wrecked Roland's only spare tube. Happily, I had a spare of the right size but by now it was beginning to get late, and we knew that there were no hotels for another fifty kilometres. It started raining again

We took off into the traffic, set on making it to the next town before dark, but it wasn't going to be easy. Where earlier in the day we'd felt like we were dancing with the trucks as we were scooting along and overtaking them, with the onset of heavy rain, muddy water was beginning to flow across the road. The spray from the trucks was horrible and muddy water obscured my visor. Overtaking became a bit of a gamble, and for Sophie this ride through the rain was just about the last straw for her. We decided that Roland should take the lead as he would then be able to judge how Sophie was doing, and go at a pace she would be able to manage.

Darkness came faster than we had anticipated and the rain continued to fall. Now, overtaking wasn't an option, and dazzling headlights coming towards us were the finishing touch. We settled in behind a big truck that at least had all its lights working, and accepted that the only thing to do was to keep following it until we got to a town of some sort. When we got to a town, the first hotels were firmly closed and I hated to think what either Sophie or Caroline was thinking. I was knackered and Roland looked on his last legs. When we did find a hotel we didn't move more than a hundred metres from it for thirty-six hours.

131

One of the things that I really liked about travelling by bike in Thailand was the opportunity to stop and eat at one of the many food stalls. On the main roads these cater to both locals and the truck drivers alike. We steered clear of the stalls where the buses stopped because they were so busy, but any that had trucks crowded around turned out to be good bets. Most of the time I had no real idea about what I was eating, and sometimes it felt as if it was best not to know. But the flavours were wonderful, and the food always seemed piping hot, sometimes it was piping spicy hot too! I rather enjoyed not knowing what the food would taste like in advance – sometimes even the smell of food wasn't enough to give a clue.

We were heading for Phet Buri and the rough roads of the previous days turned into smooth, immaculate asphalt that was almost a holiday to ride on. I was delighted for Sophie, who had been quite stoic about the disaster day. Inevitably we got lost but each time we did, the locals put us on the right route, and the day eased on by. We arrived in the town at midday, and though it was the hottest hour, it allowed us plenty of time to find somewhere cheap to stay. A local chap on a moped saw us looking and offered to show us what he said was, "Very good, very cheap, very nice." He wasn't wrong, and we had the peace of mind of off-road parking again.

We'd come to Phet Buri because we all wanted to see the caves of Buddha, which were just five kilometres outside town. These historic caves are full of candle-lit statues of Buddha, many of which are coated with gold leaf and sit clustered in darkened recesses. There's quite an odd feeling in the caves; the respect that the locals must have showed them over the hundreds of years made it feel, I thought, as if the rocky walls had soaked up an aura of total calm and peace. My skin tingled.

In the late afternoon we set off to explore the town itself and to our delight, didn't see any other tourists at all. A wide, muddy-coloured river flows through this unspoiled town and it seemed as if all life centred on its banks. Long slim wooden boats, rather like overgrown canoes, blasted up and down the waters. These were powered by overgrown engines that had probably not seen silencers since they had been salvaged from whatever truck or other that could no longer support them.

The banks were covered with wooden houses that hung in defiance of gravity right out over the river, and in their open bases we could see life in the raw. Men were welding, a woman was plucking a duck, two others were hanging up washing; one man was butchering some sort of animal, others were playing cards with great enthusiasm, and some were sitting reading in cool shade. Some were squatting with their backsides out over the water, adding to the sewage that was already there. At the end of the day, the winding narrow streets came alive with lamp-lit food stalls that wafted an array of wonderful scents into the air.

The road suddenly changed again at Phet Buri. Now we were on a dual carriageway and without the need to battle with lumbering trucks all the time, we zipped along at a much more comfortable pace. The traffic got denser as we neared Bangkok, but it was still manageable to ride in and it wasn't long before I realised that Bangkok drivers use the same driving style as the Romans. In Rome, drivers concentrate on what is happening immediately in front and ten degrees to either side – they never look in their mirrors, trusting that the person behind is obeying the rules too. This driving style meant that there were few accidents and everyone could zip along at a greater speed than I'd normally think was sane.

I asked a van driver at traffic lights for directions to the Banglampu area of the city and with true Thai hospitality, he ended up leading us there before carrying on with his own journey. Banglampu is home to the famous Kho San Road and we knew that if we wanted somewhere cheap to stay this was where we had to head. It was also relatively close to the Indian Embassy and I needed to start organising my visa. As always, I had no idea how long this would take to do, but I wanted to allow plenty of time.

The Kho San Road is a blitz of backpacker hostels, moneychangers, restaurants, travel agents, clothes shops, tourist shops and market stalls selling everything from T-shirts to black market cassette tapes. To my surprise nothing was cheap, but as Caroline and I explored, we realised that the streets behind the Kho San Road held the same sorts of goodies, but that the further we got away from the road, the lower the prices became and the more the stallholders were prepared to bargain. I treated myself to a new pair of jeans, at roughly a fifth of the price I would have been charged at home. I was chuffed with my find as my bike jeans had just about had it. They had been ripped by thorns in Africa, and had coped with all of my fall-offs there; they'd been washed by being beaten on river rocks, they had been bleached to pale beige by the months of sun and were now held together with a patchwork of whatever material had come to hand along the way. Each patch told a story of the road and in a way it was sad to have to bin them, but they were no longer safe enough to wear on the bike, and not smart enough to be worn at border crossings.

At the end of the day, the food stalls came alive and once again Caroline and I were spoilt for choice. The food was incredibly cheap and I decided I was going to have an eating campaign. I was still dangerously skinny from the dengue fever bout and had to get some more meat on my bones. I was still struggling a little from the effects of the bug and tired easily, and I was also having trouble with my back again. I'd not been able to do my exercises for the weeks that I'd been ill, and for the past days I'd been too tired to go out and walk as much as I should have. I was now getting warning twinges.

Bangkok traffic is so dense that the city is considered to have the most polluted air in Asia. As the population and prosperity of the city has grown, so has the intensity of the pollution. The small three-wheeler rickshaws were supposed to be one of the biggest contributors to the fumes, but for my money the smoke-belching trucks and buses made the most visible addition to the layer of carbon monoxide that hung in the humid city air. My mouth held the taste of the fumes and my skin was always greasy within an hour of getting up and about. Much of the traffic is made up of small scooters and mopeds, which duck and dive their way through the traffic like a swarm of angry bees. The locals use them to the extreme, and I wondered what the traffic authorities at home would have to say I saw men on two scooters, one each end of a fifteen-metre pipe as they rode through the traffic looking as if they were characters from a Laurel and Hardy movie. Another bloke had three giant gas cylinders strapped to his scooter, making his overloaded tyres look as if they'd been drawn by a cartoonist. One man was running a barbecue business from his bike and he rode with smoke and glowing cinders trailing behind him. Another was a window cleaner, but didn't have a collapsible ladder strapped to his bike; he had the real thing – made of bamboo and very long! A seller of plastic goods had his bike loaded up so high with red, yellow, blue and green buckets, bowls, water jugs, spatulas and washing up brushes that I couldn't tell if he was on a scooter or a moped. And of course a scooter is the main form of family transport for many – it was quite usual to see Dad riding a scooter with a child sitting on the handlebars, another standing between his legs, Mum sitting elegantly sidesaddle behind him holding a baby, and the final child sitting on the luggage rack behind her. It made my worries about being overloaded seem quite ridiculous.

I surprised myself by really liking Bangkok. There was a lot to see and do. I even got used to the noise and the traffic fumes. I was also offered a job that would pay me two hundred pounds a week, so I was told. Teaching English is a traditional job for travellers in Thailand and now I could see why. If the money really was that good then it would be worth stopping for a while. But I had a problem. I knew that Caroline would be quite happy to link up with some other travellers to see some of the north, but what to do about Jan? I had no way of getting in touch with her. If she stayed with Boong then I'd need every penny I could earn to help me get home, but she would worry if she didn't hear from me. But would she stay with him? At that stage I really didn't think so. I was pretty sure that she'd be ready to go again by the time I got back, and then all our plans would be back on track. The night before we left, Jan had had a blazing row with Boong and had almost left him then. I decided to ride on, but with my fingers crossed that her wish to travel would be stronger than her wish to settle down.

Motorcycles weren't allowed on the motorways in Thailand, but we didn't know that. I hadn't asked the question because it had never entered my mind. So when we were stopped by flashing blue lights on the motorway north out of Bangkok, we were a bit gobsmacked. There wasn't even the remotest trace of biker camaraderie. The motorcycle policeman was one of those that I'd been warned about. He wanted our money, for his pocket. I'd no doubt, despite the language barrier, that this was what was going on. He leisurely switched off his bike, kicked out the side stand and climbed off. As he stood, he hooked his thumbs into his belt and strutted over towards us, looking at us through his mirrored aviator sunglasses. He and his 250cc cruiser looked like a mini version of an American bike cop and his Harley. I'd watched my reflection grow in the lenses of his shades as he got closer - the curve made me look as if I was standing in some sort of weird hall of mirrors. My brain turned into sludge by this unexpected turn of events, so when my driving licence was demanded I stupidly handed over the real one. Roland was far quicker-witted, and handed over his fake. I had to pay to get mine back, but Roland told the policeman to get lost – we were just five hundred metres from the end of the motorway. This was the first time in two and a half years that I'd had to pay a bribe. I'd just handed over my budget for three days.

Then the rain started again, and this time it was out to cause some real damage. The water sheeted down, causing mini-rivers to form by the roadside, and collecting in dips in the road where there was just enough water to make the bike feel like it was about to aquaplane. This is a very unsettling feeling and completely different from anything I'd had to deal with before, but I was very glad I wasn't on a dirt road. The rain intensified and by this time we were soaked through. Rainwater had found its way through even the smallest gaps in our clothing and I could feel it running down my back. Our boots were sodden, and I could feel water sloshing back and forth in mine as I shifted my feet around to brake or to change gear. Paddy fields stretched away from the roadsides, and within half an hour of the rain starting they were all flooded. Even the earthen walls between them could no longer be seen. Small farms and villages were flooding too, and none of the houses were up on stilts so I wondered if this amount of rain was unusual – there was real misery being caused. There was no shelter for us either, so we rode on. Where the road dipped, it was now flooded, sometimes at least half a metre deep, and through my rain-streaked visor I couldn't see where this was happening until the last minute, unless a vehicle coming towards us hit it first. When one did and the driver hadn't guessed how deep it was, great sprays of water would shoot out, and those just added to our wretchedness when we were zapped by one.

Then the rain stopped, suddenly! We'd been pounded incessantly by it for three hours and then, as if we had ridden from one stage setting to another, we were in the dry and the sun was out. Behind us the sky remained angry and tons of water were still plummeting to the ground.

By the time we made it to Suhkothai, 'the city of happiness', my indicators had decided to stop working. I never knew whether Thai drivers paid any attention to them, but for my own peace of mind I always used them. If I was going to have an accident, it wasn't going to be because I hadn't warned that I, the foreigner, was about to do something that may not fit in with what was expected by the local drivers. But I'm no bike electrician and that night I simply could not find out what was wrong. My throttle had also suddenly become so stiff during the day that at one stage it had almost jammed, though that I could fix. I had spare cables tied into place along the frame and if needed, all I had to do was to release the old ones and connect on the new. But, I decided that I would try to dribble oil down inside the cable sleeves in case that would do the trick, and it did. I also took the chance to change Libby's engine oil. The last time I'd done that was at Three Ways on the Darwin road, and we had covered a lot of kilometres in pretty intense heat since then. We rode on to Chang Mai the next day with Libby almost purring with the luxury of new oil, and Caroline dealing with the task of hand signals!

I was on autopilot by the time we made it to Chang Mai. We'd got lost far too many times, the road had been rough as guts and I'd pulled something in my back when I'd been working on the bike the previous night. A good day's riding distance turned into a nightmare and by the time we found somewhere to stay I could hardly climb off the bike. If we'd had to ride for another fifteen minutes, I'm not sure that I'd have been able to.

Lying in bed that night I began to wonder if I'd made a major mistake by travelling with three people I didn't know. They were all on holiday and were trying to have as relaxed and as carefree a time as they possibly could. I was slowing them down and making their lives more difficult. I needed to do an hour of physio exercises each day, and walk for at least another hour. So as not to hold the others back, I'd always be up early in the morning to do my exercises, but then I'd have to wait around for them to get on the move. Sometimes this wouldn't be until the middle of the day, when my riding ability was already on the wane. My back seemed to be fine in the mornings but by mid-afternoon, it was aching warnings at me. Three hundred kilometres worked fine, but if the traffic was intense, or we got lost and the kilometres piled up, then I was skating on the edge of trouble. Chang Mai was potentially going to be a turning point for me, and I debated whether to tell Roland, Sophie and Caroline that I could no longer travel on with them. This was the first time my back had felt so grim since I'd first arrived back into Indonesia and if it was going to take as long to get fit again then I'd have no choice. Roland and Sophie would be fine together and I was still sure that Caroline would have no problem linking up with other travellers. But I was getting a little worried about her. Over the weeks I'd discovered that she was addicted to dope and that she had just about run out. She was getting very edgy indeed and Chang Mai was not the safest place to try to get hold of more.

Poste Restante had letters for me – two from Birgit and one from Mike and Sally, who had bad news. They'd had an accident and Sally had been flown home. They didn't give me any details but it seemed that someone had ridden into them and Sally had ended up with broken bones. I could imagine what that would have done to her. When I'd ridden with them, she'd always been very brave, but not completely at home on the pillion seat. Mike was now just a month ahead of me – perhaps I'd meet up with him somewhere in India.

I wrote to Birgit and asked her if she would still like to link up with me for a while in India or Nepal, which seemed like a really good idea. I knew that she would be happy to travel to each day's destination by bus and the thought of being able to spend time with her felt like it was exactly the right thing for us to be doing. I tried not to listen to the little voice in the back of my mind that was telling me that bus travel might not be an issue anyway, as Jan might well not be around by then.

The indicator problem still bothered me and as part of my getting fit again campaign I spent hours searching for and talking to the bike shops in Chang Mai with no luck. None of them knew anything about BMWs and weren't prepared to attempt to work out what the problem was. But an auto electrical repair shop was and soon discovered a blown relay. They had nothing suitable in stock and BMW in Bangkok didn't either, but I could get hold of a Harley-Davidson relay, so Libby became a BMW/Harley/Jawa/Land Rover. She was now collecting quite a lot of spares that had no right being on a BMW, but I liked the story that was attached to each modification.

The other problem I had travelling with others was my budget. I couldn't be seen as a party pooper, and that meant I was spending too much on beer and better quality food. I had been putting on a good amount of weight, but could have been doing that with less expensive nosh, and my budget was pretty much blown. The repair to Libby had hurt it too, as had the amount of money I was spending on camera film and developing. But I simply couldn't resist taking pictures in this beautiful country. I'd also had to spend a couple of hundred pounds on a new lens for my camera. I'd been battling with the old one for months – dust, heat and humidity had not combined well with all the bashing the camera had been taking from daily life on the road. That expense pretty much made the decision for me. I was going to stay with the guys for as long as they could hack being with me, but I was going to be completely up front about the effects of late starts and too long days. In the end, they would have to decide if they wanted me to stay with them!

The road to the town of Mai Sai on the border between Thailand, Laos and Burma looped away from Chang Mai through hours of swooping curves edged by lush, forested mountains. The forests were steaming from the combination of the intense rain and the subsequent sunny day we were having. Clouds of steam rose to hang above the forest like opaque space ships that were sucking fuel in columns from the trees below. I'd never seen anything like it, and could imagine that the clouds would have many a legend about them.

I'd dreamt of going through Burma to India. No one had done this since the '60s, but the political situation had been a little calmer in recent months and I'd hoped to be able to quietly slip across the border for what had to be an excellent adventure. From what I'd read, Burma sounded fascinating, and what a wonderful way to arrive in India. This route also meant that there was a very good chance that I'd be able to ride the bike all the way back to the UK – a fantastic achievement if possible, and a lot cheaper than shipping the bike to India from SE Asia. But it was not to be – I couldn't get a permit, however hard I tried and however many doors I knocked on.

It still rankled a little that I'd not been able to get the bike into the country, and had I been able to do so, I'd have been setting off from Mai Sai, so the thought of being able to go there on foot at least, was a consolation. A visa wasn't needed for a day visit but visitors have to lodge their passports with Thai immigration before setting out across the steel girder bridge to Burma.

The bridge is a really busy thoroughfare, with trucks and cars, bicycles and handcarts pushing their way back and forth. At first glance, Burma wasn't any different from Thailand, but the buildings did seem to be going up at an even faster rate. The streets that angled away into town from the bridge were full of market stalls which seemed to stock exactly the same merchandise as those on the other side of the river. All the trading was done in bhat too. "Burma money no good." one of the traders told me. The atmosphere of the market streets was fun, a lot less frenetic than the Thai markets I'd been to, though I could see no real reason why that should be. There was certainly the same number of customers floating around. The traders were really friendly and I found that a far greater number spoke English, which was a throwback I supposed, to the days of colonialism. The people looked quite different from Thais, and they all seemed, except for the Chinese, to have longer, straighter noses. The stalls stocked all sorts of goods – sarongs, electrical goods, watches, cheap plastic toys, medicines, snake whiskey and local carvings. The backpackers' info network had advised that I should try Chinese beer while I was there. It's incredibly cheap in comparison to Thai beer and was supposed to have a unique taste all of its own. In fact, the Tsingtao tasted very much like the beer I'd been drinking in central Africa – slightly flat, sweet and strong.

Many of the locals were wearing a pale yellow cream on their faces, which reminded me of the way my last girlfriend looked when she was wearing a face pack. The man on the table next to ours in the bar was wearing the cream, but didn't speak enough English to explain what it was. He had been hitting the whisky rather hard though, and that meant he had no qualms about reaching across and smearing Caroline's face with the stuff. She looked momentarily shocked, and then disgusted with us as we couldn't help but laugh. The landlady had been listening to and watching our group. We couldn't speak to her, but I liked her a lot, she was one of those people who managed to combine an air of being as hard as nails and someone not to mess with, and a kindly, jolly nature that was almost motherly. I'd been watching her as she had been ordering the men in the bar around and smacking the large brown bottles of beer out onto their tables. She obviously had quite a sense of humour and was into the part of 'mine host' as if she had been born to it. But I also noticed the respect she received from the drinkers.

She brought out a large round grinding stone and what looked like a chunk of tree bark. At that moment we were rescued by a young chap who told us that his name was Ali. He wanted to practise his English and, "Would we like know what the yellow cream was?" The landlady took the bark, which Ali told us came from the Tamackha tree, and ground it hard on the stone. The resulting powder was added to water and turned into the yellow cream. "This is used to protect the skin from the sun." Ali told us. By this time all other conversation in the bar had stopped and everyone was laughing and joking with us. I liked Burma (or Mayanmar as it was officially called).

Quite a few of the people in the market area were Karen tribesmen, Ali told us. They were wearing traditional robes and chain-puffed big fat green cigar-like smokes. "They come down from the hills to sell their produce, and then they use much of their money to stock up on these things. I don't like them though, they don't taste so good."

I was eager to carry on exploring but the guys were happy with the pub and the Tsingtao, so I left them to it. Ali came along as my guide, and offered to take me to a gambling den. I really wasn't sure. Was Ali genuine or was a scam about to start? I'd had a couple of beers and the humid heat was getting to me a bit, but it was broad daylight and I had plenty of time, so I decided to trust him.

We wound through the maze of back streets, every so often coming to a small dirty square before angling off down another alley. The walkways were earth that had been beaten smooth by hundreds of bare and sandal shod feet, and the gutters heaped with rubbish in the squares, but the alleys were surprisingly clean. The buildings were single storey and either rough concrete rendered or smoothed over earth. No one had much time for paint so all were shades of greys and yellow browns. I was beginning to get just a tad worried when Ali turned to me and said, "This is it." In front of us, in an area of wasteland where a few goats were keeping the weeds and the rubbish down, stood a low-roofed building, roughly twenty metres long. A raggedy palm thatch porch area ran along the side of the hut, and inside in the gloomy light I could see clusters of men crouching on wooden benches around tables that were lit from above by bare, low-wattage electric light bulbs. A burly, squat man with a flattened nose was standing guard at the entrance. Ali spoke to him. The guard wasn't happy as he looked me up and down, but Ali was persuasive and all was apparently well. Ali gestured to me to come on inside. As I passed the guard, he ignored me completely, as if I was no longer worth a jot of his attention, but once I passed him, he turned to stare. In the gloom no one took any notice of me, lost in concentration on the games they were playing, which were either cards of some sort, or to do with yellowed white chips that looked something like domino pieces. The air was filled with

142

cigarette smoke which drifted through the barely lit air above each table. The men, and there were only men in the den, seemed from all sorts of backgrounds. Some wore suits and had flashy gold rings on pudgy fingers, some looked as if they were office workers who had escaped to try their luck in their lunch breaks, and some were so poorly dressed they looked as if they had just come in from the fields. The one thing that they had in common was the excited enthusiasm that permeated the air, along with a sense of dread and tension. A few of the men though, played with stony expressionless faces. Ali whispered to me, "Those are the big bosses, you can tell, no?"

The other thing I liked about the little corner of Burma I'd been lucky enough to see, was the number of ancient British motorbikes that were still being used. They smoked like mad and were dropping oil wherever they went, but they sounded wonderful. They were a significant indication of the Burmese people's ability to make and mend, as I was sure that no one would have been able to afford to buy new spare parts, even if they had been available. That night, when I was talking to the owner of our hostel, he told me that he had a sideline business that was far more profitable than running a hostel for backpackers. He was a smuggler of British bikes. He would bring them across the river from Burma in small boats and then would container them out to countries like Norway and Sweden where, he said, there was a good market for them. "And regardless of their condition too." he said. "I don't have to do anything with them, but I always do what I can to make them look better; some are very old and these Burmese people don't know how to look after them!"

Roland wanted to head south through the jungle to a remote area along the border with Burma. Now I was worried. My map said that this was a dirt road and I suspected that all the recent heavy rain would have played havoc with it, but Roland wasn't convinced. He'd been told that it was good riding all the way – we could but try.

At Chang Rai we turned off towards the mountains along a superb road, and it looked as if I'd been worrying for nothing. We cruised through the rain, and at this altitude it was cold too – after all the months in the heat it was quite a strange feeling. But we rode up and out through the top of the rain clouds into patchy sunshine – in the dry season the views must have been spectacular. But our ride took us past dripping trees that were strung with damp thick vines that looked like the jute hawsers on cargo ships, and through villages which seemed to nestle in puffs of cotton wool. Cows stood looking damp, skinny and miserable by the roadside, and packs of wet shaggy dogs stared at us disconsolately from whatever overhang they had managed to shelter under. It started to rain again and I began to get an uneasy feeling. The asphalt was still very good, but why had we not seen any traffic for the past hour? There'd been nothing coming towards us at all. Around a swooping corner a great boulder had tumbled off the cliff face to sit in the middle of the road, which made me even more uneasy – no one had cleared it away. Then the road abruptly changed from asphalt to gravel. The riding was ok at first, until we found the reason why there'd been no traffic. Around a corner, the road changed into a red porridge like mud that had great gullies slashed across it by whatever truck had last braved the road. It disappeared round a bend on the mountainside, which meant that we couldn't tell how far the mud would go on for.

We stood looking at the mud, with the rain dripping off our clothes onto the hot exhaust pipes, sending little puffs of steam skywards. I had Caroline on the back of my bike and I wasn't sure how she would do on mud like this, let alone how my back would cope if we fell off. And I was sure that was going to happen. Sophie looked scared, but Roland was full of enthusiasm.

He took the lead and masterfully dealt with the ruts, his bike slipping and sliding as they went, while Sophie hung on for dear life. I was suddenly envious of his Teneré, which was a good forty kilos lighter than mine. Caroline and I set off into the gloop and at the third major rut we took a sliding, slow-motion tumble. It's not fun picking a heavy bike up in those conditions but it was a joy to have Caroline there to help. Roland meantime had reached the corner and was yelling back that not only did the mud continue for as far as he could see, but that it got worse. At that moment, two locals on 90cc Honda step-through bounced past us, slipping and sliding as they went, but without even the most remote indication that they would fall off. I felt totally embarrassed and my pride had just taken a big dent. Caroline and I just looked at each other through the rain. We didn't speak. I nodded to the good road behind us and she nodded yes.

Back in Chang Mai, Caroline waited until I had washed all the mud off Libby, and then told me that while I had been doing that, she'd been out and bought herself a bus ticket back to Kho Samui. She was fed up with sitting in the rain, she hadn't realised how expensive fuel for the bike would be and she had run out of dope three days before. She'd had enough.

One hundred and forty seven dogs tried to run out on us the day we rode to Kanchanaburi, the home of the bridge over the River Kwai. But the sun was out in a perfectly blue sky, and the scenery was stunning. The land had soaked up all the rain and the world had taken on one hundred and one hues of green. Plants were all freshly washed, revived from the dry season, and just a few flowers were beginning to pop their heads out of the vegetation. The truck drivers had all been to gentleman driver school and the asphalt was a dream. I was just a little sad that Caroline was no longer around to see what biking is really all about. The day felt as if we were being rewarded for the wet hassles of the past weeks.

Kanchanaburi hopped. It was a real tourist town, but to my delight, most of the tourists were Thais and other Asians. The hostels down by the river – or floating on it – didn't look to promise a restful night. They were next to floating discos, and bamboo isn't the best sound barrier. Half a kilometre downstream though was the perfect spot. Good price, good location, clean, and with off-road parking. I was even able to get a single room for exactly half the price of a double, a rarity in itself. It had opaque almost see-though paper walls and I liked the soft, cool feeling these walls gave to the space. I spent the last of the daylight hours sitting on the riverbank watching life on the river as the sun set golden yellow on the horizon. It was warm enough for me to be sitting in just a T-shirt and my shorts. Laughing boys swung out over the river in an old truck tyre that was suspended on a rope from a tree; wooden cargo boats chugged along peacefully on the current as they made their way downriver; long-tailed craft roared their noisy way up and down the waters; and in the distance, I could just hear the first floating disco waking up for the night.

The next morning there was bad news – Sophie was ill. It looked very much as if she had picked up a bout of dengue fever. She and Roland were going to be stuck for quite some time, but at least after my experience I could tell Roland exactly what was going to happen, and what he had to do. But I couldn't wait for them – I wanted to see the bridge and the prisoner of war cemetery and had to head south if I was going to link up with Jan at the time we had agreed. Roland was concerned about me going as I was the only one of us with spare inner tubes and after blowing two in a day, he was worried about not having mine to rely on.

None of the local bike shops seemed to understand what we needed and one even tried to sell us a tube of the wrong size. It's strange how often when you are on the road, and just as you are beginning to struggle, help miraculously appears – Jack, on holiday from Bangkok, persuaded the bike shop guys not to be so difficult and a couple of spare tubes were sent up from Bangkok the next day.

Jack and I spent the next couple of days together. We explored the town and I really enjoyed the chance, through him, to be able to talk to the locals. I'd found that most of the guys who could speak English only wanted to sell something. Of course, I couldn't blame them but I had missed the chance to talk to everyday people. I liked Jack too – his ambition in life was to be the first Thai man to ride around the world on a bike. He wanted to know what I thought was the best bike to use for the trip – he thought a Yamaha Teneré would suit him and had been admiring Rolands. He wanted to know about kit to take, visas, spares, sponsorship, carnets, availability of food and in fact, all of the sorts of questions that I would have loved to be able to ask someone before I'd set off.

"I have a fine dream," he said. "Perhaps it will remain a dream, but it's good to have one that I must stretch for, and who knows? Maybe it will come true one day." I didn't often give out my home address to people I'd just met, but with Jack I did. I told him that if he managed to make his dream happen then he should come and stay with me, wherever I might be in the world.

After I'd seen the bridge over the River Kwai (which isn't the original, or anything like the one in the movie) and had visited the very moving cemetery, Jack wanted me to see the floating meditation lady. I went along with this only because Jack was so keen, but was glad that I did. The woman was amazing. Very gracefully, she went through a series of yoga positions while floating in the river, and was never at risk of getting her face wet! She also claimed to be able to cure back problems, but I was still too nervous for that. Jack had a go and when she pushed, pulled and pummelled him I was very glad I hadn't risked it. If what she did was supposed to be either healthy or pleasurable, I couldn't see it. Now if I'd been in a torture chamber...

I was sad to leave Roland and Sophie, but in a way my decision had been made for me. And, blow the expense, I was really looking forward to being on my own again. Jack came to say goodbye, and I was off running for the south. I'm still hoping he'll knock on my door one day.

This was how I liked to travel – an early start, with all the pieces falling into place with the minimum of fuss. Libby seemed to sense my mood and felt better than she had in days. At last my destiny felt like it was my own to discover. I didn't have to worry about anyone else or fit in with any one else's routines. I almost felt guilty at suddenly having so much freedom, but it was an opportunity, if Jan was going to continue on with me, then I would lose some of this freedom again. That was a price I had to pay, and I knew that in spite of Jan being different to me, I'd been lucky to link up with her as a travel partner.

The ride back to Kho Samui went like a happy dream – nothing and no one bothered me. My back was feeling great again and I kept on meeting interesting people. As I wasn't part of a group – that apparently self-sufficient unit – people would come and talk to me. Even Thai women would try to talk to me, something that had never happened before. Again, I wished I could speak more Thai than the thirty or so words I'd been able to pick up to date.

I dropped down into the resort town of Hua Hin, definitely not the sort of place that I'd want to stay, but it was interesting to see how the world worked in this much-westernised resort. Perhaps this was one of the places under siege from the drunks. All I saw were rows of high-rise modern hotels, with the inevitable clothes shops, travel agents, bars and restaurants, all were of a decidedly higher class than the places I'd been frequenting. I arrived on a day of celebration, the streets were lined with people and a grand procession was underway with schoolchildren forming the bulk of the marchers. Each group was dressed smartly in its own brightly-coloured football shirt, and the procession was led by a lad on a very large, healthy looking horse. The marching beat was supplied by a brass band that sounded as if all the instruments had been jumped on, though the kids all looked as if they were thoroughly enjoying themselves.

Just as I made it back to Surat Thani to catch the ferry over to Kho Samui, it started raining – I should have taken it as an omen. When I hunted Jan down, after a few moments of pleasantries, she told me she was staying in Thailand. Though I'd been expecting it, I felt as if the remainder of the trip had instantly crumbled into no more than a mad dash back across Asia to home.

It seemed like the dream was dead, and I asked myself how I could have been so loyal to Jan once I'd made the offer, when I knew that Birgit would have come. To make things worse, Jan added that she was not going to pay her full share of the costs incurred to date. Now this was really frustrating, to make space for Jan and her kit, in Singapore I'd sent home the vital items of basic kit that would have helped me to save costs – I no longer had my tent, my sleeping mat, my cooker or my pans.

The next day Jan had a change of mind. She told me that she would pay me the full costs after all, but she could only pay two-thirds of it straight away, and I could only have it in Bhat, which meant that I'd have to pay the commission on the exchange. But that didn't matter, all of a sudden life started to look up again and I stopped thinking quite so many black thoughts about her. I hoped that things between her and Boong would work out OK.

With this change in circumstance, I needed a day to rethink. I'd been carefully not thinking 'what if?' thoughts, they would have spoiled the past weeks of travel, but now I had to make a plan. What route to take, to where? How long to get there? And, what on earth was my new budget going to look like?

It had to be Penang to catch the ferry to Madras, as quickly as possible. I'd scoot down the west coast of Thailand past Phuket and Krabi. I'd have no money to hang around down there, but at least I'd have had a taste of them. Four days to do the ride would be about right and as for the budget, I wasn't going to do one – I'd just go for the cheapest of everything. No more beer, and I could find cheaper places to stay – they'd be ratty, but still a roof. I'd stop treating myself to the odd western meal, and stick only to whatever was the cheapest local dish on a menu. It felt like a completely new challenge and I knew that somehow it would work out. What was going to happen next? Whatever happened, Penang was going to be the start to a new adventure.

Chapter 8

Unexpected Adventure

'Again the pages turn and inevitably a new chapter begins. For once I look
forward to what lies ahead and no longer really fear the unknown.'

Flores

I'd heard that sometimes a ferry ran to Madras. If that wasn't
going to happen then, as Penang is such a large port, it might just be
possible to snag a ride across on a cargo ship. What I didn't want to do
was to airfreight the bike to Madras; the cost of doing that just didn't
work with the money I had left, whichever way I jiggled the figures.

Penang is a wonderful city and I found a hostel which had a yard
to the rear where I could get the bike off the street. This was always a
priority and I'd slept in some dog-rough hotels in the past, purely so that
I could keep the bike as safe as possible. I shared the room with Nathan,
an Australian who was on his way to India to buy a locally made Enfield
Bullet motorcycle. He planned to spend six months touring through
the country, and also hoped to get up to Nepal. At that stage I didn't
envy him the battle he faced to buy a second hand bike in good enough
condition to do this, without too many mechanical hassles. He didn't
envy me trying to get my bike into India!

On day three of my stay in Penang I discovered that the ferry to
Madras no longer ran. The ship had had a major fire and was supposedly
out of service forever. I talked to a local man who had done this trip
several times. Yang told me that he wasn't surprised that the fire had
happened. The ship was always overloaded with people and their
belongings. Many entrepreneurs used the route to trade back and forth
between India and Malaysia, with many of the traders heading further
on into Indonesia. To save costs, most of the passengers would cook
their own food, often over the heavy brass primus stoves that India still
makes, or over charcoal braziers. Just the sound of this gave me the
jitters and I began to think that perhaps it was a good thing I couldn't
take the ferry, though it would have been a great people-watching
opportunity, and very easy to get the bike off at the other end. The key

150

was to arrive on the same vessel as the bike. No crate to worry about or to pay for and a far easier set of customs rules to deal with.

The loss of the ferry was quite a blow though as all other options were going to be expensive. I wondered how the traders were doing and if they had found another way to get their goods across. No one could tell me, and Yang was nowhere to be found. I tried all of his haunts, most of which were small cafés. Penang is famous for its variety of really good quality food that is incredibly cheap, and as in many parts of the world cafés are the centre of daily life for aspiring entrepreneurs.

I'd originally met Yang in his favourite café. The streets of Penang are laid out in the main on British colonial lines, and the city is an amazing cross match of cultures. It's historically and geographically a crossroads between those cultures and the population is a rather eclectic blend of people from Malaysia, Burma, Indonesia, China and India, with a few westerners thrown in for added character. Each has made their mark on the city with its buildings, foods and businesses. The streets almost throb with the sound of wheeling, dealing and fortunes being made. Rollers, Mercs and Bentleys run the roads alongside rickshaws and a never-ending stream of panel vans. Eateries range from street stalls, to cafés to swank plate-glass and chrome restaurants. Palm trees and bougainvillea soften the edges of it all. The street stalls are superb places for travellers to eat – the food is cooked on the spot and the variety is enormous. You can wander through the stalls having a starter from Thailand, a main course from India and a dessert from Indonesia. The cost? Buttons, in real terms.

In status, Yang's favourite haunt was up a level from the stalls, just a little. But the café itself was set down a couple of steps from street level, which meant that from window tables you were watching legs and torsos, but hardly ever got a glimpse of a face. The owner was Chinese, a tubby, greasy-haired, raucous chap who loved his own jokes. He took the mickey out of everyone and everything, and seemed to be quite merciless about doing so. He had a go at me within seconds of my first visit, everyone turned towards me and laughter was unrestrained. It was quite a disconcerting feeling, but I knew that the laughter wasn't malicious. You share tables quite automatically in cafés such as this and I had the good fortune to sit next to Yang. He had shoulder-length jet-black hair, and was wearing immaculate black business trousers, a crisp blue shirt and a red tie, perfectly knotted. Others in the café were dressed much more casually or in grimy working clothes. Yang looked at me and said, "You mustn't mind you know, this is his way and people love him for it. Many drink and eat here only for the entertainment. They don't come for the quality of the food that's for sure. I suggest you just have coffee, and those cakes over there are very good." He then turned away from me and carried on his conversation with the other man at the table.

I returned to the café to be abused several more times, though I took Yang's advice and never went there hungry. Yang seemed to partly live in the place and I soon clicked that this was his unofficial office. I was sad that I didn't understand much Bahasa. This is the language that both Malaysians and Indonesians speak, though with different dialects. In a way though, not understanding the language was interesting. It meant that as Yang was doing his deals, I had to concentrate on facial expressions and body movements. They speak a language all of their own. No details, but with most of his clients I could tell how the deal was going. I never could with Yang as he had the ability to maintain a poker face regardless of how excited or angry the other person got. Some, particularly the Chinese, were quite flamboyant!

Through one of Yang's contacts I had some great news. I heard about an onion cargo ship that travelled back and forth across the Bay of Bengal, and the whisper had it that I might be able to get the bike and myself on board. The fee sounded as if it might be considerably more expensive than the ferry, but at least I'd still be arriving on the same vessel.

I found the shipping agent's office and after many cups of tea over several days, I'd done it. In fact the agent seemed positively delighted at being involved in something completely different from his usual business duties. I was introduced to the First Mate, who dealt with the Captain for me. Yup, no problem. I couldn't go on this sailing,

I was too late, but I could go on the next in two weeks' time. Terrific. I settled back to enjoy Penang.

The delay meant that I was going to be in the city for Chinese New Year. With such a large percentage of the population being Chinese, this has real impact on the city. Banners are hung from building to building across the streets. Lampposts are decorated, giant one and a half metre long joss sticks are lit at the temples, ancient eggs are cracked open, restaurants put on special menus, families get together and a nighttime parade is organised. On the night of the parade fireworks lit the sky, and excitement filled the air to blend with the smell and smoke of gunpowder. The parade represents all parts of the Chinese community. Businesses were there, and schoolchildren paraded with paper lanterns in shapes of tigers, ships and peacocks. Families paraded in vintage motorcars and the local bike club rode their throbbing gleaming Harley Davidsons and Honda Goldwings, blipping their throttles as they cruised slowly on by. Dancers twisted and whirled in their traditional costumes, and scary faced ten-people-long dragons ducked and dived their way through the palm-lined streets. Delight and good humour shone on the faces of those lining the streets watching this quite wonderful spectacle.

But for me, disaster struck. I was lying on my bunk in the hotel, with my head propped up on my hand, and all of a sudden the wooden slats gave way. I crashed through onto the lower bunk. It was a moment of absolute agony. Off and on I was still struggled with back pain, but as the days had been going by, it had been easing. In fact the past days of exploring Penang on foot had done my back a power of good. But all of that instantly went by the way, and I knew at that moment that I wasn't going to catch the next sailing of the onion cargo ship. Now I felt miserable. It felt as if there was some sort of conspiracy against me – perhaps I wasn't supposed to go to India at all. Pain, sudden frustrating inactivity and a series of defeats can make you think such things. I was confined to my bunk for a week and that is a lot of time to think miserable thoughts. To make it worse I was then told that the

153

onion ship's Captain had changed his mind – I wasn't to be allowed to go across on his ship, at any time.

Well, there are worse places than Penang to be laid up, and the enforced stay meant that after that first week I was able to explore the city in greater depth. I found a man who made wood and paper fans for a living. He described himself as an 'Old Fashioned Fan Maker' but with all the power tools he had lying about it was tempting to dispute that. He was however an interesting character whose job, sitting in front of his street-side workshop, afforded him a ringside seat on the world. His workshop was filled with bundles of cane, stacked against the wall like rolls of tan-coloured carpet. He also had a workbench, but seemed to regard that as being a pretty useless piece of furniture as he obviously enjoyed working at street level. One of the things that I really enjoy about long distance travel is that you can make time to enjoy people and learn from them by being a sort of fly on the wall. The fan maker called me over; he told me he enjoyed people watching too and that he was aware of what I'd been doing. He was astute, and at our first meeting he told me that I was, 'living with great disappointment'.

I squatted next to him and he very respectfully asked what my problems were. He didn't meet my eye, but carried on gluing almost opaque paper to the cane skeleton of the fan he was making. I told him some of my tale, trying to be cheerful about the whole business, and that I was sure a solution would present itself. He just nodded, and carried on with his work. We chatted some more but my back made it pretty obvious after a while that I should get up and move around. I shook his hand, said goodbye and turned to go. He said, "See you tomorrow", quite certain that I would be back.

I did just that the next day and he had a surprise for me. He knew a shipping agent who could arrange for the bike to be shipped to Madras via Singapore. And as this was the long way round the fare was really good value. In spite of the dogleg route it would take just two weeks. He also had a carpenter friend who would do me a good price on a crate. "I'm afraid I can't help you to get to Madras though", he said. "This you must make happen yourself." All of a sudden life was back on the up

154

The direct airfare to Madras was incredibly expensive; more than double the price of shipping the bike, so there was nothing for it but to take the long way round myself. The cheapest way meant catching a train to Bangkok, flying from there to Calcutta and then catching a train down to Madras – a massive U-shaped journey. A new adventure was about to begin and the bonuses were obvious. I'd not been on a train in Malaysia or Thailand before, I liked Bangkok and was happy to go back for a day or two, and the thought of a few days in Calcutta suddenly seemed like icing on the cake. The extra days would also give my back a little more time to recover before riding the bike again.

The 'International Express' left from Butterworth, the town on the mainland adjacent to Penang. I'd booked myself a second-class fan cooled sleeper berth, for the same price as an air-conditioned bus to Bangkok. Though the compartment wasn't spotlessly clean, the seats were wide and well spaced, and every fan worked. With a shuddering roar of diesel and a blast on the horn, we were off. The track was well maintained and the train ran smoothly past the neat and tidy houses in small villages. Every so often we would stop at small stations and a rush of families would climb aboard, loaded down with string-tied packages. As they settled, Malay, Chinese and Thai voices echoed shrilly up and down the carriage. As we moved off, an air of stunned peace would settle over the carriage.

The border crossing was conducted with practised ease, though two of the Thai officials had shiftily accepted a discreet payment from one of the men in my compartment. Within an hour we were on our way, the engine now straining to pull the weight of the laden carriages. When the breeze was in the right direction heavy diesel fumes blasted in through the open windows, leaving our faces feeling dingy and greasy, but that was a small price to pay for the ability to smell the ever-changing scents as we rolled through the Thai countryside. Rich musty smells from the jungle, the faint whiff of burning metal when the train piled on its brakes, the manure smells of the paddy fields and every so often a sudden inrush of scent from the banks of flowering shrubs that sporadically lined the tracks. The sun dropped behind silhouetted palm

trees and suddenly it was dark. In spite of the warning sign under the window, 'Do not open while asleep', no one made an attempt to close it, and the smells of the day changed into cooler nighttime scents. Dinner was served through the window by one of the Thai ladies who rush up and down the platform selling food when a train comes in. I didn't need to understand Thai to make my order as all the food was carried in large open plastic or enamel bowls. I settled on chicken drumsticks and the sticky rice that Thais love so much. Without asking, she had splashed a very hot chilli sauce across the rice.

I woke to shrill shouting from my neighbours. We had stopped in a big station and everyone was getting off. Not a sign said 'Bangkok', but along with everyone else, I got off too. It was Bangkok, and outside the railway station a tuk-tuk driver touted for me to ride to the Banglampu area in his rickshaw. We bargained the price and set off. In the middle of what was nowhere to me, he stopped and told me that the price was now three times the amount we had agreed. No amount of arguing would get the price back down, but I was blowed if I was going to pay the inflated price. I got out and started walking through the streets. Dawn was just breaking and the walk was a bonus as the city was still at peace and it was easy to head in roughly the right direction, taking my lead from the rising sun. At the river I found a taxi boat to go the last stretch. These river taxis are also called 'long tails' because of the two or three metre long shafts that take the power from the large noisy engines to the propellers. The boats are narrow and low. They cut through the very murky waters at speed, and at times we only just made it under the low-slung wooden bridges.

The journey to Bangkok was worth it. The Indian Airways ticket was a quarter of the price of the direct flight from Penang to Madras. Even with the train tickets, accommodation and taxi costs, I was going to get to Madras for less than half the price.

I arrived in Calcutta with a blood orange sun dropping down into India's haze of dust and wood smoke-filled air. The world had taken on a bright glow as if someone had spilt a giant tin of orange paint over the trees, roads and buildings. By the time I'd cleared immigration, the orange glow had changed to misty shades of mauves and purples, and just a faint hint of cool was in the air. The ramshackle buildings still radiated heat from the day as I stood waiting for a taxi. I didn't have to wait long before a beaten up, bright yellow Ambassador taxi screeched to a halt in front of me. It did so with a dash of style that fitted with the driver's immaculate but rather showy clothes perfectly.

Babu was a character! Dark skin, the whitest teeth I have ever seen, and his almost non-stop chatter was accompanied by enthusiastic head wiggles whenever he wanted to make a point. As the car bumped and rattled over the bricked roads and potholes, he was absolutely adamant that I mustn't try to stay in the Salvation Army Guesthouse. "Very dirty Sah", he kept on turning round for far too long to tell me. But this was the cheapest place in Calcutta I knew of and my budget had taken a big dent, so I was determined. Babu spat a great red gob of betel nut juice out of the window, sulking. But his sulk didn't last long and soon he was back to chattering enthusiastically. When he wasn't leaning on his horn as if he was sure that all other traffic would part before him like the Red Sea, if he did it long and hard enough, he was leaning out of the window to yell and curse at other drivers.

There didn't seem to be any system. The traffic appeared to have no rules other than 'go forward somehow'. Battered Ambassadors heaved their heavy rounded bodies forward, lumbering around potholes. Three-wheeler rickshaws buzzed like demented flies, darting and ducking past the other road users. Big, beaten up buses

 belched clouds of smoke over everyone, and bullied their way along with a rather solid superiority. Their windows were decorated with shiny pictures of the gods Ganesh and Shiva or fat, non-smiling Buddhas. They had glittery tassels hanging and swinging like some sort of freak belly dance as the bus thumped through yet another hole. Garlands of bright orange marigolds framed the windows, and bold

157

signs stated warnings and religious confidence. 'Sound Horn Please' and 'God Is With Me'. Big Tata trucks, subservient only to the almost kamikaze behaviour of the buses, arrogantly elbowed their way through the mess. Only fools, buses and cows got in their way. People-power rickshaws scuttled their sweaty way through the chaos, battling for tiny spaces. The rickshaw men looking wide-eyed at the constant mash of ever-changing threats, all of which had the power to crush them and their passengers out of existence as one would do with an irritating bug. Cyclists were next down the food chain, with pedestrians being the lowest form of life. The latter though, still had to cross the street and did so with a combination of fatalism and pro-rugby agility as they handed off cars in their dash from one side to the other. The amazing thing was that it all seemed to work, until a cow got in the way that is. Cows are holy and know that they can get away with anything, so they did. They would aimlessly wander out into the snarling mess of the traffic, and the 'flow' really did somehow miraculously part for them. Perhaps in a past life Babu had been a cow, or perhaps, living on the taxi driver's edge of life he was already dreaming of the form he would like to take in the next one.

Eventually he bumped the taxi down Sudder Street and pulled to a halt outside the Salvation Army Guest House. I breathed a sigh of relief, wondering how I was going to cope with riding the bike in this sort of traffic. In a way, arriving in India without my bike was yet another bonus. There had to be some sort of a system to the driving and as a temporary backpacker I might have the chance to learn how it all worked before hitting the roads myself.

Before accepting the fare, Babu made one final attempt to get me to stay somewhere else. "The Central Guest House, very good Sah and cheap too – very good place, very safe." He also volunteered his services as my driver and guide for the time I was to be in Calcutta. If I'd had more money then I would have taken him up on it. A good local driver can really help you to learn the ways of a big city, and Babu had already proved to me that the gods were with him, and his taxi! But neither was to be. With a philosophical head wiggle and a, 'You'll be sorry' look at me, he accepted the fare, a cup of tea sized tip and headed off to find his next customer.

The Salvation Army Hostel was a dark, dank and dingy building. The staff didn't seem to care about anything and certainly not about their guests. The shared bunk room I was shown to had a small sealed window, a 40 watt light bulb that seemed to have been restricted to just 20 watts, and a rough beaten floor that could have had paint on it at sometime but now just had layers of sticky grime. All except one of the bunks had rumpled sweat-stained sheets, and were surrounded by travellers' clutter. At a glance I could tell that nothing of real value lay there for the world to see. On one bunk a tall very thin man lay in an almost comatose state with sweat pouring off him. On one corner of my bunk was a pile of two sheets that had probably not seen an iron for years. They looked as if they had started off life with bright pink and white stripes. Now they were so faded and stained that the only way I could tell they had once been this way, was where one of the seams had become unstitched.

I was tired and after all the travelling my back was sore. I lay on the saggy bunk with a sense of relief. At last I had made it to India and though not particularly pleasant, this was to be my home for the next few days of exploring. I had four days to take a look at Calcutta and to find out about getting a train down to Madras, to get me to the port at the time my ship should be docking.

The sick man was called Billy. He was Australian, travelling on his own and a bout of malaria had just hit him. He'd been in Africa some years before, where like many, he had caught malaria and still struggled with occasional attacks of it. My medical kit still had paludrine and chloroquin, so I handed them over and set off into the streets to find bottled water and a couple of bottles of 'Tumbs Up', India's very, very sweet version of Coca Cola. The two mixed together would help Billy re-hydrate, and the drugs take the edge off his malaria.

Corner shops are not hard to find and where there are hostels for backpackers you can be sure that they will sell bottled water, fizzy drinks, biscuits and loo paper. Tired, I snacked on biscuits and painkillers, and fell into bed. In spite of the dank heat, sleep came quickly.

In the morning, over breakfast at the Blue Sky Café, I met Sev and Jo. One of the reasons I love to travel so much is that I am far more likely to come across kindred spirits than I am when I'm working at home. Every so often I'd meet people whom I clicked with instantly,  as if I'd known them for years. Sev was a tall very good-looking Australian of Italian extraction and Jo was a very pretty British girl with long brown hair. The two of them seemed perfectly matched and travelled in complete harmony. A bonus of meeting them was that they'd been in India for quite a few weeks by this time and knew how things worked a darned sight better than I did. They didn't make me feel like one, but I was an India rookie and they were happy to share what they'd learned, which made my life considerably easier, and cheaper!

After breakfast we walked through the packed streets and crowded pavements together. Beggars struggled to find shade amongst the stalls that lined the pavement edges. A shoe repairer had set up next to a man who was making sugar cane juice drinks. The drink maker wore only a T-shirt and beige trousers, both of which were stained from the juice that squirted out from the old clothes mangle he was using to squeeze the long yellow and green stems of the cane. Next to him was a seller of underwear. This man displayed Y-fronts that looked big enough for a teenager to use as a hammock, and next to these giant briefs he displayed soft lilac, pink and orange coloured bloomers. He also, tucked to one side of his stall, had a range of decidedly tiny ladies knickers in scarlet and black. When he saw me noticing those, he picked a pair up and winking, nodded towards Jo. Along from him was a vendor of hardboiled eggs, a samosa seller who was dunking the pastry triangles onto a vat of shimmering yellow oil, and along from him a seller of cakes that looked as if they held enough sugar calories to deal with my weekly intake.

160

On my first trip to India in the early '80s, buying a railway ticket had been a time-consuming chore, though the exercise had always been an excellent 'people-watching' opportunity. It would often take three days to complete and that would have included queuing up in at least four different offices in different parts of a city. You needed to get a permit to get the next permit, to get permission to have the ticket and then, a queue for the ticket itself. Times had changed and this time the whole exercise took just an hour in an air-conditioned office. To travel two-thirds of the length of a sub-continent, the ticket cost me just $10.

A couple of days later I had my first experience of a strike in India. I woke to near silence and at first thought that it was early. There was a strike on and almost miraculously the traffic was virtually all gone. There were no street vendors touting their wares and the chai stand on the street corner was deserted. The strange calm didn't at first seem to sit well on the city. Noise and the frenetic mass of people movement were the lifeblood of Calcutta.

With the strike, exploring on foot was suddenly made easy. For once I could look up as I walked. Until now my eyes had had to concentrate on where I was going. Pavements weren't even; there was rubbish to fall over everywhere, dogs and people used the streets as toilets and dead animals in the gutters weren't unusual. I'd started to develop the agility of a ballet dancer with my attempts at dealing with the constant heaving mass of people and traffic.

Now I had time to look at the tops of the buildings, where old colonial traces could still be seen. I had time to take in the ramshackle electrical wires that hung like a mad woman's knitting from the sides of the buildings and spread like giant black cobwebs across the streets. And, I could even see from one end of a street to another! Above the cinema hung a huge brightly coloured hand painted mural that, with an eclectic clash of violence and romance, advertised the latest Bollywood epic. It sold pure escapism and the scenes portrayed in the patchwork of the film seemed to be as far removed from everyday life on the street as it was possible to go. The gun-toting men were all

161

heroes with bright handsome faces and the women pictures of vibrancy, flesh and flirtation.

Around a corner I heard a familiar sound which, had I been a cricket enthusiast, I would have recognised instantly. Ragged children had turned the empty street into a cricket ground and a crowd had gathered to watch. It dawned on me that a general strike was as good as a bank holiday at home. Cricket was being played; families had pulled tables out into their alleyways and were enjoying having friends and family around. Instead of the city seeming to have lost its lifeblood, it seemed to be taking a big welcome breath of fresh air before the urgent rush for survival started again. I was happy too – with my ticket already bought, I wasn't in a rush, and the trains were still running. I felt lucky to have been able to see this rather wonderful city in this way.

Packed and ready to go, Billy was looking a lot better and I was now eager to get going. I like Indian trains – they are like a small city on wheels. India has the largest railway system in the world and percentage-wise it's still probably the safest way to travel, though there is supposed to be a death on the railway every day. Most of the engines are now diesel but every so often you are able to find a steam train still running and for me, when that happens, I can't help but appreciate that I am travelling with a dash of history.

First class compartments are air-conditioned, with plenty of space and have waiter service. They are not first class as we know it but they do have style and you sit with people who have status in society. I don't like it though – after 24 hours of air con you lose all mental ability to deal with the heat outside. Also because the other passengers are loathe to talk to you. Money seems to build superiority which doesn't encourage chat. It doesn't help that as a traveller you always look a little ragged and therefore, suspect. On the other hand, for once in India body space is respected.

Third class is the other end of the scale. You sit on wooden bench seats, and the windows have bars on them. Everyone spits, goats and chickens are welcome, and passengers crammed in tight form a solid human jigsaw puzzle for the whole of the journey. If I could snag a window seat then the journey would be tolerable, but anywhere else in the carriage it was incredibly uncomfortable. But of course it's cheap, and getting a seat at all is considered an achievement. So much so that there are professional (but unofficial) seat minders at terminus stations - you pay them a fee and they get to the train early, snag a seat for you and fight off all others until you get there. I'd tried that one time on a previous backpacking visit through India, just to see how the system worked and also because I had a 36 hour train ride in front of me. So, I paid my money, wondered if I'd ever seen any result from it, and got to the station an hour before the train was supposed to leave. My minder was exactly where we had agreed in the already packed carriage. I locked my pack to the overhead rack, and with my bag of food and water in hand we swapped places. I nodded a greeting to my neighbours. No goat, no chickens, and I was just one seat away from the window. That would do nicely. My neighbours were obviously uncomfortable at having me with them, but over the next half an hour or so of nodding and smiling they seemed to accept that I wasn't too weird and that they were probably safe. The next thing I knew, the seat rocked wildly, flashes of bright material appeared on either side of my head, two dusty feet appeared on my chest, and within seconds a fat, sari-clad lady had slid herself, greatly aided by gravity, between me and the back of the seat. I was no contest for her fat belly and strong thighs, and within a second I was on the floor, surrounded by sandal-clad feet and spit. The fat lady looked directly down at me with an expression on her face that said, 'So, what are you going to do about it? This seat is mine!' The other passengers' expressions ranged from outright hilarity to discreet shows of sympathy and for me the next 36 hours were not funny. Imagine 36 hours of standing on the London Underground, in mid summer at rush hour, with the 'exotic' musty scents of unwashed bodies and curry breath piped through the windows.

Train toilets are an adventure in themselves. Third class passengers either don't get a loo at all or have a hole in the floor of a tiny sweatbox of a room; whatever you do in the room drops straight through the hole onto the tracks below. Second class passengers have a stained, stainless steel moulded floor pan, with raised up foot shaped islands placed strategically in front of the hole, which also is open to the world below the train. The breeze that comes up through the hole encourages you to conduct your clean up operation as rapidly as possible. First class passengers on the other hand are treated with full respect. They have almost exactly the same facilities as second class but the loos are cleaned regularly, which is a bonus as the rocking motion of the train means that people often miss the hole. I'm not sure what happens to first class poo, but you don't see any railway sleepers down there.

Second class compartments are my favourites, and it was one of these that I had booked for myself on the 'Down' express, 'Down' being a train that was heading south. Passenger lists are located by the door on the outside of each carriage and you check here to see which seat you have been allocated, in which carriage. The lists are always an adventure because it doesn't matter that the ticket office has had sight of the spelling of your name from your passport, and that you have spelled it out for them, letter by letter. The spelling is unlikely to have more than a vague resemblance to your name. Sometime it's purely phonetic, but with an Indian accent! The trick for me was to scan the list looking for anything that didn't look Indian. Sometimes your middle name has been picked out and as before I found myself checking to make sure that I wasn't on the list as some form of Mr Nigel. But this time there it was. Manicom, and spelt absolutely correctly. Must be fate, life was on the up again. Just a few days in India and I was already considering that perhaps fate did rule life here.

Second class compartments are rather like those on carriages in old-fashioned British trains. A corridor runs the length of the carriage and off that corridor are compartments with seating space for eight people. The bench seats are comfortably padded, as are the backrests. Above the backrests are wide padded luggage racks. The seating system is a gem as it's designed to allow six people to sleep on beds. At night, luggage comes down onto the floor, making an upper bunk on either side. The backrests flip up and are locked into place roughly half way between the seats and the luggage racks. The beds are surprisingly comfortable and the best plan is to try to snag a middle bunk. It gets hot up in the top bunk and you are more likely to take a tumble out of bed if the train rattles over a rough section of track. Though there are seats for eight, two of those aren't booked for the nighttime, leaving the remaining six passengers with their beds.

The people who travel in second class are inevitably interesting, and interested in you. Given a bit of encouragement it never seems to take long before conversations are struck up and life stories are being told. Food is also shared and when you are new to train travel, the other passengers are always pleased to show you how things work. I've sat with schoolteachers, mid-level businessmen and their families, students from reasonably well to do families and so on. One big advantage is that there are inevitably people amongst a group like this who can speak good English.

The windows still have bars on them, but that works well as it means you have a chance of a breeze blowing through all the time, which helps to counteract the body-generated heat, the heat of the day, plus the heat that seems to be collected magnetically by the roofs of the train carriages. The bars also help stop people reaching in to pinch things when the train stops at a station at nighttime, and they prevent desperate people from attempting to climb in to grab a seat. But I have seen people get on board by somehow wiggling through the bars in Third Class. My only worry is that I'm too fat to get through them in an emergency, as are many middle class Indian people. It's a fate thing again.

Arriving in a station is an event. When no train is in, the stations tend to be fairly sleepy places. Trains never seem to be early but they run predictably to schedule so passengers inevitably have time on their hands before their train arrives, and often slip into some sort of dozy hibernation as they wait in whatever shade they can find. When the train arrives though, all hell breaks loose. Whistles blow, porters shout, people grab bags and battle towards the train, carriage doors slam open allowing outgoing passengers to pile off. Food vendors wander along the side of the carriages offering their wares up to those in second and third class.

Samosas, barbecued meat on mini skewers, nan breads, chapattis, fruit, nuts, bowls of rice and whatever the dish of the day is. Tea sellers rush up and down yelling, "Chai, coffee, coffee, chai". The tea sellers juggle tall stacks of cups over their shoulders, and lug large battered and blackened aluminium teapots in their fists.

Chai is India's version of tea and it's superb. It's normally very safe to drink too as the preparation is quite particular – it's not simply a case of dunking a tea bag in a mug of boiling water. That wouldn't be tea at all to an Indian; it'd be tasteless dingy coloured hot water. To make real chai you take one large pot and a heat source. Add water and lots of thick un-pasteurised milk from the local holy cow. Add loose tea, some spices and a ton of sugar – a veritable mountain of the stuff is dumped into the mix. Then boil the living daylights out of it until it becomes a thick really refreshing but very sweet drink. Because it's been bubbling for hours, you know that even though it looks like a cup of liquid mud, the chai is going to be safe to drink. And once you've told your brain that it's not to expect tea, chai tastes superb – quite delicious and surprisingly thirst quenching, the perfect match for the heat of a curry and the heat of the day.

As a passenger, all you have to do is lean out of the window and chai, lunch or dinner just comes to you. As a second-class passenger you can also order your food from the conductor, who orders it from the next station ahead. These meals are served on large aluminium or stainless steel trays that have indentations for the different types of food. One dent for rice, another dent for vegetables, a dent for curried potatoes and a dent for whatever stringy meat is available that day. You inevitably get a slice or two of nan bread or a chapatti on the side, and you eat it all with your fingers. The food is piping hot but no way as much fun as buying it through the windows which means you can see in advance what you are getting. I always had the feeling that if it looked safe and interesting then it probably was.

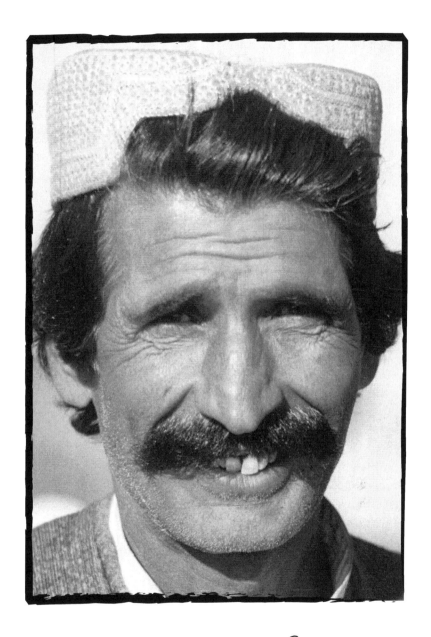

LEVEL CROSSING OPERATOR - BALUCHISTAN

THE TEMPLE OF BOROBADUR

FULL MOON PARTY - THAILAND

THE FAN MAKER - PENANG

THAI PADDY FIELDS

PETROL STATION IN THAI MOUNTAINS

CHINESE NEW YEAR

TYPICAL COURTYARD

FRESH FRUIT DELIVERY

BACK IN TIME

STREETLIFE

COLONIAL INFLUENCE

A GREAT WAY TO GET AROUND

CALM WATERS

STREET DINING

ASIAN VARIETY

RETURNING WITH THE CATCH

IT MUST HAVE BEEN SOMETHING I SAID!

BOTTLED WATER DELIVERY

SHOPPING EXPEDITION

CALCUTTA TRAFFIC

DELHI TAXI

DELHI TRAFFIC AT RUSH HOUR

THE INDIAN ARMY ON PARADE — DELHI

COUNTRY RAILWAY WAIT

DELHI BOBBY

THE SCHOOL RUN

BIG CITY RAILWAY WAIT

INDIA FACTS:

- THERE ARE 7,000 KM OF COASTLINE, WITH 6 BORDER COUNTRIES
- INDIA HAS 63,230 KM OF RAILWAY LINE
- IT ALSO HAS 3,383,344 KM OF ROAD, OF WHICH 1,779,639 KM ARE UNPAVED
- THE POPULATION OF INDIA IS NOW WELL OVER A BILLION

THE BIKE COVER MAN   THE BARBER

THE MARKET TRADER — VARANASI

TEMPLE CALM

DAWN ON THE GANGES

DAWN TRAFFIC ON THE
GRAND TRUNK ROAD — PUNJAB - INDIA

SADHU — HOLY MAN

SWAYAMBHUNATH TEMPLE

PAKISTANI TRAFFIC - SIND DESERT   QUETTA MAIN STREET - PAKISTAN

IN THE CALM OF THE DAWN

STREET MECHANICS
EVERYWHERE

BACKROAD FUN!

THE QUETTA TO TAFTAN ROAD

TRUCK LOADING AT THE BORDER

OVER THE BORDER INTO IRAN

'SPEED BUMP' WARNINGS

'PIGGY-BACKING' THROUGH THE SNOW - TURKISH MOUNTAINS

Chapter 9

Red Tape and Farce

'Go confidently in the direction of your dreams. Live the life you have imagined.'

Henry David Thoreau

By the time I arrived in Madras (now called Chennai), it was hot and humid and in spite of having slept really well, I felt tired and very sticky. But that didn't matter. Finally I was in Madras, and with luck my bike's container had been swung off the ship that very day.

The rickshaw rank outside the station was a yellow and black swarm of three-wheeled bees, and I soon had three drivers trying to persuade me that they knew the way, that their rickshaw was the fastest and that they were the safest driver. At that stage I hadn't even told them where I wanted to go! It was the Broadlands guesthouse. Back in Calcutta, Billy had said that this was a perfect spot for me: clean and well run, cheap and, better still, it had three courtyards. Billy had been certain that I'd be able to get the bike in off the street. As a bonus there were good cheap restaurants nearby and it was a short rickshaw ride away from the port. I later learned that the Broadlands is run and staffed by retired railway workers, which explained why it was to such a high standard. The only downside to the place was that the staff were said to be racist towards other Indians and I worried that this might mean I'd have to move on.

Traffic is less frenetic in Madras, and my driver rickshaw'd me to the Broadlands in a few minutes. On spelling my name the reception clerk looked up at me over his glasses. "Mister, you are not Indian." I explained that I was not and handed over my passport. I wasn't quite sure what was happening but wondered if this was somehow something to do with the racism I'd heard of. Not the case at all. I discovered that I have a Tamil name. Manicom in the Tamil language means, 'The eight precious stones' and it was quite an odd feeling to find that people of a completely different race shared the name. I wondered if there was any sort of historical connection and made a mental note to someday try to find out.

Over the coming weeks I grew ever more grateful to Billy for putting me on to Broadlands. It became a quiet haven at the end of each day of chaos and frustration at the port – I was still intending to extract the bike myself.

Day one saw me down at the port trying to get someone, anyone, to explain to me where I had to go and what I had to do to start the process. By chance I could see my  container from the road – I could clearly see the registration marks and knew that unless something dramatic had gone wrong I was little more than 100 metres from my bike.

But by day three I'd given up. I'd walked miles, begged and pleaded, demanded and insisted, and had been treated with complete lack of interest. I was going to have to find myself a shipping agent and see if we could come to some sort of deal. I hoped I'd find one who would, for a fee, guide me through the red tape and confusion, whilst leaving me to do the running. For three more days I knocked on doors and waited in sweaty corridors. No one was interested in helping me at all. Most of the agents, when I eventually made it through the layers of junior staff, said that they had no idea about getting foreigners' bikes out of the port and that anyway, they were too busy.

Back at the Broadlands, and too exhausted to go out to get food, I asked one of the staff to go for me. I'd noted on previous days that this could be done for a small fee, but had never taken advantage of the opportunity because everyday on the street was a chance to explore. Within minutes I was sitting at one of the wooden tables in the courtyard with a very good thali in front of me. A thali is a collection of curries and sauces served with rice. It's usually vegetarian and in Madras, if you ate in a local restaurant it would be served on a fresh banana leaf instead of a plate. The curries aren't hot but are full of flavour. The sweetness of chai washes a thali down very well and by the time I'd eaten I was feeling a bit more human.

At that moment a stocky, moustached, blonde man of about 28 or 29 marched into the courtyard, swearing furiously in German. He strode up and down the courtyard tense with rage and frustration at something. As he swore and raved, he slipped between German and English and I began to get the picture. He too was a biker and he had been in Madras trying to get his bike out of the port a week longer than I had. Things were going as wrong for him as they were for me, and he had had enough of India.

I introduced myself. Karsten was just about ready to kill people he was so frustrated, but he gradually began to calm down, in part I think because he realised that I was in the same boat.

Red tape in India was introduced in the days of the Raj and the East India Company, and I suspected that it is almost as frustrating for Indians to deal with as it is for a foreigner. The difference being that after over one hundred and fifty years it was all they were used to, so just got on with it. I'd been dealing with customs and immigration officials for more than two years of travel through Africa and Asia by this time, so I wasn't quite so fazed. Just confused as to what could be done about it.

<u>4 People</u> – *A wall sign in the Madras Post Office.*

This is the story about 4 people named 'Everybody', 'Somebody', 'Anybody' and 'Nobody'.
There was an important job to be done, and Everybody was sure that Somebody would do it.
Anybody could have done it, but Nobody did it.
Somebody got angry about that because it was Everybody's job.
Everybody thought that Anybody could do it.
Nobody realised that Everybody would not do it.
It ended up that Everybody blamed Somebody, when Nobody actually accused Anybody.

Karsten told me that he had found a shipping agent who had accepted the task of getting his bike out of the port. "Nice people", he said. "But they do nothing!" When he mentioned the name of the company I knew that I had heard of them before at some time, but I'd duly forgotten the name. Winnies Shipping had a good reputation on the bikers' circuit and at that moment, as I cursed myself for not writing their name down when I'd heard it, I knew that things had taken a positive step forward. Karsten and I sat under the purple and pink bougainvillea in the courtyard, talking things through until the early hours of the next day. As the night cooled, so did he, a little. We decided that I would go with him to Winnies on the Monday, this being a Friday night, and I would try to get them to take my work on too.

The weekend was time to relax and prepare. We talked bikes and travel. We drank endless cups of chai and I walked the beach. Fishermen worked there, pushing their wooden boats out through the murky surf. Sari-clad women strolled amongst the line of man-made refuse that the sea had rejected. And seashell sellers pestered

anyone they could find, blowing their conch shells as they strolled the beach, making a quite eerie sound that floated across the sands. One came and sat quietly by me, offering me a beedie cigarette. I shared my fruit with him and the two of us sat watching the waves roll onto the sand. Further down the beach, a herd of water buffalo had been brought down to the water for a bath, and the fishermen sat mending nets that had been hung up to dry on low wooden frameworks. Church bells tolled in the background (it was Sunday) and the buzz of the city seemed just a little quieter than on a weekday. I'd read that a good percentage of people in this area were Christians and the sound of the bells in this very different part of the world was rather reassuring.

The mini holiday of the weekend came to a close too quickly in one way but in another I was raring to go. Even Karsten seemed slightly less negative. I just hoped that something positive would happen for him as I didn't much want to be a witness to murder.

The day started well when it clicked that we would be able to share the cost of a rickshaw each day – we were both sure that there were going to be quite a few more trips to the port. Karsten took me into the shipping office, past guards who looked the other way when we strode in. Up a flight of dimly lit stairs that were lined by waiting men, into a small waiting room, which Karsten ignored, and straight on into a large, open plan office. Sixteen desks were lined up, neatly set at ninety degrees angle to one large desk at the side. The big one, whose top was held up on either side by sets of drawers, was flanked by two four-drawer grey/green filing cabinets, upon which were stacks of wire in-trays. The surface of the desk was covered in papers and half-drunk polystyrene cups of tea and coffee. Behind the desk sat a well-dressed beardless man whose hair was slicked back neatly with some sort of oil. He wore an expression on his face that was a combination of tired, kind and resigned. He greeted Karsten with a polite handshake, and a face that said 'bad news, and I don't know how to give it'. He greeted me with interest while one of his staff pulled across an extra chair for me. Once we were settled, Mr Johns got it over and done with. "Mr Karsten, your motorcycle will not be free today. I am hoping that this may be possible by the end of the week". Thankfully Karsten did not blow up. Mr Johns was unable to offer an explanation other than, "This is India my friend, we are working hard for you".

That gave me the opportunity to explain the reason for my being there, and after an hour of discussion, three cups of chai, and a further half an hour of document reviewing, Mr Johns agreed to take the work on. Though he told me, "You will need to be patient you know", and glanced across at Karsten. He sent one of his staff down the street to get photocopies of my papers, and then sent us on our way.

We were at Mr Johns office everyday for the next two weeks. We tried enthusing and buying the chai. We tried gentle pushing – nothing seemed to work. We sat hour after hour in the waiting room next to Mr Johns office, and became as much a part of the office as the dead flies hanging from cobwebs in front of the dust-stained windows.

Regular clients began to greet us; the guards started to welcome us as if we were part of the family, but still nothing happened. All Mr Johns could say was, "It is all moving forward, we are getting there". Karsten flickered between rage and an almost comatose acceptance. But even in the latter state, I knew that there was a volcano bubbling below the surface, so kept a close watch on him.

Then all of a sudden I'd had enough and knew I needed a break. So I got a job. Actually the job found me. I was sitting chatting in the back courtyard with a Dutch girl called Nanda. She had just come down from Tibet where she had managed to get over the border from Nepal and had spent nearly a month hitchhiking around the country. This was quite a rare feat and to have done it as a woman on her own made it even more special. Nanda was a sparkly, friendly person who bubbled enthusiasm – her positive way was infectious. We had word that a movie tout was looking for extra's and for the hell of it we decided to go to see what was up. Others were muttering that the extra's were for a blue movie. There had been rumours floating around that porn was a thriving business in Madras, which holds the second largest filming business in India, second only to Bombay. Neither of us was interested in that type of work, but it was worth listening, just in case.

The deal was all expenses paid to travel to the hill station of Ooty where a crew was filming an African Safari movie in the wildlife park there. We were supposed to get dressed up as rich western tourists and to mooch around in the background of the hotel, or to be filmed belting around the bush in a Land Rover, supposedly taking pictures of the elephants and lions. We were told that genuine African footage of lions was going to be spliced into the movie at a later date. The elephants were going to be Indian elephants – well, no one would notice the difference would they? It all sounded delightfully bizarre, and when they said that not only would we get food and accommodation but we'd get paid for the work too, it seemed too good a chance to miss. We signed up, stored our kit and the next day set off with the agent.

172

We were supposed to travel by train but at short notice the agent hadn't managed to get tickets for the five of us – two other travellers had also signed up. We piled aboard a bus and travelled white-knuckled for the better part of a day until we could get on a train, which took us further up into the hills. The final leg of the journey through lush tea plantations was by a narrow gauge railway, which rocked and swayed its way through an area that didn't look as if it had changed much for 50 years. Little stations, with names such as Covedale and Wellington, could have been plucked straight out of Dorset and plonked down amongst the tea plantations, the dark-skinned people, the eucalyptus trees and the dust. As we climbed higher, the temperature dropped. After months of heat, this was the coldest I'd been and it became decidedly uncomfortable. Ooty sits at the junction between Tamil Nadu, Kerala and Karnataka, and was once the summer headquarters for the government of Madras. The town still has an air of unhurried privilege with its flower gardens, single-storey stone cottages and leafy winding lanes. In amongst these are churches, parks and maharajas' summer palaces. We were told that in season the place retains little of the peace we were seeing, as large numbers of well to do families head up here to escape the heat of the lowlands, bringing with them all the requirements of modern life including ghetto blasters. It was hard to imagine the town thus transformed.

The agent had booked us in to the Tourist Lodge on the Commercial road. It was basic and cold, and I found myself wishing that I had my bike jacket and my sleeping bag, both of which were packed away with the bike. Still, the lodge was a roof over our heads and next day the sun was shining. The trouble came when the agent found out that the film crew had already found some travellers in Ooty, and the scenes we'd come up for had been shot the day before. It seemed that none of us were to become Bollywood stars after all. We all elected to stay in Ooty for a couple more days, even if we weren't going to get paid. The agent agreed to honour our return tickets to get back to Madras and the Tourist Lodge had space for us for a little longer.

Nanda and I set off to explore the hills around the town. Paths spread out and meandered over the hillsides, connecting hamlets, with fields, with woods. We found kids playing in a fresh air that was a complete contrast to that of the cities on the coast. Here the children all wanted their photos taken as they played games in the wild flowers that coated the hillsides. Old women sat outside their brick houses, sewing, grinding flour and cleaning vegetables. A man with a bright yellow turban-like head covering and a vivid pink shirt sat washing vibrantly orange carrots in a clear water stream. On the hillside, we were well away from the sounds of traffic and I realised that this, other than the sound of an axe hitting wood somewhere in the distance, was the quietest moment I'd had in a very long time. It was almost sad to have to head back to Madras and I wondered how Karsten had been coping.

Nothing seemed to have moved while I was away, other than that Karsten had progressed from chai to beer. At Winnies we tried demanding action and started to insist that we went wherever our papers went. This way we had the chance to see that things were actually happening and that our papers weren't just stuck in a back office collecting chai cup stains. Mr Johns was not happy about this, but I knew that Karsten wasn't going to stay in check for much longer, unless he saw movement of some sort, in fact any sort. I also thought it was a good opportunity for seeing more places and people that were usually hidden from the normal backpacker.

It was at this time that we discovered that Mr Johns had a taste for rum, and that when he was half cut, he would work like a lunatic for a couple of hours. Miraculously, things would seem to happen. In many parts of India booze is illegal and those that wish to drink have to qualify for a permit. The laws in Tamil Nadu had recently changed and the underground drinking dens that Mr Johns had been used to visiting for his illicit rum, were being licensed. But the atmosphere in them hadn't changed. With low lighting, they reminded me of stage sets for bars in the days of Prohibition in the USA. Though legal, the drinkers still did not meet each others' eyes and the air was furtive.

There were no women drinkers, but the men who'd had a healthy helping of booze were full of camaraderie, though they didn't stretch quite as far as singing bawdy songs. Bottles of booze were always served in brown paper bags as if the drinkers were even trying to deceive each other! A half bottle was Mr Johns daily allowance and when we were doing the buying he was happy to enjoy it. Afterwards he actually seemed to enjoy his work back in the office as well. At least for the amount of time he was able to keep at it. After a couple of hours, his eyes would begin to droop and before long his head would be down on his desktop. That was the moment for us to leave, as we knew that nothing else would happen that day, but we always left feeling a little cheered. Phone calls had been made, documents signed and rubber-stamped, and runners had been sent out with our papers in hand and looks of urgency on their faces.

Still no real progress though – the weeks frittered by, and two weeks of strikes by the customs officers and dockworkers hadn't helped either. Ships either had to lie up and wait outside the port, or were being diverted elsewhere. An expensive business for all, that was complicated with real style by the strikers. The customs officers went on strike on day one, and by the end of that day had negotiated a solution to their problem. The next day the port workers went on strike, and again, by the end of the day their strike was over. The next day the customs officers went back on strike, and so it continued. This hopscotch of industrial action stretched on day after day, leaving Karsten and me with ticking clocks and dwindling budgets. I was also due to be meeting Birgit up in Nepal, and if things didn't get sorted out fairly rapidly, that plan was dead.

To make things worse, the plague was hitting vast swathes of India and people were dropping like flies. The longer the wait went on, the more concerned we were that the plague would reach as far as Madras. If it did, we were going to be faced with either running for it without bikes, or continuing with fingers crossed that we would stay well. Neither option sat comfortably. At the time, the eminent Ayurveda expert and physician to the President, Mr Vedvrat Sharma, suggested burning cow dung cakes to keep the plague away. This was a time-tested ayurvedic remedy apparently, but it didn't inspire confidence. Meanwhile, my delay was worsened by circumstances straight out of a Laurel and Hardy script. The port's container stacking area was like a mini multicoloured city, with blocks and avenues. No trees, just miles of asphalt and rusty yellow cranes that reminded me of giant stick insects. My container was stacked in a 500-metre long row of similar containers; all of them baking in the sun, and at the end of the row stood a broken crane.

Normally that would have been no more than a hassle for the dockworkers. It wouldn't have held things up for me, however long it took for the crane's spare parts to arrive and for them to be fitted. This time, things went horribly wrong. The asphalt roadway at the other end of 'my' row collapsed and a 3 by 4 metre hole appeared. There was no way a crane could safely span this hole, and that was that. Until the hole was investigated and repaired, the only way I was going to get my bike would be to cut a bike-sized hole in the side of the container with an acetylene torch when no one was looking.

The plague was spreading; fortunately it was still a long way away but for us it added another pressure. I hated to think what hell it was playing with people's lives on the other side of India. Then Diwali happened. I think that Mr Johns had mentally donned a tin helmet before he told us that while Diwali was on, not much business would

get done. It's one of the biggest and supposedly the happiest of all the Hindu celebrations, but for us the bad news was that it would go on for five whole days! I was fairly regularly in contact with Birgit now and I could see that there was a very good chance that the cheap non-refundable ticket she had bought to enable us to link up in Nepal would be wasted.

I knew that as someone not long out of university this would be a major financial loss for her, and besides that we were both really looking forward to seeing each other. Goodness knew when the chance would happen again if this all went pear-shaped.

I tried not to sulk and knew that I was lucky to be in the country at the time of such a major celebration, but I just wanted my bike. Even I was becoming a little belligerent now!

Mr Johns advice was, "When everybody else is on holiday you must have a holiday too. Nothing is going to happen this week. Go away, be tourists, forget your troubles for a week. Go on, you are free." Karsten took that bit of advice like a mouthful of the most foul tasting medicine you can imagine, and that fact was spread all over his face. I had to physically drag him out of the office and back to the Broadlands, but that night I decided to take Mr Johns advice. I wasn't going to spend any more time sitting around in Madras waiting for something to happen. I was going to take control of life again and do something,

 anything! I asked Karsten where he really wanted to go to in India. I said, "Pretend that you will never get your bike back and you are going to have to fly home in a week. Where would you like to go?" To my surprise, instead of saying straight to the airport anyway, he said he'd like to go to Puri. It's a fairly small seaside town way up on the coast towards Calcutta. Puri is a major Hindu religious centre and the beach was supposed to be great. Karsten also told me that there were shops where you could buy grass over the counter and that he wanted to be able to do that at least once while he was in India; he liked a smoke. My guidebook said the place was interesting and I thought, if Diwali is on and it's a major religious centre, then perhaps there will be interesting things going on that are connected to the celebrations. It all depended on whether, at this late stage, we could get train tickets.

We went to the station on spec and a short time later found ourselves on the 'Up' train, with just one change to make at a junction just south of the city of Bhubaneswar. It was a long ride and the train was so packed that there wasn't even a remote chance to slot our bunk beds into position, but that was fine, the crush of people held us up for much of the journey.

In the earlier days of rail travel in India, platform food and drinks were served in biodegradable containers. A potter would sit at the end of the platform and using a foot-operated potter's wheel he'd turn out cup after cup, leaving them in the sun to bake hard. The chai sellers would slot 20 or so of these cups into each other and you could always see where the sellers were by these terracotta towers. The beauty was that when you had finished your tea you just binned your cup out of the window and the next rains would wash it back into the earth. Now the cups are polystyrene. The same sort of thing happened with bowls. These were made of large leaves that had been stitched together and dried in a bowl shaped mould. They would stay stiff long enough for you to eat your rice and whatever it was, and then you would flick the empty bowl out of the window to rot down or be munched by a holy cow. Holy cows are India's natural garbage collectors and they survive, particularly in the cities, on what humans throw away. But the bowls now are made out of tin foil. The problem is that people follow the custom of generations and everything still gets binned out of the window. As a result, the railway tracks and surrounding countryside are a mess of refuse.

I caught Karsten just too late to stop him throwing his cup out of the window. Challenged, he rather indignantly said, "The locals all do it!" I persuaded him that we should use one of our carrier bags to collect our rubbish in and rather than go to the effort of arguing, he agreed. For the next seven hours, in front of an audience of bemused fellow travellers, we carefully collected our rubbish. At major stations, small boys leap on the trains with hand brushes made out of palm leaves. Most of the boys I'd been told were orphans living on the streets. For a small amount of money, which they collect from the passengers in each compartment, they sweep out all the rubbish. The system works really well. They earn a living and the collections of orange peel, peanut shells, sweet wrappers and so on are regularly cleared away. Thinking that I was helping, and had found a way to get rid of our carrier bag of rubbish without losing my seat, I gave the nearest boy the bag and a rupee. He looked in the bag, looked at me, looked back in the bag, shook his head as if confused, walked over to the window and threw the bag out, leaving Karsten laughing harder than I seen him do since I'd met him!

We eventually arrived in Puri and as we'd agreed, we telephoned Mr Johns 'just in case'. "Ahh Mr Sam", Mr Johns said, "Great news, come in to the office tomorrow. You can have your motorcycles!"

We were stunned. It had been a very long backside-numbing journey and we had to decide what to do. Stay for a couple of days now we had come this far, or scoot back to Madras as quickly as possible before whatever had suddenly gone right, went wrong again. Would we get train tickets anyway? We stayed the night. Karsten bought his grass and proceeded to fumigate the room, and then we crashed. In the morning he said, "I'm going back, today, even if I have to fight for a ticket or ride on the roof!" But there were no seats to be had for the next 3 days and even third class was fully booked, though the ticket man took pity on us for some reason and sold us 'second class standing' tickets. We'd never heard of those before but grabbed them gratefully.

We were on the next train, the fullest I'd ever been on – it was more 'crush' than 'standing'. With a delay between trains in Bhubaneswar, we just had time to get to one of India's most famous zoos. It's one of the few places where you can see white tigers and though I don't like zoos much, it was too good an opportunity to miss. The zoo though was pretty grim. It looked unkempt and so did the tigers, magnificent though they still were. But the saddest thing about the visit came from learning that one of the tigers had incarcerated himself. He'd been a wild tiger but had leapt into the zoo's tiger compound in search of a mate. He'd found one, but then couldn't get back out!

When the Madras Down train arrived at the station, it was even more crowded than the Puri train had been. The only relatively free space to stand or squat was immediately outside one of the toilets, which already stank. The regular roll of the train would flap the toilet door open to allow the hole in the floor to gust stench over us. It was hard not to be sick and my back was complaining at the jolting abuse the long distance standing was giving it. To add spice to the journey, the train suddenly stopped in the middle of nowhere. The wheels from the carriages in front of us had suddenly started making a weird noise and the train's crew had piled on the brakes. The train sat for an hour, with no information being passed as to what the problem was. The packed-in people started to get very restless and many piled off the train and down onto the tracks. After another half an hour, we did too. At least it was a chance to get some fresh air and a stretch; the air around the toilets was now ever more fetid as the heat in the standing carriage grew. A crowd of men, excitedly offering advice, clustered around the underside of a carriage further up the train. Somehow, the joint in the rails that the train was now straddling had opened a gap of more than thirty centimetres. That accounted for the strange noise, but what were the crew going to do now - we had been incredibly lucky not to derail. With the overcrowded state of the train it would have been a major disaster. The solution, a further hour later when it was obvious that no help was coming, was to start the engine and drive on – very slowly. Our carriage shook violently as each of the big metal wheels clunked into the gap.

Madras is a golden city after a journey like that and Broadlands was like a palace. We showered, discussed burning our clothes and then fell into our beds. My alarm went off three hours later to tell us that Winnies would be open in forty-five minutes. We had time for chai and then for the rickshaw dash to the office. Karsten was wide-awake and bouncing from one foot to the other as he gulped his chai and implored me to drink the scalding liquid faster.

At the shipping office Mr Johns, grave faced, invited us to sit in front of his desk. "I have bad news for you", he said. "We made a mistake; we do not yet know when you can have your motorcycles". Karsten flipped. He'd sat with his legs under Mr Johns desk and with one almighty heave and a furious bellow he kicked the underside of the desk so hard that the whole thing lifted off the ground. Half-drunk chais and coffees spilt all over the official looking papers and behind us, all typewriting stopped.

Every set of eyes turned towards us as Karsten stood, now speechless with rage. Mr Johns looked at me and said, "Mr Karsten is upset, he mustn't be upset, what is the problem?" I explained in my best British voice of reserve, "You are right Mr Johns, he is now very upset, perhaps it really is time to make something happen to get him his motorcycle. It is like being without his wife for him you know." At that moment, Mr Johns boss came out of his office and beckoned the agent across. The two of them conferred, with eyes flicking from each other to Karsten as they talked.

By the time Mr Johns had returned to us, and the typewriters were clacking importantly again, the plan that we should become temporary shipping agents had been hatched. With them we could try to get in to see the port manager. This was the only way that we could get the whole thing jump-started. At that moment we would have tried just about anything and the level of risk to all involved was never even discussed. Mr Johns was confident and we assumed that he had the backing of his boss.

We never dreamt that the plan would result in Mr Johns and I being arrested. If we'd been aware that Karsten was going to have to resort to hitting port policemen to escape, then we would never have gone along with the idea, but by then we'd been battling with Indian red tape and procedure for nearly six weeks.

My original idea that as I'd already experienced clearing my bike from ports a couple of times, I could save money and do it myself in Madras too, without paying for an agent, was a case of ignorance is bliss. I'd been in India before on a couple of trips with a backpack, so I thought I knew enough to be realistic. I knew that it would probably take me two to three weeks to find my way around and to work my way through the usual red tape. In retrospect, the daftness of this thought was quite sublime!

Madras port reeked with the smells of diesel, sun-baked concrete, unwashed bodies, and the collected grime of a century or more. All of this was spiced by the tang of sea and the rich curry scents from the food stalls outside the gates. The humidity floated this heavy load through the air with an effort that just added to the lazy torpor of the midday heat in Southern India.

But I wasn't bothered. We'd done it. We had actually blagged our way in to see the manager of the harbour. At last things seemed to be on the move. Perhaps finally we'd get our bikes. The manager's desk was covered in glass paperweights. These seemed to act as a visible sign of rank – the more a person had, the higher up the scale he was, but they also stopped the paper chaos that covered his desk from being wafted out of his window onto the water of the harbour below. Not that they would have been noticed down there. The rolling waters were covered in a collection of a working harbour's waste. Polystyrene cups bobbed alongside oil-stained wood, bits of old rope, torn cardboard, food packaging, a dead cat, and a chunk of seaweed that had probably regretted losing its footing on the harbour bed. All of these slopped lazily in a rainbow of spilt oil.

His office was not what I'd expected for a man of such a high position. The décor was worn out minimalist. The paint on the walls a pale green gloss, and peeling up towards the ceiling. The floor was grey painted concrete and his desk was a basic metal affair, but with a very large top. The manager had been surprised to see us but had recovered quickly. It couldn't be often that his day would be invaded by two European motorcyclists pretending to work for a shipping agent, and the shipping agent himself.

The agent had almost grovelled in his respect for this very powerful man. It was only at that moment that I realised just how far Mr Johns had stuck his neck out to get us into the port, and to this office. The manager sat back in his creaky chair, and looked at the three of us with an air of concern. Surely this had to be a good sign. With not a moment to lose, I stepped forward to tell our tale, before Karsten could. Karsten had had enough of India, of delays, the heat and the constant hassle. He had ceased to be even remotely tactful and I knew that if I wasn't quick enough, all the effort to get us in would have been a sweaty waste of time.

The manager listened carefully and with a sudden burst of action, surprised even Mr Johns by grabbing a thin sheet of paper from one of the piles. With his fountain pen he scribbled a paragraph of words. He then grabbed a couple of rubber stamps, with which he thumped an inkpad and then the sheet of paper with heavy-handed enthusiasm. He looked up, smiled, apologised for the delay and then turned away from us as if we had already vanished from the room.

Outside the office Mr Johns read the sheet, and with almost boyish excitement he said, "This is it, very wonderful, you will have your motorcycles by the end of the week." Karsten's expression was extremely cynical. After all, we'd heard this before. During the six weeks we'd been trying to get our bikes released from the port, this had almost become a catchphrase. I tried to be a little more positive. The sheet had been signed by the port manager himself, and it had those still-damp rubber stamps all over it.

We headed back out into the glaring sunshine and started the long walk over the dusty railway tracks, through the loading yards, past the labourers resting in the shade of a warehouse, and across the baking heat of the main entrance area. The port is guarded by two fences. The outer fence had a guard post manned by pristine, khaki-clad men who toted rifles and behaved with arrogant officiousness. Their job was to check that those entering the port had the right to do so. We'd been checked on the way in, and it had been a 'fingers crossed' moment. Our papers were rather dodgy documents stating that we were temporary shipping agents and that we had an 'appointment' with the port manager. The reality was that we were nothing of the sort, and didn't have a firm appointment, though Mr John's had managed to get us permission to get as far as the boss's secretary. The papers had worked well enough and we had been impatiently waved through. Now, on the way out, we had to deal with the guards on the inner gate. Their job was to make sure that no one was taking anything out of the port that they shouldn't have been, and I suppose making sure that no one was slipping illegally into India.

One of the guards squinted towards Mr Johns and me as we approached the gate. As he did so, he lowered his rifle so that it pointed at us. This did not look good. Karsten was 15 metres behind us as we moved closer to the guard. The guard spoke imperiously and aggressively at Mr Johns, who put a slightly shaky hand on my arm to hold me where I was. A rapid and very furious argument followed. With much arm-waving my permit and passport were studied as a crowd collected around us. Suddenly I felt like a Martian, and I didn't need to speak Tamil to know that somehow we'd been rumbled. The fact that I was suddenly being poked in the ribs with the rifle, made it all the more obvious that we were in trouble.

At that moment Karsten came running straight past us, almost thumping his way through the crowd. The inner gate guards were too stunned to do anything for a moment, but were soon shouting words to the effect of 'Stop that man!' to the outer guards. But they were too late, as with a final shove of a man who had the misfortune to get in the way Karsten was out of the gate and running through the crowded street. Much later he told me that he'd forgotten to take any ID documents with him and realised that the treatment we were getting would probably intensify ten-fold when he was stopped.

Our guards were incensed. Mr Johns and I were pushed and shoved across the entrance yard, past the first warehouses and into a small office in which not a jot of air moved. The fan wasn't working and the men sat quietly on wooden benches with sweat pouring down their faces. The man sitting behind an enormous wooden desk, totally out of proportion to the size of the office, had large sweat marks under his arms and across the chest of his uniform. He was one of the largest men I had seen in southern India so far, and he must have been suffering miserably. We were like a mini explosion into this sleepy uncomfortable little office. Moments later, after much shouting, with red betel nut spit flying enthusiastically from the lips of our guard, Mr Johns and I were thrust roughly into a small room. The door was locked, leaving us to look at each other with slight disbelief. We sat listening to the continued shouting from the outside office.

Moments later, a guard burst in, grabbed Mr Johns by the arm and pulled him out of the room. That was the last I saw of him for four days. It took that long for the shipping company to bribe him free. It turned out that Mr Johns was in deep trouble and I felt incredibly uncomfortable about it. For us it had been a bit of an adventure and potentially the end of a very long and frustrating wait to get the bikes out of the harbour.

I was released by the port police within a few hours, but it was several days before Mr Johns was able to start work for us again. Now he worked quietly. He'd had a big fright and I think he simply wanted to get rid of us. I felt a little sad. Over the weeks we'd got to know a lot about this kind, friendly man and his family, and now I felt that it was we who had let him down. It wasn't his fault that he was stuck working in a system that seemed about as functional as a pen with no ink. It was definitely time to move on. Karsten got his hands on his bike just two days later, and he transformed from being one very angry biker into a man with few cares, but the experience had led him to a real hatred of all things Indian.

It was another four days before I was told that my container had been pulled out of the row and that it was about to be unloaded. This time I was back in the port with the right papers and thankfully 'my' guard didn't seem to be on duty. The container stood on its own on the back of a trailer in the yard, and I looked for a forklift of some sort. I'd no idea where the bike had been stashed in the container but knew that the dockyard workers who'd come to unload the container wouldn't be expecting the bike to be so heavy. Mr John's had told them what I was there for.

The workers were scrawny, dhoti-clad men who seemed as interested in what they were about to do as they were at the thought of lifting themselves from their shady spots. A headman of some sort tried to drum up some enthusiasm, and failed miserably. But the men did get up and a customs officer broke the seal on the container. The rusty door creaked open and there was my crate, right at the front, but it had been packed at the top. That made it roughly two and a half meters off the ground. I couldn't see how they were going to wrestle it out without a forklift. I didn't speak the language, and had no way of stopping what happened next. With surprising speed a large empty crate was pulled in front of the trailer, four men stood on top and with equally surprising strength they pulled my crate out towards them. The crate fell out of the container scattering the workers, and hit the ground with a horrible crunch. It shattered the crate the workers had been standing on, and the force of the impact smashed my crate open. It had landed at a forty-five degree angle on one corner, and at that moment I was sure that I had a dead motorcycle on my hands. I was angry with the workers, but at the same time very happy that none of them had been caught under the crate. If they had been they would have been in a real mess. I stood, quite stunned, for what seemed a very long time. This was big time trouble.

The crew helped me break the rest of the crate open. As we did so I was really thankful that the fan maker's mate in Penang knew his business. The bike had been incredibly well supported inside, though with the front wheel off to cut bulk, most of the impact seemed to have been taken by the bike's forks. That was either good news, as the springs would have absorbed a lot of the impact, or grim news if the forks were bent. They looked bent. The bike had twisted free of its straps and bracing points, with a good amount of weight landing on the front brake disc – the wheel had been strapped into place next to the forks. The mudguard was cracked, an indicator had snapped off and so had a mirror, but the forks had only twisted in the head brace, or so it appeared. The men helped me to lift the wheel back between the forks and once bolted into place I loosened off the head brace which allowed me to use the wheel to lever the forks a little more into position. So far so good, but when I turned the wheel it looked as if the disc had been bent. This would make for interesting braking, though perhaps not bad enough to have a new disc sent out from home. The men watched shamefaced as I put the rest of the bike together, collected up the broken parts and loaded the luggage onto the racks. Now she looked like a bike, but I was worried. She'd had a long fall and

I had no idea what other damage there was. I tried to put things into perspective by thinking about the number of times I'd fallen off the bike in Africa, and that she had survived those. Surely this impact had been no worse.

I didn't feel able to tip the workers, though I knew that in reality, what had happened wasn't their fault. It was just life. I rode out of the harbour gates and within seconds realised that I really was free. I'd done it. I had my bike back. I was a good month behind schedule, but that didn't matter. A plan could be made. What did matter was that I had my freedom back, India stretched before me and if I got a scoot on I could still make it to Kathmandu in time to meet up with Birgit. With all these thoughts in mind I hardly noticed that I was riding in Indian traffic!

Long after the adventures in Madras port, I discovered that in total it wouldn't have cost much more to fly the bike to India from Penang, and I also discovered that getting your bike out of an airport in India can often be done in just a day or two.

Chapter 10

Dynamite!

'If you reject the food, ignore the customs, fear the religion and avoid the
people, you might better stay home.'

James Michener

At last I was riding away from the port in Madras, two months behind schedule, but I was free, and that was the last time the bike would have to be shipped anywhere – I hoped. In a perverse sort of way, clearing the bike through the port had been fun. It had certainly been an experience which had me involved in a set of adventures I couldn't have imagined. I'd made new friends and seen a side of India that was going to stand me in good stead for the rest of my time in the country. I also learned that I had a pretty high tolerance of delay, and that in India patience really is a virtue. But I was still happy at the thought that I wouldn't have to go through anything like that again. Now I had lots of riding to do, and the mysteries of India lay before me waiting to be explored, tasted and experienced.

On a whim, Karsten had decided to ride to Nepal, and against my better judgement I agreed that we should ride together. He still had plenty of money left and didn't want to head back to Germany, but wanted to be out of India as quickly as he could – Nepal seemed like the logical option.

We arrived in Varanasi, the ancient city of Benares, in the dark and it was only the fact that Karsten had very loud horns on his bike that persuaded the staff of the Dak hostel to let us in. This persistent, impatient, demanding blasting of his horns was typical of Karsten. He was angry with Indians after the weeks of red tape from the Madras port and had become more abusive on the way up. He had a short fuse and not a jot of patience left. If it wasn't for the fact that Varanasi was to be the last major port of call in India, I'd have split from him then. But I felt a sense of loyalty towards Karsten – we had dealt with the Madras officials together. In any case, we had naturally fallen into a 'good guy – bad guy' routine whilst getting the bikes out of the port, which seemed to work, and I was concerned that if I wasn't with him, to round off the edges of his behaviour, then he'd get himself into real trouble. He was past caring and seemed to be actually looking out for confrontation. A part of me also disliked the way he was portraying western tourists, and I'd thought that if I remained with him then perhaps I could dilute that image too. I had a feeling that outside of India he was a good bloke, but now he needed a little protection from himself. The Indians, with their exuberant, happy-go-lucky, 'in your face' attitude, certainly needed protection from him!

I wanted to go out on the river Ganges at dawn, the perfect way to start a visit to this ancient religious city. The sun comes up on the far side of the river, highlighting the buildings with a warm glow. Most of the buildings along the ghats (an area where broad flights of steps lead down to a river) are palaces of ancient Maharajas, and their sandstone reds and creams virtually shine in the early morning sun. Dawn is also the time of great activity – the Ganges is a holy river to Hindus and it's the dream of many to make a pilgrimage to the city to bathe in its fabled waters. The water from the Ganges is quite literally the source of life for many. At dawn, the steps down to the river fill with men clad only in dhotis, a sort of loincloth, or long-sleeved knee-length cotton shirts. Women come to bathe too, but custom requires that they are dressed with proper clothing, so you see them lowering themselves into the water dressed in full saris. It's a colourful sight.

I was confused though. Didn't the pilgrims realise that in modern India, the Ganges, on its way down from the Himalayas, meandered past farms and took on chemical seepage from all the fertilisers and insecticides? Did they not realise that there were factories up river that dumped all their untreated effluent straight into the water? Surely they must be aware that the city's sewers emptied into the river too, and that the dead bodies floating in the water were a major hazard to health?

Not only did people come to bathe in the water, but they drank it too. Sahdus are men who have given their lives over to pilgrimage and these men too come to drink the water, though I never saw one taking a bath! It is said that if you drink water from the holy river, you will have a long life. People would bring bottles down to fill, so they could take water home for consumption if they became sick at some time in the future. You could even buy tiny clear glass bottles of souvenir Ganges water to take home with you. The dead bodies were in the water because it is a strong belief that if you are cremated beside the river and your ashes are scattered over the water, you will achieve great rewards in the next life. If you can't afford the wood

 to do the cremation then the next best thing is to throw the whole body into the river, and let it float away. As we sat in a boat, a head and a pair of knees bobbed by, causing three sets of ripples on the glowing river. A whole body was below the head and knees, and in a sitting position those were the only parts that broke the surface. Moments later, a tiny baby floated past us, a purple shape set in orange. The baby floated just feet away from a man who was dipping his toothbrush into the water before brushing his teeth.

As I watched the pilgrims washing in and drinking the water, I said to our boatman, "Don't these people realise how dirty this water is?" "Oh Mister", he replied with a convincing sideways waggle of his head. "This water is not dirty, just looking dirty."

Around us, other people in boats were setting loose garlands of bright orange marigolds, and floating off candles burning soft yellow flames, in small boats made of leaves. The tiny flames of hundreds of these candles twinkled like fairy lights as they were eased downstream on the gentle current. On the shore, the burning ghat was in full smoky flow and at the dhobi ghat, brightly clad women were washing clothes by soaping and then beating them against rocks or the stone steps.

The backstreets of Varanasi are a maze that felt as if it had been randomly designed by the passing of time. Small cobbled or earthen pathways pass between tall flat-topped buildings and once off the touristy main walkways, it's a chance to see real life India. Great thick wooden doors are set with iron studs and massive wrought iron hinges. Walls are painted pale terracottas, creams and umbers, sometimes with murals of the gods and animals and flowers. I was told that one was painted because the daughter of the house was just about to get married.

Small boys latched onto us, dancing around and pulling our sleeves at every chance they got. "Where are you coming from?" "Where are you going?" "What are you doing in Varanasi?" "Are you married?" "Do you have children?" "Give me money." "Of what age are you?" "Do you have a sister for me?" And the latter question was asked by a cheeky, grubby-faced urchin who didn't look as if he was long enough away from his mother's breast to be asking such questions. "We will show you around," they said. "Only nothing rupees!" the cheeky one said, making the others giggle.

Even Karsten had to grin, and we let them take us to the Golden Temple, whose site was disputed as a religious land by both Hindus and Moslems, and has a roof that's reputed to be of pure gold. Not that I'm an expert, but it certainly had the rich glowing yellow with a tinge of red that I associate with gold, so who knows? As non-Hindus, we weren't allowed in, but the boys took us on a climb through buildings, along landings and up stairs on the outside walls, to a vantage point where we could see the whole temple. It was worth the climb and I was rather pleased with the boys for allowing us this chance. We wouldn't have found it on our own.

They then wanted to take us to a silk sari shop, another of Asia's colour riots. I loved saris and how elegant they would make Indian women look. The range of colours on offer was stunning, and even a rainbow couldn't compete with the vibrant offerings. There were many different qualities from practical low-cost cotton to heavily-jewelled, gold-encrusted silks. Saris are usually a full six and a half metres long and to my eye, such elegance was at the price of comfort. The irreverent in me wondered how on earth the women went for a pee when they were wrapped in so many layers.

The next stop was a 'factory' that was far more to Karsten's taste. They made fireworks in a small room that obviously doubled as someone's living room, and Karsten immediately latched onto the biggest bangers I have ever seen. These twenty-centimetre long, dusky red cardboard tubes looked just like mini sticks of dynamite, and as the boys clustered excitedly around Karsten, he bargained for his purchase. I kept out of the way and sat on a sweaty burgundy vinyl sofa, which had lace doilies across the back; a grey Formica, marble-topped, gold-rimmed coffee table had a couple of blown glass elephants on it, one in red and the other in green; on the wall was a picture of the elephant god Ganesh, and around its gold-coloured frame hung purple Christmas tree tinsel. The factory  boss organised cups of chai and turned on the TV so I could watch cricket while he and Karsten were working. He obviously thought that as an Englishman, if I missed the cricket I'd be getting withdrawal symptoms. I liked him for his consideration and wondered if he'd ever had a couple of tourists in his living room factory like this before.

Back at the hostel, I threatened Karsten that he'd be in big trouble if he let the fireworks off anywhere near me. I thought he had got the message.

Ten minutes later, when I was lying on my bed reading, a lit stick of dynamite bounced across the floor with a venomous hissing sound. Seconds later it exploded with a bang that was so loud the light bulb in the room broke, the light fitting in the hallway fell from the ceiling, and my ears were ringing so hard that I wondered if I'd ever hear again properly. Karsten was on his bed roaring with laughter, I think, and tears were rolling down his face. For him, it was the best prank ever!

Within minutes, the whole staff of the hostel and most of the guests had come running into our room. They found the two of us on the floor, with me beating Karsten with every bit of strength shock and anger gave me. I thought he'd got that message too, at the time.

One of the things that I did like about Karsten was that he was an early riser and was always organised enough to be ready for the road at the time we'd agreed. He was meticulous with his packing and took care of his bike as if it was his best mate. Though he called it Gustav, he treated it as if he was married to it, and I understood how he felt. You do build a close relationship with your wheels when you are on the road for a long time.

One or two people have called me a sentimental idiot and asked me if I realised that I was giving personality to a set of nuts and bolts. Of course I did, but I was sure that each bike would have its own quirks that would be the equivalent of a personality. I knew what speeds my bike liked best; I knew what suspension setting she should have for what load and what road conditions, and I knew what she'd be like if I got those things wrong – she would do a bike's version of a sulk. I knew what tyre pressure she liked best, because by the way she felt, she told me. Libby liked to have her services done, and always sounded and felt better to ride afterwards. When you spend many hours a day on a bike on your own, it's easy to start to treat it as a friend, and a reliable bike can be one of the few constants in a never-ending voyage of discovery, full of surprises, both good and bad. The bike, like any person, can get you into trouble and out of it again. Libby did just that.

Perhaps the only thing that Karsten and I had in common – and this was of real value at the time – was the way we both cared so passionately about our bikes. In spite of the fact that we'd been virtually thrown out of the hostel, it was this which made me decide to carry on riding with him. Sometimes he was like a big enthusiastic puppy dog, and with a great grin on his face would leap and bound into things with little thought for the consequences. He certainly got me into adventures that I'd never have experienced had I been on my own. Other times he was like someone who had been scarred by growing up the hard way – his learning time in India had been hard. Sitting on the bike thinking about this, I decided that travelling with Karsten was perfect for India. You love it or you hate it – there is very little in between.

I was almost out of time to get to Kathmandu before Birgit flew in, and was happy for Karsten to ride in front as that way I could easily see what he was up to, instead of having to worry about what was going on behind me. His riding style was simple: thumb on the horn and go for it! To my surprise he told me that in spite of liking big bangs, he wasn't so happy about all the noise he was making while riding, but it gave him a sense of security. One of the things about our bikes was that the horns sounded completely different from any of the local vehicles, and that made us stand out – if people notice you when you are on the road in India, that's a good thing. He wasn't doing anything he shouldn't have been though. Even the trucks and buses had big signs on their rears stating, 'Blow Horn!' There was so much noise on the road that I sometimes wondered if all drivers were blind, and were finding their way by noise alone!

The road northwards from Garakpur was littered with truck wrecks. They lay stranded by the roadsides, sometimes for weeks until they could be repaired, acting as a constant warning when on the road; you have to have your wits about you all the time.

Being noticed on the road was a safety factor, but not such a good thing when stopped. Every time we pulled over to grab a cup of chai, or even for a simple bum rest, we'd be instantly surrounded by people. Sometimes there'd be upwards of a hundred watching how we drank our chai. Even when we stopped on an open bit of road, with apparently no one around, we'd be at the centre of a crowd within seconds.

One such roadside stop made me ill. Not the crowd of people, and not even the fact that Indian people have no sense that there is anything wrong with them touching your bike, twisting the throttle, pulling in on the brake or clutch, or twiddling the switches. It was the food. Chappatis and dhal are normally safe to eat and this truck stop looked OK – there were plenty of people using it, and that's normally a good sign.

But by the time we had reached Kushmaga, the place where Buddha is supposed to have died, I was feeling pretty close to death myself. Whatever it was at lunchtime that had got me, it was the fastest acting bug I'd come across. As I was feeling so grim, we decided to head for the International Lodge, which is run by Buddhist monks – better to be ill in a place where people, as a result of their religion, would care.

On a previous visit to India my girlfriend and I had almost died in our room. We'd both picked up dysentery, but didn't know that when we'd booked in. We had felt unusually tired but put that down to the long train ride we'd just done. Planning to rest, we stocked up on oranges, nan bread and bottles of water – so we wouldn't have to go out later on a food hunt. We'd gone straight to bed in a room that was easily one of the dirtiest we'd stayed in. The sheets were old and so sweat-stained that we could see the stark outlines of the people who had used the bed before us. Families had obviously used the room – there were four, head-to-toe sweat shapes imprinted indelibly onto the sheet. Too tired to care abut that, or about the pile of fruit peel in the corner of the room, we crashed. We were too poorly to get up the next day and by day two, we were too ill to get out of bed to get more water. Overnight we'd become so weak that neither of us could even to make it to the toilet, and we lay in our own mess, unable to move. We'd both got to the stage during the night where we simply didn't care what happened to us next. When we'd arrived, we hadn't said anything to anyone other than the lad who booked us in, so no one was expecting us, or would notice that we weren't around. It was only because another guest had complained about the smell from our room that the owner had let himself in, and had found us before it was too late. He was incredibly kind, and along with gentle help from his mother, nursed us back to health.

Karsten wasn't ill, but as we'd both eaten the same thing at lunchtime, I was keen that we wouldn't fall into the same trap. He didn't get ill, but that didn't stop the monks from trying to take advantage of us. When we got settled and I was too ill to move, they raised the price of the room. They then tried to preach Buddhism to me as I lay on my bed between rushes to the toilet to projectile vomit from both ends. The toilet, thankfully, was one of the best I'd seen in India. Instead of the usual rough concrete walls that may or may not have paint on them, the walls in this bathroom were covered in shiny, dark green tiles from floor to ceiling. It had the usual porcelain squat toilet, that works quite well when you are erupting in two directions at the same time, but in my weakened state it was a major effort to stand up

195

again once I'd drained myself of whatever it was my body didn't like at that moment. Each visit began with an urgent dash, and ended with a slow shattered crawl back to bed. But Karsten did a great job of taking care of me – he showed me a compassionate side of his personality that I hadn't known was there, and I would have been in far more trouble without him. It was yet another situation where something goes badly wrong, and there's a kind human being there, offering to help.

Thirty-six hours later, my fever had broken and the immodium was doing a good blocking job. I felt incredibly weak, but there was such a bad atmosphere in the International we couldn't wait to get away. We loaded and left, with me glad to follow Karsten. He was a good rider too, and today he was obviously making an effort to make life on the road easy for me. He bargained at the truck stops for chapattis and bottles of water. He asked the way, dealt with paying at the filling station, and found a hotel at the end of the day.

He left me sitting knackered on my bike, like a mini island amidst flowing chaos, while he rode round the beat-up desperate-looking border town of Rauxul Bazar. The buildings were ramshackle and though most had been painted at some time, all were stained by dripping rusty water, mud splashes and years of collected grime. Dodgy characters slouched around in doorways, looking like faded, timeworn opportunists that were down on their quota of opportunities. Garish advertising posters hung, either in tatters from the walls, or flapped gently in the listless breeze. Mangy scabby dogs slunk scavenging hopefully for a meal, from one rubbish pile to the next. Penny-sized black flies buzzed like miniature bomber planes from piles of shit in the street, to land on chunks of meat that hung under the faded awnings of the food stalls. Biting midges clustered around the moisture of children's snotty running noses and rusting, wrecked, cannibalised trucks and cars lay by the roadsides. Even the holy cows looked as if they had been mentally afflicted by the dodgy air of this border town.

As a sort of reward for Karsten's hotel hunt, fate that night found a use for the fireworks he'd bought. There was a festival going on in the bazaar area the inevitable crowd grew around this strange tourist who was celebrating with them, with his loud bangers. The darkness hid the filth, scars and lethargy of the day, and this night Rauxal Bazar rocked. Karsten's last night in India looked as if it was going to be a happy one and it would have been, had we not been plagued by mosquitoes.

For a change there weren't any mosquito nets provided in the room, and we paid the price. Our room was dark and damp, and we seemed to attract hoards of these whining, buzzing, bloodsuckers. Mosquito repellent was useless and by one thirty in the morning, Karsten was fully at war with the things, fighting a battle King Canute would have been proud of. In the morning we'd had so little sleep we should have stayed where we were, but this night had been the last straw for Karsten. I didn't bother to try to explain that mosquitoes wouldn't recognise the borderline. No, we had to get out of India, that day.

We set off down the alleyway from the hotel and out into the congestion of the main street, weaving our way through the collection of trucks, buses, pick up trucks and men piled high with packages, and we bumped over railway tracks, along which steam trains still run. The border was a shambles, with no real sign of the border point at all, and we rode gently through the mass of people on the move, past what was the immigration hut. There were no signs at all but the officials were obviously used to people doing this. One of them came running down the rutted and rubbish-strewn street after us. While one of the officers tried to work out what to do with us, the other stripped to the waist outside the window, and balancing on two bricks in the mud, proceeded to wash himself under a standpipe.

After the hour and a half that was required to stamp our exit permits in our passports, we were free for the next stage – customs. Yes, we were in the right place, yes they were open and yes they would like to help us but oh dear, the man with they key to the cupboard where the manual on how to deal with carnets was kept, was missing. "We are having no idea when this man will be coming, but not to worry Sah, we are sending a man to find the man. This will all be very quick for you Sah." Eventually the senior customs officer arrived, but not before I had laid down on the floor in the office to rest. There were no seats on our side of the counter, so I had no choice. By this time my bowels were rumbling again and the loss of a night's sleep, plus the increasing heat, were taking their toll. The customs officer leant out over the counter and looked down at me saying, "Sah, Sah, you cannot be lying on the floor Sah. What is being the problem Sah?" "I'm sick, we have been here one hour, and your man is still not here. I simply must rest." I replied from the floor. Another runner was sent, and ten minutes later the man with the key came back, pointing out that the manual had been sitting on his desk all the time! It was a shame really, as the officers were in fact really nice blokes and had genuinely wanted to get things moving.

Moments later we were riding across the bridge into Nepal. The Nepalese officials were incredibly efficient and within forty minutes we were through, legal and stamped. Murphy's Law struck then. It was a national holiday and we'd forgotten to check. All the banks were closed, so Karsten strode off to change some money on the black market. The customs officer had told him where to go! He came back twenty minutes later with loot, a bottle of water and two one-litre bottles of beer. He'd been hanging out for Nepalese beer for the last month, almost drooling over the thought. Though the bottle for me was a kind thought, I was in no fit state to celebrate being out of India with him. No problem – he knocked both back himself, and then set off into the traffic with such enthusiasm he was scattering people around him as he went. Fortunately, Nepalese people are pretty nimble.

In my befuddled state I tried to keep up with him, but I didn't have a chance as people moved back into his wake to watch him. They paid no attention at all to me, following behind. I dodged, weaved, used my horn, all the time losing ground. Then I saw enormous teeth, foaming, sneering lips and giant rolling eyes bearing down on me. There was such a crush of people and cars I had nowhere to go. BANG! The cart of a runaway horse hammered into one of my panniers and the bike and I were instantly thrown to the ground, Libby's engine screaming as I involuntarily opened the throttle. Thankfully everyone was able to get out of our way as we crunched down. My stomach squirmed, and for a moment I caught the sight of a small man hanging onto the horse's reins for dear life, but without any effect at all. I lay stunned, listening to the sound of shod hooves and metal wheel rims clattering off down the road, still out of control. Meantime, Karsten was blissfully riding on.

Until a policeman arrived, as far as the crowd was concerned the accident had been my fault, or so it seemed. Then the mood dramatically changed and the nearest people helped me pick Libby up. She'd lost some more paint, but that I didn't mind; they were travel battle-scars. What I did mind was that on closer inspection, not only was my aluminium pannier bent, but the luggage rack itself had snapped in two places. The pannier wasn't a problem as it was just bent, and the rack had performed exactly how I hoped it would. It had absorbed the bulk of the impact and it had broken, protecting the frame of the bike. That would have been a much bigger problem – the rack would be easy to weld. Using luggage straps and duct tape, I

 fastened the box onto the bike as best I could and wobbled out into the traffic again. I found Karsten waiting impatiently for me by the roadside about a kilometre further along. From the expression on his face he looked as if he thought I'd stopped to do a quick bit of souvenir shopping! With just enough time for me to catch up, he shot out into the traffic, and knocked a cyclist over. The man was furious, and things were getting nasty when 'my' policeman arrived on the scene. He calmed the cyclist – no damage had been done – the policeman waggled a finger at Karsten, who then set off just like a rocket again. I caught up with him sitting cooling off by the roadside, about half an hour later.

The potholed asphalt turned into a dirt road, and my heart sank. I didn't have the energy to deal with dirt, but the next village was seventy kilometres away, so I had no choice. Other than loose gravel, hairpin bends, potholes and mini waterfalls that came down over the road, I don't remember anything at all of the next two hours of riding. That night, I climbed under a duvet in a mountain lodge and slept instantly. This sleep of the dead lasted until sunrise when the local rooster yelled in his own unique way: "Come on, get up! It's a new day! You're missing out!

Chapter 11

The Top of the World

'A journey is best measured in friends rather than miles.'

Tim Cahill

The rooster was right, and to my amazement I felt almost completely well after a deep night's sleep. The air on the village hillside was chill from the altitude, but the mountains and forests around us were sharply detailed in the clear, clean morning light. I felt as if I'd woken up in a different world.

Over the past months I'd been able to remain terribly British as far as breakfast was concerned. If I'd not been in a place where I could buy 'pordge', 'corn flaks', 'aigs' or 'tost', I'd managed to buy bread and jam. My head simply wasn't able to get around the idea of curry for breakfast, and these touches of home to start the days off gave me the mental as well as physical energy to face whatever the day had to throw at me. 'Pordge', when I could find it, was always perfectly cooked. 'Corn Flaks' were inevitably a bit soggy, and never tasted quite right with hot milk, but that was a small concession in the fight against stomach lurgies. 'Aigs', could be fried, poached, scrambled or boiled, and again were always perfectly cooked, though the pale yokes looked an anaemic almost beige colour. And 'tost'? That was always a white bread treat which, even though the little foil-wrapped butter slabs were almost always slightly rancid, gave a day a good start. This morning I was out of luck, but with the new world I'd woken up to it seemed only right that I should be eating some sort of thick dhal soup for breakfast. It was incredibly cheap, and kept me feeling full right the way through the morning. It was probably also just the right thing to be putting into my still rather sensitive stomach.

As we rode that morning, in the distance we could see Mount Everest, a phenomenal sight and yet another very physical sign that we were in a different world. The Nepalese people we'd met to date were smaller than

Indians, and had rounder faces with small, almost slit, eyes that were set wide into their faces. They nodded as we went past and would talk to us if we talked to them first. It was only when we made an approach that their faces would come alive, and their enthusiasm would shine. Karsten was delighted and rode around with a permanent grin on his face.

By lunchtime we'd made it to the main road that runs down through the Kathmandu valley to the city itself. We'd just stopped to admire the view down the valley, when a Dane and a Swiss pulled up next to us on their bikes. These guys were the first biking overlanders we'd seen since arriving in Madras and we'd actually begun to wonder if there was anyone else out there. They were heading away from Kathmandu which was a great shame, but they did pass on the name of the Everest Hotel, which they said was perfect for bikes. They also let us know that there were some other bikers there. Karsten grinned at that, and I could see him thinking, 'Party time'.

My first impressions of Kathmandu were sad. When the city finally came into view, we realised that it was sitting in a yellow cloud of pollution. The city sits in a one thousand three hundred metre high bowl between the mountains, and as the carbon monoxide fumes are so much heavier than the thinner air at this altitude, they sink to the lowest point. That was Kathmandu. I'd not had any preconceived ideas of what the city would look like, but I did have a picture of a relatively carefree place that would have been much affected by hippies. The smog simply didn't fit with that picture at all, unless of course the bulk of the fug was caused by a generation of dope smokers!

Kathmandu is technically made up of three cities that are spread through the one hundred and thirty five square kilometres of the valley.

 Patan sits just over the river from Kathmandu city, and Bhaktapur is a few kilometres to the east. At one time these were small city-states, and competition between them was fierce. Status symbols were key to this and as a result

the valley has one hundred and thirty monuments. The whole valley is a World Heritage Site – it's thought that there have been people living in there since 900BC, but the oldest building is 'just' one thousand years old. The valley is prone to earthquakes, and in 1934 a massive 'quake destroyed many of the ancient buildings.

The name Kathmandu comes from the Sanskrit name for the two-storey wooden pagoda that stands in the city's heart, the Durbar Square. It has no iron nails and no other metal supports whatsoever - legend has it that the structure was made from the wood of just one tree. Its name, Kaasthamandap, means literally 'wood-covered shelter'.

Kathmandu is the capital and largest city of a country that only relatively recently opened its borders to the outside world. Its rulers and kings had been reclusive, in spite of the fact that Nepal stands at a crossroads in Asia, something obvious in the people themselves. Many have Mongoloid features and most of the others seem to be of Indo-Aryan extraction – Nepal is a bit of a cultural and racial melting pot.

But the late 1930s and '40s saw a change. The kings discovered the outside world which they started to explore for themselves, at the cost of their subjects. The dramatic change though, came in the late '50s and early '60s when they opened the country up and development aid money began to pour in. Until then the way of life had developed very little from the Middle Ages, and many people still live as they would have in those times. But with the influx of aid workers, the opening of the borders and the building of roads, came tourism. At first most of the tourists were hippies in search of cheap living and enlightenment. Kathmandu became a key stop on the hippy trail, and the centre for the hippies was 'Freak Street', a mix of beauty and squalor that smelled of incense and before long was lined with small shops set up selling enlightenment. A mini-industry was built around the hippies to serve their basic needs, and Nepal's position as a crossroads in Asia played a major part. Just about every narcotic known to man at that time was available in one form or another.

I liked the fact that the inhabitants of Eugene in Oregon, and Minsk in Belarus, had the good taste to twin their cities with

Kathmandu, but I wondered how that had come about, bearing in mind its hippy history! Perhaps they'd bred large numbers of hippies, or perhaps they were simply, already enlightened.

The hotel had plenty of space for our bikes in their gated, flower-filled courtyard, and they had room for us. Karsten leapt off his bike hooting with laughter – one of the bikes parked there belonged to a friend of his! One of the other bikes belonged to an amiable bear of a German called Ben. When Ben sat on his BMW, it almost disappeared under his bulk. Ben had his priorities sorted and to keep his sturdy figure, he liked to eat, a lot. With that in mind his prized cooking utensil was a giant cast iron frying pan, which weighed a ton – I suspected that if he ever got hammered by a runaway horse and cart, the cart would come off worse if it hit that pan of his!

The next day, after I'd changed money and collected my post from the zoo-like Poste Restante, Ben helped me work on the bike. Even though by this time I'd ridden just over eighty thousand miles, because Libby had been so reliable, I'd hardly had to do anything with her other than basic servicing. In no way was I complaining, but there were jobs that I really should have known how to do. Ben set to teaching me the skill of stripping down and cleaning the carburettors. "I think they are a little overdue to be done Sam," he said diplomatically. He also helped me to change my front tyre – I'd been carrying a spare all the way from Australia, but with Birgit about to arrive, I wanted to lighten the load a little. She was bringing back out my tent and petrol cooker, so I needed to compensate for their weight, and bulk. That night, as a reward, Ben and I went to eat Buffalo steak, and when Ben's extra large steak arrived I was most impressed – I wouldn't have been able to put away even half of the thing.

The day finally arrived. It was Monday the seventh of November and Birgit's plane was due to land at the Kathmandu airport. She arrived with her helmet, her old burgundy leather bike jacket, a small pack and a big grin. This was the first time she had been to a Third World country so her eyes were wide open from the moment she stepped out of the plane. Watching her reminded me that one of the things I'd found so fascinating was her insatiable curiosity. Because of language, I was the odd one out with the welcoming party for her from the other bikers that night. Karsten, Jurgen, Tomel, Franz, and Ben were all German. The lads had laid on booze, nibbles and a very warm 'Willkommen' for her. It was one of those moments when the amazing camaraderie of the road shone out. The Everest Hotel for all of us was a mini oasis in Asia; in a way, it was our own crossroads.

Then French Eric arrived on his BMW. By this time there were seven BMWs in the courtyard, but Eric's was decidedly different, as was the man himself. Eric had set off from France with a sidecar attached to his bike, and his girlfriend inside. To help gather funds for his trip he'd sold every part off the bike that wasn't required to make it work, and had built replacements for those parts himself. He'd made an enormous fuel tank that dwarfed the bike. Everything was hand painted black, and he was carrying pots of paint so that he could paint the flag of each country he passed through onto his tank. He also carried a 'ghetto blaster' and an amazing collection of cassette tapes – when I saw how much kit he was carrying I stopped muttering 'must get the weight down' about my bike. Eric, in spite of such flamboyant travel style, was a quiet, rather laconic person. I also thought that he was lonely, but after his girlfriend had gone home in disgust, he seemed to prefer travelling on his own. Eric's girlfriend had left him after the sidecar had separated from the bike, to leave the two of them going in different directions.

The following days were flurries of more work servicing the bike, most of which Birgit did for the first time, finding a welding workshop to fix the rack and strolling the streets of Kathmandu. It's a city that encourages strolling, and in spite of the fumes, it's easy to wander, and around every corner is something new to look at. Birgs and I played tourist to our hearts' content and along the way we visited temples, meandered the cobbled back streets, strolled the famous Freak Street and yes, we shopped. Nepalese are craftsmen and women, and the fabrics, leatherwork and jewellery on show were irresistible.

We sat on the stone steps of the old Royal Palace in Durbar square, just watching life go by in the gentle sunshine. Men rode bicycles loaded high with goods; women walked hand in hand with children; wooden carts with wooden wheels were stacked high with piles of fruit and vegetables; men sold roasted peanuts in newspaper cones; and the sadhus strode around mostly oblivious to the rest of us in their own mystical world.

I liked watching the sadhus. Though some live completely naked, most of these guys dressed in vivid reds, yellows and oranges, and here many of them also painted their bodies white. They let their beards grow long and teased their hair into dreadlocks that, had they been clean, Bob Marley would have been impressed with. Sadhus, to the Hindu religion, are the equivalent of living saints. But when a man becomes a sadhu, his family will actually mourn him as being dead. He is certainly lost to them as he steps into a life where he abandons everything to be able to concentrate on devotions, meditations and seeking 'the way'. Large amounts of ganja help them to do all of those things. They survive by begging, but it didn't seem like begging (except around tourists). Hindus feel that it is a privilege to feed them.

Near the Pashupatinath temple, the sadhus also painted their faces in bright yellows and reds, which made me think of the aboriginals I'd seen in Australia. The temple sits on the banks of the Bagmati River, and it's considered to be the most sacred temple in the world for the Hindu god, Shiva. Its flat roofs are copper-clad and yes, this time were definitely coated in real gold. I had that on good authority from one of the sadhus, whom we sat and talked to for a while. I was looking for a taste of enlightenment myself, and thought that I might learn a little from him. He was interesting at first, but I soon got the feeling that he was working the crowd, which we were just part of. He seemed to be sick and the only enlightenment I gleaned from him was that he was unhappy with his life, which wasn't what I'd expected at all. To see what would happen, I slipped him some rupees, and as soon as I'd done so, he stood and left.

205

Birgit and I watched life swirling on round the temple, but both of us felt uncomfortable. The river is a rubbish tip, even by the steps up to the temple itself, and on the street side of the temple were market stalls that obviously catered for tourists. A small corner was selling religious dyes and cloths, but the rest was tat which didn't seem to fit with the mystical feeling I'd anticipated having. I'd had that feeling in churches, libraries and giant old buildings in so many other countries, but not here. When we saw crowds of tourists being encouraged to watch a cremation on the Arya Ghat, we'd had enough. We walked past the six-foot high, gold-covered bull, the giant silver-plated doors, and left.

The monkey temple was a different ballgame altogether. Yes it was still touristy, but this time the whole set up had style, and the tourism didn't seem to interfere with the beauty and mystical feeling the Swayambhunath temple retained. The temple is a good walk out of the city, but neither of us minded that – it was cheaper than getting a rickshaw and we were more likely to see things of interest as we strolled. The walk starts by crossing a large bridge, over a slow-moving dirty river. Neither the children that were playing in the mud, nor the fat hairy hogs that were wallowing in it, seemed to mind the fact that they were enjoying themselves in a watery open landfill. The streets were strung crisscross with runs of little flags in yellows, reds and white. If you could block out the noise from the vendors, the cows in the street, the rickshaws, the buses and the bicycle bells, then the flapping sound from the flags could very easily have come from a yacht marina. Grubby brown-skinned kids played with puppy dogs in the roadside grime; men and women worked teasing burrs out of bundles of knotted untreated wool; goats fed and beggars begged. There are lots of beggars in Kathmandu but unlike in India, they are patient and not in the least bit pushy. Here people actually talked to them and gave them money, rather than treating them as if they were scabs on society, or something awful that they had trodden in.

As we cleared the main city, we were walking on grassy, stone-walled country lanes between villages, with their blocky rough concrete or mud-walled buildings with either flat or corrugated iron roofs. Paint was not something that was a necessity of life, but it didn't matter as the buildings seemed to blend into each other, as if they were never designed to be daubed in pigment. The monkey temple sits on top of a mound rather like an island rising out of an almost flat plain. As you climb the steps, trees and bushes line the sides of the mound. The steps were an impromptu meeting place-cum-market. Craft sellers plied their wares, beggars begged, and men played board games in the sunshine. One of the games looked like it was a combination of snooker and shove ha'penny.

The ganja sellers were there, though discreetly. One approached us with a whole carrier bag full of grass to sell. We were told that most of these guys are traditional farmers who supplement what they grow to eat, by cultivating a bit of grass to sell on the side to tourists. The money they made, we were told, paid for such luxuries as education for their kids and medical treatment. I'd no idea how much truth there was in that, but the bloke who tried to sell to us fitted easily into that image.

Swayambhunath is the temple that we see in so many photos of Nepal, the one with the giant painted eyes of Buddha. The temple is on a sort of dome that is supposed to signify the world, and on top of the dome is a cubed tower that's topped off with a cone-shaped roof. The eyes are painted onto the four sides of the cube so they can look out over the whole world. It's a site also revered by Hindus, and was busy with mostly Asian tourists or pilgrims. Monkeys inhabit the temple, and though most of them don't deign to have anything to do with visitors, preferring to pick over the offerings left by the pilgrims, one or two had to be watched. They weren't pickpockets in the traditional sense, but if you had any food tucked away, they'd know it!

Franz had steering head bearing problems with his bike. He told me that it had got so bad, that straight was the only comfortable riding line, which must have been a nightmare in traffic. He finally managed to track down some replacement bearings and was heading off to a mechanic's yard to fit them – I'd never seen this done before so I went along to watch.

The yard bore no resemblance to any yard I'd been to in England. It looked African with ramshackle corrugated huts lining two sides of the dusty oil-laden space, full of cannibalised vehicles and buses that were being rejuvenated on a shoestring. A welder was hard at work, without any eye protection, and mechanics hurried around in oil-drenched overalls, carrying themselves with the air of magicians. They worked hard and fast at each repair. I liked the atmosphere, and the feeling that these guys could fix disaster cases, however bad. Many of the vehicles should have been in a scrap yard, but I knew that within days they'd be back out on the road, belching smoke and earning their owners a living.

Tucked away on one side of the yard was a sort of bus I'd never seen before, and though battered, it looked in far better condition than anything else in the yard. It was an old Setra school bus from Germany. Its owners had bought the bus when it had been retired, done it up, painted it burgundy and cream, and converted it into a home on six wheels. Dirk and Jens had travelled out from Germany, paying their way as they went. Before setting off they had been round the local scrap yards and had bought up fuel pumps for Mercedes and BMW cars. They'd renovated them and had sold them as they were going along through Iran and Pakistan. They'd also bought up old water pumps and sold those too. But the gem in their tale was that they had covered the roof of the bus with dumped fridges. They'd cleaned and tarted them up, and then had sold them along the way. Again, I was reminded of how much we throw away in our home countries, which in fact can still do the job – fashion has a lot to answer for. Every so often Dirk and Jens would take a paying passenger, and between those things they had both covered their costs and earned enough money not only to keep the bus maintained but also for a shopping spree. They were buying carpets and hookah pipes to take back to Germany to sell – they hoped to cover their costs for the return journey.

Eric had worked out a master plan for earning a living on the road too. He'd signed himself up for training with a business that embroidered the designs on the front of the T-shirts that Kathmandu is famous for. I'd given Birgit one with a map of the world embroidered on it for her birthday. Eric's plan was to learn how to do the designs, and how to use the special sewing machine needed to do the work. He was then going to buy himself a machine, and the threads he'd need. All of these were going to be strapped to the back of his bike, along with the rest of his bizarre collection of kit, and he was going to set up shop wherever he went. We thought that he was nutty enough to do it, and make it work. For a while his enthusiasm rubbed off on me and I started to see the possibilities too...

Birgit was ill. It started off something like flu, and rapidly progressed to the stage where she had no energy and a harsh hacking cough. We let it ride for a few days, thinking that it was just a cold, but as she got steadily worse, we decided to head for a doctor. The thin air, the very cold nights and the pollution, had combined to give her a full-blown lung infection. Even with medication the bug dragged on and I worried. The only thing for it, I'd thought, was to get her out of Kathmandu and away from the filthy air. But the problem was, how long would it be before she was fit enough to move, let alone ride on the back of the bike. If we didn't just get on with it, would she stay the same, or even get worse?

We decided to move on to Pokara, a much smaller city, with cleaner air, and both of us had dreams of going trekking up Annapurna. The Annapurna circuit is one of the world's great treks and we felt it was something we both could manage and enjoy. It's supposed to be difficult enough to keep a hardened and fit trekker entertained, but easy enough for those less experienced to have a go at. I wasn't in very good shape, having spent so much time sitting on the bike, so it sounded just right for us. We knew that we wouldn't have enough time to do the whole circuit, but a few days on the trail would have been magic. But first, Birgit had to get fit again.

We said goodbye to Karsten, who by this time had decided that he was going to fly to Bangkok from Kathmandu to join up with Jurgen, Franz and Tomil. He was absolutely determined that there was no way he was ever going to roll his wheels on India again! "Never,

ever, ever again!" he said. "Indians – pah, crazy people!" As he said this, he jabbed his middle finger against the centre of his forehead.

Birgs and I had been to the airport with them when Jurgen, Franz, Tomil and some friends of theirs were crating their bikes up to send. The flight from Kathmandu was amazingly cheap and the customs officers were as helpful and as well trained as those at the border had been – the agent had even provided crates to send the bikes with Thai airways. This was the easiest option, but relatively expensive – I'd met other bikers who'd bought the wood and made their own crates. If I were ever to fly my bike to Bangkok, I'd do the same, but the hardest thing seemed to have been to find anyone who had wood to sell – there aren't many trees in Nepal.

Seeing the bikes off had been a petrol bonus for me. The guys had to empty their tanks before they could be flown, and with a forty-three litre tank I was on hand to help – not that the local guys who were hanging around with empty jerry cans and hopeful expressions were too pleased with me.

We had a big party the night before the guys were supposed to leave, and that led into disaster. Three of the partygoers were arrested by the police on their way back to the hotel because (we later found out) our German friend had been with two Nepalese guys. He'd been drunk and they were helping him back. The police hadn't accepted that – it seemed to be taboo for Nepalese men to drink, let alone associate with a drunken tourist. Even the German embassy got involved with the attempts to get them out, but seemed to do very little and when we saw our friend again, he'd been badly beaten by the police and had paid a 'fine' of $3,000 US for them all to be released.

The journey away from Kathmandu was a mini hell ride for Birgit. The traffic out of the city was bad and the trucks and buses belched their noxious fumes at us as we wove our way through. The road ranged from immaculate asphalt, to rough, potholed asphalt, to walnut sized gravel. The gravel was made by groups of men and women who sat in the riverbeds with hammers, beating the rocks, one by one, into just the right size to be used on the road. We'd done a little riding around the Kathmandu valley but this was the first time Birgit had been on the bike for a full day. The bus drivers on the route all seemed to have death wishes, and seemed to take great delight in waiting for corners or brows of hills before overtaking us. I'm not really sure how she hung on for the day, but she managed, and thankfully the guesthouse in Pokara, that Eric had recommended, had space for us.

By the time Birgit was well again – and it did happen quite quickly in the clean air – our visas were running out. Then I caught guardiasis again. Between us we'd been on a sickness saga, but a sick bed with a view of the snowy-topped Annapurna was the best I'd ever had. And this time, I knew what medication to take. The bug killer worked and with a four-day extension to my visa, we didn't get to trek this magnificent mountain, but we did make it to the border on time.

The first riding day was only going to be 165kms, but as we set off it felt as if it was going to a long one. Both of us were still feeling battered but the winding road was easy and fun, and the views fabulous. Small villages, that had been laid out to catch the most of any day's sunshine, were dotted along the roadside. The children knew that we were leaving, and in each of the villages they would run out to wave and call 'Goodbye' to us. I would miss the way Nepalese people managed to mix curiosity, friendship and respect.

Chapter 12
Fate Addicts and Karma Junkies
"Perhaps travel cannot prevent bigotry, but by demonstrating that all peoples cry, laugh, eat, worry, and die, it can introduce the idea that if we try to understand each other, we may even become friends."

Maya Angelou

Small black pigs hurtled out of the scrub at us like fat hairy-legged bullets, and as we got lower out of the mountains the road got worse – much worse. There'd been landslides and they looked as if they'd been there a long time. We could see that in the rainy season there would have been waterfalls gushing across the road at those points. The surface was very slippery and badly rutted, and of course we kept on getting stuck behind lumbering trucks and coaches. This was dangerous riding as these monsters, though moving slowly, threw up a thick cloud of dust that would trail for hundreds of metres behind. It was so thick that it was frequently impossible to tell when the next hazard was, and where the road had once been waterlogged mud, the truck tyres had dug deep ruts that we had no chance of riding in. We could only ride in the centre, but that too was crisscrossed with deep gullies where vehicles had slid around. Then around a corner, we found a bus sitting in the road in front of us, just where it was absolutely impossible for us to get off the ridge, or turn around. There was no choice – after a few minutes of staring at each other, with the bus driver apparently refusing to accept that he was going to have to be the one to move first, he revved his engine and started to hump and bump backwards. I wondered how he managed to stay upright on roads such as this. The bus had a monster roof rack that was piled a couple of metres high with people and belongings. It was crammed full inside the bus too. I supposed that it was all a matter of the driver understanding how gravity works. If he kept enough weight close to the ground, then there was less risk.

A friendly policeman in Butral showed us the way to a hostel that was reputedly biker-friendly. It stood in the narrow section of a 'Y'-

shaped junction, near the centre of the town. Though they didn't have a courtyard, they let bikers put their machines into the restaurant, which must have sparked quite a few dinnertime conversations over the years. We obviously weren't the first to have been allowed to do this.

Birgit and I were beginning to get into a teamwork routine. As I did my physio exercises each morning, she would organise and pack all our gear. When you are living out of a couple of large boxes and are on the move all the time, most of your kit gets unpacked each night. To get it all back in again, each morning, required the skills of an expert 3-D jigsaw puzzler, and Birgit was a natural. On these sorts of roads it was absolutely vital that belongings were wedged in with care. Anything sharp or fragile had to be protected. I'd failed to do that once in Africa and had ended up with a pannier full of water from a bottle that had a hole rubbed into it, and soggy, semi inflated pasta that was ground and mixed in with several packet soups and a bag of red-skinned peanuts. By the time I discovered the mess it looked like someone had vomited into my pannier. With Birgit's packing skill we were able to be on the road early in the morning before the traffic built to a stage that could only start a day off with hassle. Seven-thirty am departures would allow us to ride through towns when window shutters were only just going up, when breakfast fires were being lit and people were wandering around brushing their teeth.

The road this day was superb. The asphalt was perfect and the early light gave a special crispness to the world we were riding through. This low sunlight, which would always disappear as the sun rose higher, cast itself over a colourful blend of mustards and sages that spread across the now more level land towards gently rolling hills, which were back-dropped by the distant craggy, snow-topped mountains. The other bonus was that there was hardly any traffic, which should have been a worry; it probably meant that the road was closed, or even that we were on the wrong one, but we cruised on regardless. As we carried on south, losing height as we neared the Indian border, the temperature rose comfortably. The riding was so good that we didn't stop to take photos when we should have. Men and women were heading towards the border town on foot, and all were carrying huge bundles on their heads.

The easy riding abruptly changed when the road split in two at a roundabout on the edge of Nepal Ganj. This town is a major border crossing back into India and it looked like it – mad, crazy, busy, but not as decrepit as Roxaul Bazar had been. It was a proper town with laid-out streets and concrete buildings, and we didn't feel as if we were in Nepal any more. The town felt more like India, but here at least there was space between the buildings. The rubble and rubbish-filled spaces looked like empty plots waiting to be developed, but in the meantime they allowed light to reach through to the streets.

Thanks to Brigit's eagle eye we found the Punjab Hotel quite quickly. Having two sets of eyes to deal with map reading, road signs, and hotel hunts was a real bonus, and unlike Jan, Birgit knew her left from her right. We'd soon fallen into the routine of a thump on the left shoulder for a left turn coming up, and a thump on the right shoulder for a right turn – simple but effective directions.

The Punjab was good value, and with its walled courtyard it felt like a mini-fortress. That night, we were glad it was. The warm air was tense in the town and as we looked to be the only tourists, we attracted a lot of attention. In the main it was natural curiosity, and neither of us minded that. As we were still in Nepal it wasn't uncomfortable – just strangely increased in intensity after Kathmandu and Pokara. The number of men hanging around surprised us though, and the amount of police in full riot gear was worrying. We wondered what we'd ridden into.

Nepal Ganj stayed quiet until the middle of the night, but at just after one in the morning it erupted. The first thing we knew that something really was wrong, was when shouting began between men in the corridor outside our room. We'd gone to sleep with earplugs in because of the constant banging of people's room doors. The corridors were totally bare of furnishings, so any sounds made there were amplified. The noise got louder, and it sounded as if the number of men doing the shouting was growing. Below our first floor window there was the sound of running feet, wood being banged on corrugated

214

iron, shouting, and gunfire, and then screams penetrated our earplugs. I looked out, and the sky over the town was a flickering orange, the stench of burning rubber wafting in through our open window. In a quiet moment we heard panicked footsteps scurrying past; the runner was breathing in short hard bursts. He stopped for a few moments at the side of the hotel and then, as we heard more running feet and the shouting coming closer, he took off again. We sat in bed looking at each other, wondering what was going to happen next. Even the mosquitoes seemed to have taken cover.

I got up to check that Libby was OK. Other semi-clad male guests and the hotel staff were milling around in the courtyard, casting nervous glances towards the tall, metal-covered gates. Not far away a burning building collapsed with a crash, and sparks shot skywards. Then suddenly, there was silence. It was as if someone had flicked the off switch. All that remained to remind us that we hadn't been hearing things was the smell of burning rubber and scorched wood. The crowded courtyard emptied, with people casting wide-eyed and nervous glances at each other. One of the staff told me with an almost apologetic tone that Muslim and Hindu youths had been fighting.

There were power cuts in the morning but that didn't matter, we wanted to head away from the border as quickly as possible. The air in Nepal Ganj was still tense, with people on the street watching each other warily. Just to underline the point that we had to leave, Birgit's visa had expired and mine was about to, so we headed for India as fast as we could go. The Nepalese customs and immigration were very efficient yet again, and everything was done in an hour. They acted as if nothing strange at all had happened the night before. The immigration officer had waggled a finger at Birgit about her visa, but that was it – a final police checkpoint and then, no more Nepal. In spite of our both having spent so much time unwell, we were going to miss this stunning country and its friendly people. If anything, being ill in such a poor country had shown us both how well off we were, and how kind a people who have so little, can be to strangers.

A fat, sleek-bearded officer sat at a desk outside the immigration office on the Indian side of the border. It was still chilly after the night and he'd positioned his grey metal-legged desk to catch the early sun. He had an audience of two, who actively participated and cheered on his performance. This man could make delays over paperwork last a day, and could earn a living for his skill in procrastination. He was pompous and condescending, and though we'd shown him complete respect from the outset, he treated us with the scornful distaste of a high-caste Brahmin confronted by an Untouchable. It was only 9am, but he was already having a bad day. I had the feeling that had he not had a two person, wide-eyed audience sucking up to him, he wouldn't have done anything for us at all. For Birgit, it was an eye-opener.

Customs were completely different, and the officer here was very pleasant. We worked well together through the mountain of forms that he had to fill in, and Birgit and I were on our way before ten. I hadn't won the issue over my remaining spare tyre though. I'd tried to get him to mark the carnet that I'd not brought one into India. I intended to change the tyre shortly and knew that there would be hassle if I no longer had a spare when I exited. No luck, which meant that I'd either have to sort something out later, or carry the old tyre until I left. While we'd been talking, the officer had pointed over at two bikes that were set up for overlanding. They were covered in a layer of beige-coloured dust that was so thick I'd not noticed them. A rust, emerald and midnight blue-feathered cockerel stood on one of them, surveying his kingdom as his bright red crest wobbled with each jerky flick of his head. The customs officer nodded at the bikes with his chin and said, "These men are having counterfeit carnets don't you know. Now they are not having motorcycles." We'd heard quite a bit in Nepal about the availability of fake carnets, which were supposed to be very convincing, and cheap. For some long-distance travellers the temptation to save a considerable amount of money must have been strong.

Free of the hassle and with the day still cool, we made a mistake. The bank wasn't open until eleven, and though we needed rupees, we elected to ride on to the next town. I had enough rupees left to buy petrol, but not enough to eat or pay for a room. 'No problem', we thought.

Our first day, due to my impatience, turned into a massively hard thing to get through. I wouldn't have been surprised if Birgit had said, 'That's it. If this is what it's going to be like every day, then I'm off'. But she didn't. She's made of sterner stuff, though I suspected that I wasn't going to be allowed to make bank decisions on my own in the future!

Petrol was cheaper in India than in Nepal so we filled up before leaving the town, and then asked for directions to Larkinpur. Asking directions in India is nearly always an adventure, and even when you think you have the right answer, you're never really quite sure. I'd learnt that when saying, 'Is this the way to...?' whilst pointing in the direction that I thought was correct, I'd always get an "Oh yes Sah, this is very much being the right direction for you Sah." It almost never was the right way.

It wasn't that the people were being deliberately difficult, quite the opposite. They were being too helpful, and saving face. They wanted to help so much, that when they didn't know the right direction, they would point you somewhere that might possibly be correct, just in case. But whatever, at least they had done something to help you, the visitor to their country. It also never paid to let anyone see a map. People were fascinated by maps, but the majority couldn't read them and that just confused matters even more.

It was far better to ask, 'Which is the way to...?' whilst keeping my hands down by my sides. Even when asking for directions in the correct way, I would still have to ask at least five very different people, and then take the route that most people said. Frequently they'd be right. But the best option of all was to go into a pharmacy, and ask the pharmacist for directions. They were always well educated, had travelled and could speak excellent English. Not one time did I have a wrong set of directions from a pharmacist.

The road the pharmacist set us out on was rough, but it was asphalt although mainly single-track. This made life interesting when another vehicle came towards us, especially as buses worked on the premise that as they were bigger than us and had louder horns, they had right of way. Rarely did they hop two wheels off the asphalt for us, and during the course of the day we were bullied off the road completely, twelve times. Mostly it was quite manageable, but sometimes the rough-edged asphalt would be rimming a drop of thirty or forty centimetres. With a fully laden bike, two up, those were a bit of a worry. Libby managed them though and Birgit did really well. Some novice pillions panic when something potentially dire is happening. When they panic they grip on tight and do anything their self-preservation instincts tell them to do. Birgit was totally calm and kept her instincts under control so I could deal with keeping the bike up, without any scary wobbles or being grabbed at the wrong moment.

This business of rules of the road was a lesson well learned. The two main rules in India are quite simply: 'I'm bigger than you are, so I go first', and 'I was here first, so I go first.' I can understand both of those and where everyone is obeying those rules and acting accordingly, then it's not too bad. The third rule though explains some of the cacophony of noise that you find on India roads: 'My horn is louder than yours, so I go first!' In the end, for a biker, it's better to let every one else go first, (except bicycles because one does have a certain amount of pride you know). Any sense of machismo should be left at home when you are faced with the fate and karma junkies that populate India's roads.

One friend managed to beat the system by making rule three work for him. He junked everything out of one of his panniers and filled that with a couple of car batteries. Attached to those batteries were air horns off a train. When riding with him, even the biggest trucks pulled out of his way to let us overtake. It was nice to wave as we rode past.

Rule one was the scariest though. On one occasion I was riding alone on single-lane asphalt through a canyon. The asphalt had just enough loose sand and gravel to each side to allow a couple of big vehicles to pass, with a bit of room to spare, it frequently had my name on it. This day, I was happily cruising along, when the truck coming towards me hopped two tyres off the asphalt, leaving me thinking that

I'd found one of the few gentleman truck drivers in India. I soon realised that out of his dust was nosing a truck that, having a louder horn, was overtaking. I started to panic a bit as thorn bushes were growing in the space that was left on the verges, then I too became a temporary believer in karma – behind the first two trucks was another one who was also trying to overtake. I had nowhere to go, and they weren't slowing down at all. I knew I'd had it, so decided not to watch. I pointed the bike between two of the trucks, closed my eyes and held on for dear life. I was buffeted madly in a sand storm for a few seconds, and then amazingly I was through. I'd no idea how I'd done it, but behind me the roaring orange Tata trucks had flattened every bush. I stopped, got off the bike and shook for an age before having the courage to carry on.

Weeks later I heard the tale of another biker who hadn't been so lucky. He'd lived, but badly shattered both his arms, and smashed his legs so severely that no one ever expected him to walk again. His bike had been written off, with one cylinder ripped right away, and the other one forced up into the main engine block by the strength of the impact.

There's sometimes a sense of camaraderie between local bikers and motorcycling visitors. Riding away from Nepal Ganj, Birgit and I were bumping along the potholed, heat-warped asphalt, when two lads joined us on their Royal Enfield Bullet. This made-in-India, 350cc bike was much smaller than Libby, and its suspension made Libby's look as if it was off a Rolls-Royce – we glided through the bumps, they hammered their way through. With each bump, the two of them would be airborne, the pillion passenger bouncing so high that he looked as if he was riding in a rodeo, rather than hanging on to the back of a bike. But still they tried to keep up, buzzing around us like a puppy dog chasing its mother. The lads, without helmets or protective gear, were grinning and shouting to us excitedly. They were enjoying the race, though in fact we were simply cruising. After a while I felt I had to open the throttle and leave them behind. They were getting carried away with their enthusiasm and it was beginning to be dangerous. Just a few weeks before the same sort of thing had happened, but the rider had got too close to me and had hooked one of his big chrome crash bars onto the front of Libby's pannier. He nearly threw us both off our bikes.

Every so often we'd come across a bridge. Some were impressive, steel girder jobs, often with a toll. On a bike you don't normally get stopped for this, and locals on bikes don't either. But this time as we slowly rode to the front of the queue, a man leapt out in front of us with his hand held up, palm towards us. My first thought was that we were about to be taken advantage of. The precedent had been set on the quieter country roads where it was normal to find that a group of men had stretched an old rope across the road as a moving barrier. They would be attempting to collect a 'safety tax' or a 'road tax'. Sometimes, after the rope, there would even be men working to fill potholes in the road, but most of the time it seemed to be simply a money-making scam.

On the bridge, I wasn't going to ride off and pretend I hadn't seen this man. He was pretty obvious and in any event, the traffic was so dense it wasn't going anywhere quickly. "Mister, Mister, Sah," the man said. "Please be coming inside." We went with him and were greeted by a smart middle-aged man in European dress. "Welcome, come and drink chai with us. We have sent out for cakes too." He showed us through into a small sitting room behind the toll office. Large green painted windows looked out over a small yard where flowering plants were growing in old powdered milk tins. Another man was sitting there and we were invited to sit too. The second man was dressed in more traditional robes, and was somewhat older. The chai arrived and we got talking. At this point I still wasn't sure if there was a scam underway, but what was happening was interesting. The men wouldn't speak to Birgit, though they had acknowledged her. "Where are you coming from?" "Where are you going?" "How big is your motorcycle?" "Do you believe in God?" The usual list of questions went, but in a very unpushy atmosphere. The cakes, which were almost pure sugar, arrived. The men still didn't speak directly to Birgit, but addressed their questions to her through me. I could feel her itching at this and I teased her later that it's more normal that the women do all the talking – I was thumped for that quip! Suddenly the conversation stopped. The two men looked at each other, and then the older man peered across at us and said, "You know, this is a very special day in my life. Here we are. I am a Muslim, my friend here is a Hindu and you are Christians. Is this not a fine thing that we are sitting here together, drinking chai as friends?"

He was right. It was special and I sat quietly kicking myself for being so cynical – trusting first normally works, and this stop with our new friends certainly relegated the night in Nepal Ganj to where it should remain – a sad memory that was based in reality, but not the norm for most people. Violent mobs live everywhere in this world, but they do not rule the minds of those who keep theirs open.

We were later told that in India it's a sign of complete disrespect for a man to talk to a woman he doesn't know. Until custom says it's possible, then it shouldn't happen. This knowledge was helpful on many occasions, as it helped us to realise when we were dealing with someone who looked kosher, but was dodgy because of his lack of respect.

We still hadn't found a bank, and time was getting on. The day was beginning to stretch out and the pressure of the road was already telling on us. In Sharjhampur, the bank wouldn't change either travellers' cheques, dollars or let us use our credit cards. Now

worried, we rode on towards Bareilly, with two lads on a moped showing us the way through the town. The roads were a maze and it didn't help that we got stuck in a water buffalo jam. On the outskirts of Sharjhampur we found a hotel with its name up in English, but no, they wouldn't let us pay for our room and a meal with any form of funding we'd got. But the manager was a very helpful chap and told us that another hotel in the group probably would let us pay in the morning after we'd found a bank. He phoned them, got the go ahead, and booked us a room. He also kindly wrote down the name and address of the hotel in both English and Hindi.

It was dark by the time we arrived in Bareilly, and if we hadn't had that note, we'd have had a hard time finding the hotel. I dislike riding in the dark at the best of times, but in India its lunacy. The traffic doesn't seem to ease up until very late at night, so you are riding with all the same problems, but with one vital sense working on just half power. If you can't see whatever the problem is, you can't avoid it. Judging the speed of other vehicles and distances in the dark on this road was virtually impossible and donkey carts were invisible. Indian drivers must eat a lot of carrots, as many of them wouldn't turn their lights on until they absolutely had to.

The hotel was expensive and the room adequate. The shower didn't work, but by then we were past caring. The bonus, besides safe parking, was that the hotel had a restaurant, which meant that we didn't need to cook food for ourselves, and in any case we'd still no money to buy anything outside the hotel. The restaurant was a dingy, deserted room that had us both wondering what the food would be like. The bar in the corner had no alcohol on display – just a selection of vividly coloured soft drinks. The tables were all Formica, which made me think of a 1960s café, and the vinyl floor was sticky to walk on. When they came, the portions of something interesting but nameless, were small, but that didn't matter, and with food and a roof over our heads we finally started to relax.

Changing money in a bank that isn't used to dealing with tourists is a far more interesting thing to do than in one that is. The first two banks I got the rickshaw driver to take me to in the morning wouldn't change anything at all for me. I'd taken a rickshaw, leaving Birgit and Libby as a sort of collateral for the hotel manager. If we'd left together he might have thought that we were doing a runner, and neither of us wanted that to happen, especially after he'd helped us out so much. By the time I'd left the second bank, shaking my head in concern, the rickshaw driver was getting worried that he wasn't going to get paid. I'd asked him to wait for me each time I went into a bank, and had explained that he needed to do that because I had no money. It was a tremendous act of faith on his part that he had been prepared to go along with it.

By mid-morning we'd found the Bank of India, and after queuing for an hour I was told that no, they wouldn't change travellers cheques, and no they couldn't do anything with my credit card. But yes, they would change dollars. I was queue-jumped to the front of another desk by the courteous assistant, who explained to the very smart man behind the desk what was wanted. He took my passport to inspect. As I'd been around a bit by then, my passport was filled with stamps from all sorts of exotic places, and a crowd soon formed to admire them. Sometimes, when battling with the day in an unknown land, it was easy to forget how lucky I was.

I was given a small brass token and a form that had been completed in Hindi for me, and instructed to take these to another counter. While I was waiting in that queue I was joined by a group of engineering students. They'd heard on the street outside about this man with the full passport, and had decided that they should meet me. All were in their late teens and dressed immaculately. Their open inquisitiveness was infectious and I really valued the chance to talk with them. Then at last I had a wallet full of rupees, which made me feel both safe again, and rich.

Because of the long day we'd just had we were close enough to make it to Delhi, if everything went well. The road was mostly in much better condition, but setting off in the middle of the day threw us straight into the worst of the traffic. Even so, for some blissful spurts we managed to reach a hundred kilometres an hour, but the rest of the day ground along as a 'foot down, first gear, second gear, foot down, first gear, leap out of the way of the truck', type of day. But we were only run off the road ten times, which was a bonus!

The sun was dropping fast by the time we were thirty kilometres away from Delhi, which called for a decision. If we kept going we could park the bike and settle down for a few days of exploring on foot and by rickshaw. If we found somewhere to stay where we were, we'd have

223

to face Delhi traffic in the morning, and by now we knew enough to be sure that we could well spend the next hour trying to find somewhere to stay for the night. By this time my back was feeling pretty sore from the bumpy, stop-start day, but we decided to risk it. Surely, we thought, the way into Delhi would be clearly signposted, and we had directions from Dirk and Jens to get to the Delhi Tourist camp. The name of the place sounded awful, but the guys had assured us that we'd love it, and that we'd probably meet other bikers there. It was another of the rare crossroads for overlanders.

The sky was a deep orange colour by the time we made it to the outskirts of Delhi. Rush hour should have been over by that time, but it didn't feel like it. We battled with Dirk and Jens' directions so much that we gave up on them and started to look for a pharmacy, but there wasn't one to be seen anywhere. The second best person to ask directions from in India is an older man who is well dressed in European style clothing. Smartly dressed older people nearly always spoke English and often knew their way around. And there at the side of the road were three such men, dressed in sports trousers, business shirts, ties and all wearing what looked like Harris Tweed sports jackets. "Excuse me, could you tell us the way to the Delhi Gate please?" We'd picked on this landmark because we could see from our map that it wasn't far away from the Tourist Camp. If we could get to the gate then we could work out the next bit for ourselves. Surely, we'd thought, people would know where the Delhi Gate was, but all we got from the men were blank expressions.

We tried saying 'Delhi Gate' in every way we could think of, but with no success. My final attempt was to say, "Can you be telling us the way to the delegete please." I added on my version of the sideways head wiggle for good measure. "Oh Mister, why are you not asking before for the 'Delegete'? You must be going straight here, then left at the lights, then right at the next junction, then straight again and then finally you must be going left. Then you are there. Thank you verrry much." the oldest man said with a head waggle in return. The dim light from the street lamps combined with neon shop signs and car headlights to help us miss most of the hazards in the road as we rode on through the dark, and he was right.

By the time we pulled in through the gates of the campsite and had booked ourselves into a cabin, which turned out to be an airless cell with an iron-framed bed, I'd had it and I feared that we'd both be walking bow-legged for days. The lesson learned was: in Northern India expect to ride no more than two hundred and fifty kilometres in a day, and even that distance could take ten hours of battling to do. Riding was a lot easier way down in Southern India – it's almost a different world.

As we rolled towards the cabin, a bloke came running out towards us. "Mates, welcome." he yelled with a happy smile on his face. And so we met Mark, who turned into a lifelong friend.

Being in Delhi was how I imagined it must be in the army – 'hurry up and wait'. Birgs and I had a lot to do there. We wanted to see some of the sights, but first we had to extend her plane ticket so she could snag some more days in India. We also had to get visas for me for Pakistan, and Iran. The visa for Iran was the worry. Most people we'd spoken to had told us that it was virtually impossible to get when outside of the UK. Some travellers in the Tourist Camp had been waiting for weeks and were being told by the embassy each day, 'Come back tomorrow'. I felt as if I had been defeated by Burma and I was sad that I'd not managed to make China happen, so for me Iran was a must do – if at all possible.

However, with as much doubt hanging over the idea, I also started to investigate what would be involved with shipping the bike to Mombasa in Kenya. This would be a radical change in plan but it could work. It was now November in Delhi, a great time to be there – in summer, temperatures could reach forty-seven degrees Celsius, which would have been pretty unbearable. But Iran and Turkey were further north, and in the mountain regions it would be very cold on the bike. I'd already accepted that I'd not be going to the north of Pakistan, but had consoled myself with the thought that this would be a good reason to come back to the region at some time in the future. If I shipped the bike to Africa, I could fly back to Europe to meet up with Birgit and to earn some more money before going back to Africa.

This thought had come about because I'd asked Birgit to come with me to South America. I'd got so far round the world by this time that I was having dreams of making it all the way round. Birgit's response had been, "Yes, I'll come with you, but I want to ride my own bike, and I want to go to Africa first." She assured me that wanting her own bike had nothing to do with my riding style, more that she wanted to be in control of her own destiny. She also feared that she might get bored sitting on the back of Libby for country after country. I could understand that. At five foot one, Birgit wasn't tall enough to ride Libby and get her feet down on the ground, so we couldn't take it in turns to be pillion. In any case, I rather liked the idea of her having her own bike too. On a long trip when you are together for twenty-four hours a day, it's rather nice to have your own space, and riding separate bikes would allow for that. As for the Africa idea, well, I'd loved it there the first time and thought, 'why not?' It would be interesting to see how things had changed and it'd be great to get the chance to go places I hadn't got to the first time through. Of course being on two bikes would be far more expensive than sharing, but quality of life and the fact that we'd be travelling together seemed much more important.

The plan could work, but I told her that she'd have to maintain her own bike. In part that was because I thought that if she understood her bike then she'd be in far greater control, and that meant she wouldn't make as many mistakes as I had in my first year on the road. Keeping a bike running when it's getting this sort of life is quite a time-consuming affair and if I was looking after two bikes then there'd be less time for exploring. Also, if Birgit had a bike similar to mine, we'd be able to share knowledge when there was a problem. I already had full respect for her abilities, and suspected she was going to turn out to be a far better mechanic than I was. When she'd set the valve clearances for the first time in Kathmandu, she'd done it with confidence and as if she'd done it many times before.

Shipping agents told us that it was possible to do and quoted prices that seemed reasonable, but Pakistan, Iran and Turkey were still the first choice, and in the purple and cream fronted High Commission of Pakistan I was told that I could have my visa within four days. But the Iranians were a different ball game.

We arrived at the Iranian Embassy with Birgit walking in front of me. She was treated with a smile and full respect by the guards when they saw her German passport. And having let her through, they turned to me with an equally warm welcome, obviously thinking that I was German too. Their attitude changed faster than I could click

my fingers when they saw my Brit passport, and I was only begrudgingly let past. Inside the embassy I was treated with a calm non-committal manner by the official behind the bulletproof glass in the visa applications area. There'd been quite a queue and the waiting had made me nervous. A lot was hanging on how this official treated me and the reception at the gate hadn't started things off well. If the official didn't like what he saw, then I'd get an instant 'No'. I'd worn my best possible clothes and had made sure that everything was clean and pressed. I'd cut my beard short and had tied my ponytail so it hung neatly down the back of my neck. I'd planned an itinerary for the route across Iran, and had all the documents I needed, including a letter of recommendation from the British Embassy.

The official looked up at me over the top of his half-glasses and said, "I cannot help you now. Come back in four days. But I can tell you that it will take one month for your application to be processed. There is no guarantee. It must go to Tehran." With that he passed my documents back, and started to look at the other papers on his desk as if we had already gone.

That timescale worked if the Pakistani embassy stuck to their quoted four days, but what bothered me was the thought of being without my passport in India for a whole month. It's against the law, and if I was in an accident or got pulled over by the police, then I'd be in trouble, with arrest and jail until it got sorted out. Money wasn't going to be such a problem as I had my credit card, and I could arrange with American Express to get money without my passport. The British Embassy listened to my story, and kindly agreed to write an official letter explaining what was happening. I could carry this around with me and if there were any difficulties, I could refer whoever was causing a problem to the Embassy. Perfect, things had started to go right.

Back at the Tourist Camp, we were making new friends. Dirk and Jens, who had turned up at the camp themselves by this time, had been right. It was an overlanders' crossroads. Mark, who'd greeted us as we'd arrived, was from the UK, and on his way to Australia by bike. Paul, a Swiss chap, was there to buy his annual Enfield to explore with for a few months, and then to ride back to sell in Switzerland. "This," he said, "covers the cost of my months in India perfectly. I have a great holiday for free." Gerard, another Brit, was the character of the site, an experienced traveller who had been all over the world. He had a sense of humour that would constantly catch us unawares. Dry is not an arid enough word to describe his quirky way of looking at things, and he could be outrageously funny with his totally unconventional observations of life, people and the world. He was also the only person I'd met who'd managed to hit a water buffalo! He'd been very lucky not to have hit it harder, but even so, he'd damaged his bike. Being inventive, he'd drilled holes in the broken plastic parts and using wire, had stitched his bike back together again. The buffalo apparently, had given Gerard a look that said, 'Sahib, please be minding where you are going', and had then wandered back off into the traffic.

Martin was a German biker who didn't speak more than a couple of words of English, which was making his journey quite hard. In most countries from Europe across, there are people who speak English and you are far more likely to find an official at border crossings who speaks English than one who speaks German. Martin also had an odd load, competing strongly with French Eric, with an aluminium top box the size of a small fridge hanging off the back of his bike. He was carrying twenty T-shirts and a pair of pyjamas in here, amongst a ton of other

228

clothes. Martin was the best-dressed biker I'd come across, but also decided to carry his spare tyres looped around his handlebars! "It is very strange," he said to Birgit one day, "I keep falling off my motorcycle."

A few days later, Irish Rory turned up, having just ridden across from Italy. "Bloimey t'was cold," he said when I asked him how he'd got on. He'd bought himself a fisherman's pocket warmer, which ran on burning charcoal sticks. He'd been stuffing it down the front of his bike trousers in an attempt to keep warm. "It's brilliant, until you have to stop unexpectedly", he'd said with a rounded Irish brogue, "then you burn yer nuts off!" He went on to describe how he, with frozen fingers, had tried to get the offending burning item out of his trousers, with an audience of border police, immigration officers and those in a queue that stretched for about 50 metres. Rory also had the quietest BMW GS I'd ever heard. The bike purred, whereas mine and most others rattled and clattered away. Rory had had major problems with his bike in Italy and the BMW garage there had sorted him out, but they had also tightened his valve clearances so much that they made no sound. Damage was being done to the bike as he'd ridden it across the Middle East, and half way across Asia. Rory had also set off as a novice BMW rider, and it made a change for me to be able to help someone else – this was something I did know how to fix!

Zero was Japanese. He was riding a tiny 250cc trail bike and had it so over-laden with loosely strapped on, dusty battered kit that it looked rather like a mini-camel in a bazaar. He solved that problem by getting some steel racks and some excellent stainless steel panniers made up while he was in Delhi. Stainless steel cost buttons and the local craftsmen knew exactly what they were doing. Zero was worried though. He'd been on the road for a long time and, "I think I have changed." he confided to me one day. He'd been brought up in a very traditional Japanese family, with all the constraints that this involved. He'd almost had to run away from home to be able to live his dream. "I think that I am not going to be happy when I go to Japan," he said. "I don't know how my family will think of me. I think maybe I do not know my friends anymore, and I think maybe it is going to be very hard for me to find a job now." Zero had a thin, tanned, travel-worn face, unruly hair, oil-filled fingernails and battered clothes. "I have seen too many things", he said, "maybe my father was right, but my journey has been very good." Zero made me very conscious of how easily I was able to travel. I too had changed a lot and would continue to change, but at least my family supported me with enthusiasm, and most of my friends were travellers, so that would never be a problem.

Ian was from Australia and Caroline was from Dorset in England. They'd met on the road and romance had blossomed, but as that happened, Caroline's plans had taken a dramatic turn. Ian was intending to buy a second-hand 350cc Enfield to ride across to Europe, but neither of them liked the idea of being two-up on his bike for those sorts of distances. The only solution was for Caroline to buy a Bullet for herself, and then learn to ride it. The two of them headed off into the Karol Bagh area of Delhi on a shopping expedition, and found just the bikes they needed. Caroline's first ride was an embarrassing wobble around the Tourist Camp, but she didn't fall off and over the next days she became quite competent at forty-metre wobbles. Then she had to face her first real ride, and Delhi traffic wasn't the place I'd have chosen for such an event. So much could have gone wrong, and a nasty experience could so easily have laid their plans to rest. I admired her tremendously as she wobbled uncertainly out into the fumy rush of everyday Delhi streets. She had booked herself to take her bike test with the Indian authorities and had no choice but to break her road duck, but the test itself turned out to be amazingly simple. Could she ride one hundred metres and then turn a corner without falling off? She could, just. And days later, the two of them set off on the long ride to Europe.

The bikes had been delivered with chrome luggage racks either side of the back wheels, so all they had to do was to organise soft luggage to strap on. Their next task had been to kit themselves out with as many spare parts as they could carry. The Enfields were known to be unreliable, which wasn't a problem in India, as every town or village of any size would have an Enfield mechanic strategically placed to help out. But once they were out of India, it would be a different story altogether. Spares would be vital, and luckily in India they cost buttons. As Ian and Caroline set off in the dawn traffic, I said a little prayer that the fate and karma junkies wouldn't get them.

Delhi Tourist Camp wasn't just a crossroads for bikers though. Two couples with Land Rovers were on the site and there were a couple of Turkish blokes in a coach. Andy and Di were Brits and had had a ball coming across from England. Andy was a mechanic so had no concerns about his vehicle, and in fact spent a fair amount of time working on other people's wheels while he was at the camp. He'd changed the Land Rover's engine for a Ford Transit motor before they'd set off, and was really pleased with it. "Much cheaper to run and really quiet in comparison", he said. The two of them had had enough of foreign food though, and Di had persuaded Andy to design an oven that would work over their two-ring Calor Gas stove. "We'll invite you round for a roast dinner when it's done" she said to us.

The other people on the site were a real mix. In a way it was a cultural crossroads as well as a vehicular one. The majority of the cabins were occupied by Indian visitors to Delhi and people from the Middle East. Farad was from Iran and as I was so keen to get into his country, I thought I'd take the chance to pick his brains about places to go and things to see along the way. It would also be a useful introduction to the country to see a little of it through his eyes. He was quite open and honest about his homeland, and he talked with real pride about the beauty of the mountains, the kindness of the people, and Esfahan and its stunning blue mosque, but he was less than keen on the current regime. "I am a Persian and I'm a loyal Iranian," he said, "but the government does not respect the people. We are censored in just about everything we do and the Koran is misquoted to us at a whim." He was proud of the opportunity that Iran's oil reserves gave the people, but frustrated that so little of the money was spent on developing industry in the country. "What happens when the oil runs out?" He told me that he felt privileged to be able to travel outside Iran, as this was his opportunity to find out what was really going on in the world. "Our own press, radio and TV are so censored we don't know what the truth is." He went on to explain that many people had fixed satellite dishes so they could watch overseas TV and listen to foreign radio, but that in recent months the government had been flying helicopters over towns, locating the dishes, which had then been torn down by the police or soldiers. He said, "We knew that CNN was also censored and was biased, but at least between their news and ours we could work out something close to the truth. Your World Service is better, but we see how that is changing for the worse also." He told me that many rich people had smuggled in the technology that would allow them to turn their glass patio windows into satellite antennae. "Not so easy for the government to find those." he said with a small but triumphant smile.

Beneath his wife's black, richly shining hair, hung a large hooked nose that on a man would have looked manly, but on a woman looked like as if the gods had been in a miserable mood the day she had been formed. But for those who could see past that unfairness, it was her eyes that dominated and showed her strength of character, her humour and her intelligence. Delbar's eyes twinkled and teased without saying a word, as she watched me going through the process of getting past her barrier. She giggled and fluttered her long eyelashes when she saw that I'd made it. The age creases on her face instantly crinkled into the smile lines of someone who smiles a lot. She wore her hair pulled back behind overlarge lobed ears, from which she had hung giant tiered and filigree golden earrings, as a sort of mickey-taking challenge to the world. She drew attention to herself rather than live in the shadows, and seemed to take great delight in making the acquaintance of those who could see past the surface. She looked up and said, "You think it is a problem? Farad had a surprise when he saw past my veil on the first night of our wedding." She giggled again. "He's a good man though, and he is as proud of me as I am of him."

We'd normally find a bunch of Israelis at a good spot like the Tourist Camp, and I'd been surprised that we hadn't seen many. The ones we had seen there were not the norm; they were quiet and friendly to non-Israelis – we enjoyed their company. One of them told me that it was because it was too expensive in comparison with places in the Paraganj area of the city. In a way I was glad. Israeli travellers tend to be loud, and mostly seemed to treat the locals with minimal respect. They had a network that told them where the cheapest places to stay were, where the best places to change money were and so on. Some of the advantages to being an Israeli on the road were very handy with budget travel in mind, but I struggled to be around them for long. Everything they said seemed to be at the top of their voices. Good looking people though, the blokes mostly lean and fit, and the women were in the main, stunningly dark-haired and olive-skinned. But most seemed to have almost gone feral – they didn't seem to think that clean clothes were important and would nearly always look unkempt.

Their noisy exuberance was, I think, because for once they were outside of the stiff restraints and fear of their own country. From a very early age they are brought up to be soldiers and fed a diet of whatever disaster was going to hit the country next. Both men and women have to do national service and most Israeli travellers seem to be those that had just finished their stints. For the first time they could do what they wanted, without anyone looking over their shoulders, so they did.

But they were too over the top, and seemed to be happy to trample over others. For me, part of the buzz of travel came from the people I managed to spend time with along the way, and in fact, often I'd rather sit and chat with a local than rush around going from one thing that I 'should' see to the next. I thought that these people were missing out big time, but who was I to judge? I'd not been brought up with a gun being waved over my head all the time, and in real terms the UK allowed me to be who I wanted to be. If I wanted to be rich, I probably could be. If I wanted to be highly educated, I could be. If I wanted to travel the world on a motorcycle, I could. My passport certainly allowed me into a lot of countries that refused visas to Israelis for political reasons.

Delhi is the capital city of India, and it's big, though even at 1,483 square kilometres it's not as big as Mumbai, or Bombay as it was once known. It's built on land that has been occupied by seven different cities over hundreds of years, though the Old Delhi and New Delhi areas are the most visible chunks now. The old city was built by the Moghuls during their three-hundred year rule of Northern India, and the area known as New Delhi was built in the days of the Raj. The difference between the two is chalk and cheese. The old part is a labyrinth of small streets and alleyways, whereas the new part is full of open parks and straight streets. The city is set on an enormous plain and the one river that flows through it. The Yamuna is one of Hinduism's sacred rivers, though when you look at it, the river seems to be treated the same way as most others in the country – it's a way of getting rid of rubbish and effluent.

The city is a spectacular place though, and amazingly cosmopolitan. People from all over India have migrated here to live and work. The draws are the amount of work available, and the salary levels at two and a half times higher than most other places in the country. The mass of people stretches the city's resources to breaking point though, and in the intense heat of the summer, people die. The infrastructure can only provide two-thirds of the water that's needed, and as air conditioning gets turned on full blast 24 hours a day, power cuts are the norm. The air pollution is phenomenal, and in winter the city is prone to bouts of fog, which mixed with the air pollution, can become so dense that traffic virtually comes to a standstill. The mass of people and industry produce 8,000 tonnes of rubbish every day!

Despite a relatively high average income, fifteen percent of Delhi's population were still living below the poverty line when I was there. They were surviving, just, on three hundred rupees a month. The tourist camp daily rent alone was just under a third of that per day. Knowing this, I found it hard to haggle in the markets, but one day when I didn't bargain at all, the stallholder said to me, "You have only just arrived in India is it not? You must be bargaining here or you will be having no respect and you will be paying many many times too much. This is not good for you." This was all said with a brown-eyed seriousness above a neat grey beard, and with a pair of hands that seemed to have decided to do a bi-plane dogfight above the stall's magnificent array of prime fruits and vegetables. He then leant towards me and said conspiratorially, "These people are all thieves you know. Foreigners – you must not be trusting them." As I looked around me, the only people I could see were Indians going about their business.

As with any city, there's a dark side to Delhi, but it's a great place to get things done, and its history means that you come across interesting little nooks and crannies all the time. We loved the colourful markets and the massive variety of food from all parts of India. If something was made in India, you could find it in one or other of the markets. Some parts of the city smell really bad and there were places that we wouldn't walk in open-toed shoes because of the risk of scooping up something pretty disgusting. But the other smells of the city were of rich exotic spices, tantalising food and the scent of night flowering jasmine. It was almost as if the contrasts of the country had been collected together into one place.

Delhi is also a great kicking off point to get to the rest of the country. Its airport, one of the busiest in Asia, is the doorway to the sub-continent for many – the buses and trains taking up the task from there on. But none of those interested us. Birgit and I had submitted the application for the Pakistani visa, and had got it within the four days. The application had gone into the Iranian Embassy, and the officials had been much more positive about my application. Things were looking up, and now we had a month that we could use to go out and play on the bike in India.

Chapter 13

Indian Magic

*'I can't think of anything that excites a greater sense of childlike wonder
than to be in a country where you are ignorant of almost everything.'*
Bill Bryson

With just a month to do any exploring, we were going to be limited as to what we could see. We could spend the time pushing ourselves by diving from one sight to another, but neither of us was keen to do that. In India things take time whatever the form of transport and that would have meant spending most of our time on the road. We felt that with time and travel hassles involved, this wasn't an option we wanted to take. Instead, we decided to concentrate on Rajasthan, to the west of Delhi, but first, we decided to scoot east to Agra to see the Taj Mahal. Mark was intending to do the same thing and we decided to travel together. We'd been getting on well with him, and had been enjoying his positive enthusiasm. He had a glow of sheer joy of being on the road. He was also an experienced traveller and was on the same sort of budget as us, which helped.

Once out of Delhi, the road to Agra was mostly dual carriageway. Though busy, it was good steady riding. The morning mist was already burning off at 8.30am, and being a Saturday the traffic was lighter than it could have been. There also seemed to be less of an air of urgency about the other vehicles. The karma junkies were still playing their games, but they did so in a lackadaisical manner, rather than the 'if I'm not tempting fate then I'm not a man' type of driving we'd been dealing with to date. The fifty-vehicle army convoy we had to pass, made life much easier by parking up just before we got to them, and the road conditions were near perfect.

I felt as if we were standing still, and it was our surroundings that were doing the moving. Camels passed us, pulling loaded wooden carts on salvaged car wheels, the camels' faces expressionless as they peered down their long noses at us. A troop of dancing bears and dancing monkeys passed us – the poor things looked really ragged and unhappy, though none seemed starving. A dead cow – bloated and being lunched on by a flock of vultures passed by too, thankfully too quickly for us to smell the usual vile scent of decay. A broken-down truck, with its driver and mate having a chai break in its shade went past peacefully. A run of broken-down chai stops passed us busily, and a green and tan strip of rubbish-strewn verge went by as a ragged ribbon as we sat on the bikes. And that night, though all the hotels in Agra were full, we had a stroke of luck.

A Yamaha Teneré was parked up in the reception area of one of the hotels, and Mark recognised it as belonging to an overlander he'd met some weeks before – perhaps we could share his room. Peter was happy with that, and then to our surprise, Andy and Di turned up too. We were obviously back on the beaten track.

The Taj Mahal is delightful in every way. Set in its own red sandstone-walled water gardens, it's made of marble and semi-precious stones. It was created by 20,000 craftsmen over a twenty-two year period, and it's very pleasing to the eye, to say the least. The Taj has a fantastic history and is part of a love story. The Moghul Emperor Shah Jahan built the monument in memory of his wife Mumtaz. Legend has it that he was so devastated by her death in childbirth after producing fourteen children for him, that he wanted to build the most extravagant monument ever built for love. Afterwards he had the architect blinded so he could never produce anything as beautiful again – not quite so romantic.

As one of the most visited monuments in the world, it's very busy. Normally I'm not a great fan of rushing to see such over-visited sites, but the Taj Mahal is magnetic and as a bonus, Peter's rooftop room looked out over it. From his balcony we could watch the sun rise up over the white marble domes and minarets, while we sat eating breakfast. At the end of the day, as the sun went down, the white marble turned a magnificent shade of mother of pearl pink.

As we sat inside the grounds watching the buildings, and the expressions on people's faces as they too looked up at this stunning building, we realised that India's quirkiness was also at play. Behind us, an ox was pulling a giant lawnmower. After a while, the men operating the rig called a halt and settled down for a chai break. But, before they sat down they pulled the trough of freshly-mown grass cuttings round to the front, for the oxen to chomp on. It seemed only fair, and the perfect form of fuel efficiency.

As a town, I thought Agra was one of the most hassle-filled places I'd been to. Inevitable when big tourist bucks were pouring in every day, but the level of persistence added an unusual amount of battle to the day. To get you into one or other of the shops, or onto one of the tours of the area, the touts use every form of psychological warfare known to man! In most places I'd been to so far, if I could pretend that my skin was rhino thick, then I could float along with the guys bouncing off me like flies, but this was the first place I'd been to in India where actual physical contact was also made. I found that dark glasses and temporary deafness dealt with most of them, but I always walked away feeling as if it were I that had been incredibly rude!

The next stop for us on the tourist trail was Fatepur Sikri. Our guidebook said that this was an attraction that no one should miss, so as we were on the trail, we did as we were told. The Dargah Mosque and the old city were well worth obeying the instruction for. The mosque was built by another of the Moghul rulers, Akbar. Though a Moslem, he was one of the first great rulers in the region to try to take what he saw was the best bits of each religion, and

 attempt to amalgamate those into one faith for everyone. I wondered how different Asia and perhaps even the world might have been if he'd succeeded. The old city was almost totally deserted when we got there. We'd made it between coach parties and that helped the city to take on the air of a ghost town. The few touts were polite and friendly – they actually seemed to be enjoying themselves and none had the desperate air they often have.

Most of the buildings of Fatepur Sikri are relatively intact, though obviously time and the weather have taken their toll. They are made up of palaces, merchants' homes, a caravanserai, fine houses and

courtyards, (one of which contains a giant chessboard upon which, legend says, Akbar used slave girls as his pieces). I wondered if the tourist who had decided to strip down to a tiny bikini to sunbathe on one of the walls, was imagining herself to be one of those slaves. The guides were certainly imagining something!

When we parked the bikes at the end of each day, or were away from them for a while to look at things, Mark always covered his with a blue cloth shroud. It acted like an invisibility cloak, and suddenly no one paid his bright red BMW the slightest bit of attention. Libby, however, always underwent the full range of tweaking, twisting and twiddling, and sometime soon, someone was going to break something. I'd no doubt it would be totally unintentional, and I suspected that the culprit would feel very guilty, but I couldn't afford the hassle of trying to replace any bust bits. It was going to be bad enough if I dropped the bike and did the damage myself, but having someone else do it out of curiosity was something that didn't sit well with me at all. By the time we'd made it to the town of Barakpur, I'd made up my mind. I was going to get a cover made, just like Mark's.

It was only a kilometre from our hostel into the centre of the town, but we still ended up being hassled by rickshaw wallahs, who seemed to think that it was most unseemly for visitors to be walking anywhere – they hassled mercilessly. By the roadside, the town dentist had laid out a strip of faded blue tarpaulin. He had carefully lined up his tools on this, most of which looked more like weapons of torture than dentistry equipment. Next to his tarp was an old kitchen chair, and it was upon this that his victims sat. He worked with no anaesthetic, and because of his impressive range of angled and long necked pliers, I suspected that he pulled more teeth than he fixed. His hand painted sign showed a large white set of gnashers set into unbelievably red gums; somehow the artist had got them to smile. To me that smile looked more like a grimace of pain.

Next to him was the town barber. A line of men stood waiting their turn to be trimmed with shiny scissors and a set of hand-operated clippers. They were shaved with an old-fashioned cut-throat razor, using richly foamed soap that the barber's assistant kept ready-frothed. The white-chinned client in the chair looked at me over his shoulder in a fly-blown, silver-rimmed mirror that was hung on the crumbling graffiti-covered wall. 'Sanjay loves Lina' and 'Bappa 4 Farida'. Next to the love grafitti were hand-painted signs advertising the local hospital – useful perhaps, if the shaving didn't go too well. The painter of the sign had not been able to spell as well as he'd been able to paint, and for me, that did not inspire much confidence.

The next man along made and repaired shoes, the next sold vegetables, and the next fruits and nuts. Small boys seemed to have been recruited for the full-time job of keeping the dust cleaned off the stock on the various stalls. The only one that didn't have a boy was the dentist.

In the town centre the densely packed crowds seethed. The vibrant colours of saris, shirts and turbans, bobbed and swayed as if I was looking at a slightly out of focus world. Rich scents of sandalwood, incense and sweat mingled with the pervading smells of cooking food, dust, diesel fumes, animal dung and wood smoke. A shimmering heat  rose up from the mass of humanity, to bounce off sepia-toned walls that looked as if they had been stained by the tide. The lower levels were battered and made dingy by the press of everyday life, whilst the upper walls were stained in streaks by the grime of pollution and the baking, bleaching, sun. The walls held colours beneath the tidemarks that still clung to a faint memory of the last time a painter's brush had been there, and in an almost violent clash with the mass of people; brightly coloured signs shouted to the world the wares that were on sale, or with flamboyant pride, the names of the merchants themselves.

To my surprise the market had no suitable bike cover material at all. Everything on the stalls looked as if it would make good saris or would cover chairs, but they had nothing that combined lightweight and plain. I tried the fabric shop on the high street, nestled between a bicycle repair shop that, in bright red, yellow and blue, boldly advertised Hero bicycles, and a welding shop that had rusty chunks of metal and wire as the backdrop to the red-white sparks that were shooting out onto the street. In the other towns we'd been in, shops of one type clustered together and weren't thrown together as a mix like this. But the fabric place had a bolt of lightweight cream-coloured cloth, and there was a street tailor just around the corner. I thought that my luck was in when a man introduced himself to us. "Namaste. I am a caretaker," he said. "I am speaking verrry good English. Can I be speaking with these people for you?"

In case I'd had to do the explanation by sign language, I'd designed a simple box shape to show to the tailor, so that he could see what it was I wanted. Sadly, this confused matters even more, as the caretaker couldn't grasp the concept of the box shape, let alone a bike cover. Nor could the five other men that had instantly crowded around to give advice and assistance, whether it was needed or not! Chaos ruled. I ended up with a very happy tailor, proud assistants and a bike cover that was big enough to put two bikes under! But it would do the job, and if I ever broke down in the middle of the day or simply wanted to hide me as well as the bike, then it would do that too.

The roads between Barakpur and Jaipur were amazingly quiet, and only a few ageing trucks and buses were around to blast their horns at each other, at the camel carts and cyclists. As for Jaipur itself, it lives strongly in my mind for three things: a rickshaw ride, a 'bunch of fives' and a pink city.

We'd been instantly hassled by the rickshaw riders as soon as we set foot outside the gate to the campsite area of the Jaipur Inn. I'd had a bad night's sleep. As we were getting into Rajasthan the night air was getting far cooler and I'd actually been cold. My tent was supposed to be for two people but with Birgit and I, plus all our bike gear inside, it was far too small. I knew that it would be cramped but I'd thought that the bonus would be body heat from both of us. My now ageing sleeping bag would then be good enough to cope with the chilly desert air. It hadn't been, and I'd dozed through a very shivery night.

The rickshaw rider who hassled the most had a surprise. I grumped at him that no, I didn't want him to take me anywhere, but I'd take him! We set off with him in the back of his own bicycle rickshaw, looking very much as if he were royalty. As I pedalled the ungainly, rattling contraption away, I enjoyed the dumbfounded expressions of the other rickshaw riders.

Jaipur town is a centre of trade for the surrounding area, and as such it was incredibly busy. The traders seemed to either sell things that they had produced out on the farms, or things that those out on the farms would need. The colours were stunning: rich greens from the vegetables contrasted with bright oranges, reds, yellows and

 turquoises of women's saris, and the pink and orange walls of the city and palaces provided the perfect backdrop. All this was going on under a bright blue sky and was spiced up by selections of vivid-coloured curry powders, the sparkles from the many jewellers' shops and the gleaming white shirts that the men all seemed to favour. The streets hustled and bustled with those out shopping in the markets, the Ambassador taxis, the bicycle rickshaws, the chai sellers, the roaming stalls of stainless steel pots and pans sellers, and camels that moved imperiously through the crowds.

I watched an obviously wealthy lady doing her shopping in the market. This woman had the power that wealth brings, and she knew it. There was no hesitancy in her waddling stride and her fingers stabbed out at whatever caught her eye. She held her shoulders back and kept her chin up as she talked down to the market traders. Open fingers raised, she waggled her chubby wrists in disdain or disagreement; the traders would have touched their forelocks if that had been the custom. One stallholder, dressed in a white, loosely-wrapped turban, a long, dirty white shirt and a dhoti, bobbed and bowed at her every word as he scuttled around his wares, always making a show of selecting the best of everything. She demanded and received discounts wherever she shopped. Each purchase was thrust into the arms of the increasingly bow-legged coolie who was trailing along behind her. The crowds parted just as easily for her as they had done for the camel. She and the camels had mastered that perfect expression of superiority.

Somehow in this melée of everyday Jaipur life, Birgit had ended up walking behind Mark and I, and it wasn't until I heard a shout of pure rage from her that I realised that she was in trouble. I quickly turned round, just in time to see her punch a man on the chin, with a perfect right hook. The man's head shot back under the impact, with the expression on his face a combination of shock and fear. Around us, everyone stopped what they were doing. Shop owners sitting on their front steps stared; shoppers turned to look; stallholders watched the show and those passing on a bus swivelled to look, blank-faced, as they went past. The man had groped Birgit's breasts and no one was going to do that without her permission! She was so furious that when the man took off down the street, pushing his way frantically through the crowds, she chased after him! He was lucky she didn't catch him, and I'd just seen another side of her.

Being groped was a sign of the times – we'd been told that this sort of thing happens more and more. Not only is it embarrassing for the victim but it's against the culture of the country. There are plenty of things that happen in India which make visiting women feel uncomfortable, but actual physical contact like this must feel like a real invasion.

Body space is an issue that, when combined with curiosity, can be a problem at first. There are so many people in India that in some parts, especially in cities, body space goes down to centimetres rather than the usual metre that we are comfortable with. Birgit had bought herself a set of contact lenses. Glasses and lenses are modern, well made and incredibly cheap in India, and it had been too good an opportunity to miss, but she needed a mirror to be able to put them in. The only suitable mirror was in the unisex washrooms on the site in Delhi. I'd found her there, attempting to put the first lens in. About twenty centimetres away from her face, with total fascination, an Indian man was watching her nervous finger as it wobbled close to her eyeball.

243

All sorts of habits in India can be off-putting. One of them is the way that men constantly rearrange their 'crown jewels' in public. If they aren't rearranging them, then they are having an unconscious grope of them. It's done in a very matter-of-fact way. But the groping of women was, though not completely new, getting worse, and young Indian men in many parts of the country leer at foreign women. They stare blatantly, with salacious expressions, and quite a few even pump their hips as they are doing this. If there is a gang, then it's worse.

From an earlier section of the ride through India, I had an idea why Birgit had been groped. I'd been riding for days through a land that had made me feel like a time traveller. I was moving through the Middle Ages – for hour after hour I rode past dusty brown fields that were being ploughed by men wearing loincloths and no more. They trudged through the heat behind oxen that were pulling wooden ploughs. The villages were few and far between, and the few buildings were made of straw and mud. Many had cowpats drying on the walls. These crusty pancakes are used for fuel for cooking once they have dried; many Untouchables, or Dalits as they are now called, make their living by collecting, drying the pats, and selling them.

At around 5pm this world turned flaming orange. Everywhere was one shade of riotous orange or another, and the eerie light was only broken by the odd silhouette of a palm tree or an ox cart moving slowly across the land. This light is particular to India and it almost wraps itself around you, making you too an integral part of the scene. This light is formed by the end of day sunrays working their way through hundreds of kilometres of air filled with smoke and dust particles. So gentle is the change into night that this slow moving world feels like it's almost suspended in the glow, as if it will stay forever.

I emerged from the glow into a village. Unusually at this time of day there was hardly a soul to be seen, and for once I wasn't mobbed as I pulled to a halt. A foreign biker is always a tremendous attraction and usually far better value than TV. After all, you are live, in their world and most people don't have TV – though they know what it is. Sometimes getting mobbed is a real chore, especially if you are tired, but it's a great opportunity to give something back. The mob never wants to make trouble, they just want to 'know' everything about you, enthusiastically. If I am learning about their world then I feel it's my responsibility to answer their questions, though some are very predictable.

On this particular day I found out that I simply wasn't as good as TV. In the centre of this tiny village, almost the whole population had gathered in the dusty square, amongst the goats, chickens and the odd holy cow, to watch Dallas on satellite television. Who knows where the TV had come from, but my goodness doesn't Victoria have a chest, and didn't she share such a lot of it with us all! I wondered what thoughts were going through the villagers' minds as they settled down from their medieval chores. If this sort of stuff was being shown on TV in places such as this, I could understand why the men were beginning to think that western women were available and easy.

There was evidence of this attitude down in Madras. While trying to get my bike out of the port I'd met an Indian tour operator who specialised in taking Indians from Madras to the beaches of Goa. When they arrived he would take the men to good vantage points, and would issue them with binoculars so they could watch the tourist girls in their bikinis.

The added irritation for us after the grope was that Birgit had been appropriately dressed for India – or so we'd thought. She was wearing a long, very loose, cheesecloth skirt and a baggy long-sleeved T-shirt.

It obviously wasn't enough, so at the first opportunity she bought herself a pair of baggy Indian trousers and an akurta, which is like a knee-length baggy shirt with a small split up each side. She used her scarf from Varanasi as a dupatta over her head, and her breasts. Amazingly, with this outfit on, the leering virtually stopped and the bonus was that all of a sudden market stall traders started to take her bargaining seriously – our food bill dropped dramatically. She also successfully bargained for a quilted Rajasthan blanket for me – no more cold nights!

So far I'd not been bothered much by punctures, and in three years I'd had just three, which after all the thorns on the tracks in Africa had surprised me. Due to the style of the wheel rims, tyres were a chore to change on my bike. But India was about to change my puncture record. From the stories I'd heard, punctures seemed to fall into three categories: the quiet fizzle of a slow puncture, the soggy riding wobble of a let down, and the major blowout that happened with a bang. With the latter, a bike would leap all over the place, leaving the rider to hang on for dear life. My first punctures had been slow ones, but I'd seen the results of soggy wobbles with Roland in Thailand, and my friends Mike and Sally had suffered the big bang on the road out of the Rift Valley in Ethiopia.

My puncture the next day was in keeping – just another slow fizzle. The three of us had been out cruising around the Nahargarh Fort and the Amber Palace, and yet again I'd been feeling incredibly lucky that we had the bikes to get around on. We could go where we wanted to, when we wanted to go there. No chasing around with tours or hassle with taxis. But by the time we'd got back to the Jaipur Inn, Libby was feeling strange – the back tyre had picked up a small nail. As we battled to get the tyre off the rim I thought, 'fair enough, it was time'. But the hassle came with one of the spare inner tubes I'd been carrying. At some time, I'd packed it badly and the valve had been pulled away from the tube. The only bonus was that I'd be saving a chunk of weight by dumping it, but I was frustrated at the money I'd lost through being careless.

I broke the flow next day with yet another puncture, but in keeping with Libby's style, she didn't let it happen until we'd made it to the hotel in Bikaner. One of the problems with riding in India was the amount of rubbish lying around on the roads. Plus the fact that the traffic wouldn't let us ride where we wanted to be all the time – some of the times we were barged off the asphalt onto sandy verges probably put us at puncture risk as any number of nails could have been hiding in the sand. The cynic in me wondered if the sand was laced with spikes or nails on the approaches to the many roadside puncture repair stalls.

But today, the road this day was in good condition again – the landscape was becoming more and more desert-like as sand dunes and thorn bushes took over. Camel trains were now the norm and unfettered camels roamed the scrub, delicately grazing the green shoots from between the spikes on the thorn bushes. Groups of Rajasthani women, walking 'Red Indian' style along the roadsides, stopped to give us smiles and waves as we rode past.

We lunched on dahl, chapattis and chai at a truck stop – the more we took breaks at truck stops, the more I liked them. There were times when the usual overlanding fare of peanuts and raisins held no attraction whatsoever – nor did our lukewarm, odd-tasting water. Then we saw one, a road side truck stop. Across some tree branches that had been macheted roughly to size, strips of old sacking were strung to keep the dry, grit-laden breeze off the turbaned truck drivers. They were sitting or lying in the flapping shade on charpoys, bed-like affairs with wooden frames upon which a rough netting of sisal string is woven. The ground beneath the charpoys seemed to be layered with generations of spit, betel nut juice, old nails, bits of wire and washers. The air was full of the scents of spilt diesel, curried lentils, fresh baking chapattis and wood smoke. The fire in front of the café was loaded with a vast urn of bubbling chai. A feast with the drivers cost no more than fifteen pence, and a lot of questions.

Just before we rode into Bikaner, Mark heard a shout. David, Amy and Mattea had met Mark in Pakistan and were staying in Bikaner – yes, they'd found a great hotel, and very cheap too, so we followed them in. Like us they had a BMW R80GS, but it had been adapted to fit a sidecar. David had kept the rig so that it was still suitable to be used off road, and it was very impressive. He and Amy had met on the road, had married on the road, and Mattea had been born while they were travelling. They were all great fun and Mattea was the proverbial bright spark. At seven years old she could speak several languages and could hold very aware conversations with adults, then play happily with the local children wherever they stopped. I was impressed with the way this family had decided to live their lives and the sheer joy the three of them were getting from being and exploring together. They made me think of Michael and his two children with their bicycles in Thailand; I wondered where they were and how they were doing.

By the time we made it to the RTDC Dhoramaru hotel, Libby was feeling like a pig in a mud wallow. This time she had picked up a four-inch nail and I was sure that we'd been lucky not to have a big bang type puncture.

The next day was Christmas Eve but it didn't feel like it at all, and that being the case we decided to work on the bikes. Mark had discovered that one of the cylinder studs had sheared its thread off. Fate had played things just right for him though. Normally this would be a real problem for a BMW bike in India. Most of the Indian vehicles were based on Imperial measurements, and he needed a metric helicoil set to rethread the stud. Without one, he'd have been stuck waiting for weeks for the right parts and equipment to be couriered out from England. However, David's sidecar was like Dr Who's Tardis – he had just the right equipment, and for Mark it was Christmas after all.

It was for someone else too. I stupidly put down my second camera, a pocket sized Olympus, and left it unwatched for a few moments. It disappeared. I was sad to see this old friend of the road go missing, but hoped that someone hungry would be able to feed his family with whatever he sold it for. It was my own fault, so I could only be angry with myself, but I was sad about the film. It had thirty-five shots of Libby in unusual situations on it, and they were irreplaceable. At least the memories of the motorcycle policeman sitting on her, the sadhu on her, the Buddhist monk by her, the group of boys in Varanasi on her, the pictures of her with Everest in the background, and the shots of her at Broadlands and the port in Madras, would remain strong. Even so, feeling frustrated, I decided that I should at least report the theft to the police.

Once past the reception area of the police station, which was manned by a khaki-clad deeply tanned Errol Flynn look-alike, I was shown into a room that looked as if it had been faded by time into sepia. The yellowed walls were stained tan by the brush of generations of elbows, and doorposts had developed a patina of layered marks where they had been grabbed for support. Where thousands of hands had grasped doorknobs, the surrounding paint had been polished to a deep amber glow. The centre panel of one of the two heavy wooden doors, held a hand-painted sign which said 'Spdt Patil', in flaking gold script. A neglected, once-fleshy plant stood dust-covered and yellowing on an equally dust-covered, once-loved, table. Away from the foot-worn outline of the main walkway across the room, the cracked and curl-edged lino floor still held traces of the dark green paisley pattern that had inspired its buyer. In the corners of the walls, vivid sprays of pan juice were splattered in arches towards the floor as if a mad axe man had been at work. Those dusty corners of lino were where the more discerning pan chewers had squirted out their bloodlike spit from red lips that inevitably looked as if their owners had just stepped off an amateur dramatics stage.

Daylight struggled to make its way through high up and barred, nicotine-stained, windows and the sun that did make it through was too weak to cast shadows from the metal rods onto the respectfully hushed and listless scene inside. A faint clatter of a typewriter from behind one of the doors was the only hint that there was in fact life beyond the room. But then I noticed a man dressed in white, who sat still and almost ghostlike behind a desk, whose top had been sanded by thousands of pieces of paper and polished a sticky brown by generations of chai rings. He had a face that was scarred by the lines of a lifetime of experience. His large glasses held lenses that were so thick his eyes looked three times too big for his head. Those eyes were the only things that sparkled in a gloom where the sole movement seemed to be dust, which filtered down through a light that seemed to be exhausted as it made its way across the room, where time seemed to be standing still. Then he spoke, his deep voice flowed words out in a roll that made it seem as if each were joined together. Each 's' hissed as it passed through a set of dentures that, for some reason, had a large gap between the two front teeth. But I instantly had the feeling that I was faced by a kind man, whose aim in life was to help me. I told my tale. His big eyes blinked a slow motion shutter movement at me, and he shook his head. "Mister, I am verrry sorry to hear of your problem, and we will do what we can, but I am not holding out much hope. What is your address?" This sounded more like

'MissthterIamverrrysthorrytohearofyourproblemandwewilldo (breath) whatwecanbutIamnotholdingoutmuchhopewhatisthyouraddreth?"

Jaisalmer is a fortress town way out in the desert, and the people were the most friendly we'd met to date. They gave us no hassle whatsoever – just smiles and 'Namaste' responses to our greetings. If we wanted to try to talk, they were happy to try too. The hilltop castle was the best we'd seen – yellow sandstone walls glowed in the sunshine, and inside there were tiny cobbled streets, great old wooden doors, beautifully carved wooden windows and screens, and courtyards that had been set to catch the breeze.

One of the girls, whose dress was topped off with a beautiful saffron coloured sash, smiled openly and warmly at us. It was one of those moments when you make an instant connection with another human being and no words are needed. Her face lit up and the three of us stood silently for a moment, soaking up the sensation. I've never forgotten it and she seemed bashfully pleased when I asked if I could take a photo of her. As I took it I had my fingers mentally crossed that this shot, of all of them on the film, would come out. Picture taken, she smiled shyly and moved away across the castle yard, back into her world. That precious fleeting moment was a gem.

The surrounding desert was great to play in on the bikes. Hopeful camel riders and soft drink sellers sprung upon us as we reached the village of Sam, and even though to us they were a bit of a pain, we recognised notes of desperation in their voices. The plague that had happened just to the south had knocked tourism quite dramatically, and what had been a steady income had dried up as foreign tourists stayed away from the area. One of the camel riders even followed us out into the desert and we ended up being glad that he had. Both Mark and I managed to completely bog our bikes down in the soft sand dunes, and without him we would have been in trouble. He asked for no money but when he told us that he had a chai shop nearby, we followed along behind his jigging camel with a cuppa in mind, and we left him with a good-sized tip.

On the way back to the hotel I realised that not only was steering hard but that I'd got yet another flat tyre. The price for playing out in the desert was a thorn in the tyre, and a series of smaller thorn holes in the tube. The tube was wrecked, but it had been fun. As for the steering, it hadn't just been the tyre wobble that had been causing the problem. For some reason our games in the desert had finished off the notch that had been building in the steering head bearings. They could wait until we got back to Delhi to be sorted, but I was suddenly very glad that I'd been to watch Tomil deal with his in Kathmandu.

It was time for Birgit and me to part company with Mark. He had more time than we did and wanted to explore more of the area than we were going to be able to manage. We'd been sharing travel time and space with him for almost a month now and I felt strangely bereft as we rode away from Jaisalmer towards Jodpur and Pushkar. I wondered when, if ever, we would meet him again.

A small consolation was the condition of the road. It was absolutely immaculate two-lane asphalt, and this desert highway was virtually deserted. As the day warmed up, Libby sang in the parched breeze and with both tyres full of air, we cruised along feeling better and better as the kilometres rolled under our wheels. At a chai stop we met a couple of Australians on a red 350cc Enfield Bullet. What made them different was that they were surfers, and strapped onto special racks along the side of the bike was a full-size surfboard. It stuck out a good half metre either end of the bike, which must have made it a pig to ride in city traffic. The Aussies gave us a relaxed shrug when I asked if it was.

Later in the day, when we stopped on what we'd thought would be a quiet spot on the road for a backside rest, a white Maruti minibus came hammering past us. It screeched to a halt a hundred metres down the road, and then weaved back towards us so quickly that we didn't have time to wonder what was going on. The occupants, a large Indian family, all leapt out brandishing cameras. The head of the family yelled across as they rushed towards us, "I say, would you mind awfully if we took some photographs of you?" His upper class British accent could have been cut with a knife. Who were we to refuse, and anyway, it was payback time for all the pictures we'd been taking of people in their land.

It was time for Birgit to fly back to Germany, and the last few days we had together felt decidedly unreal. We'd spent the time pottering around Delhi's shops and bazaars so she could buy presents to take home for family and friends. We were a team and it felt quite natural to be together. I wasn't sure if I was going to like being without her. I felt pretty gloomy and as the clock ticked round, the time both dragged and zipped by far too quickly.

Ex Indian Army servicemen ran a bus service out to the airport from the Tourist Camp. The bus arrived at 11.15pm on the dot, and after we had argued a moment about the fare, we climbed aboard with Birgit's rucksack and very full kit bag. The streets out to the Indira Ghandi airport were virtually deserted; the two of us sat quietly watching Delhi winding down for the night. At the airport there wasn't anywhere to wait inside, so along with everyone else we found a place to perch in the mild air outside. With the crowds of tired people and all their bundles of luggage, we looked like refugees from some battle or famine as we squatted in the car park in front of Departures. At one-thirty it was time for her to go and check in. Birgit passed through the gate with a smile and a little wave, and then disappeared into the swirl of people.

Chapter 14

The Smugglers

"What the hell," I thought, "we'll just go with it, it'll probably be ok."

Ian Mutch

It rained solidly in Delhi for the next three days. The Tourist Camp flooded and the only power available was from the site's own erratic generator. The camp rats were flooded out of their nests and for once we could see the true level of infestation. They were bigger than the local cats, and with an apathetic mankind as their only predator, they thrived and grew fat – the wily, street-wise and battle-worn cats left them to it.

The Iranian Embassy said, "Come back tomorrow." They had said this for two weeks of on-and-off rain, and time was running out for me on my Indian visa. I felt sure that if I left Delhi, my application would be jinxed. Part of me said that if I went to the embassy everyday, then my polite persistence and enthusiasm would win me my visa. The other part of me wondered if the officials were getting sick and tired of seeing my face. My budget said that I had no money left to splurge on more exploring, until I knew what was going to happen next, but the months of being careful had paid off – I could afford the cost of the fuel and accommodation back to Europe, although if I had to ship the bike and fly myself anywhere, things would be very tight.

I spent my time working on Libby and exploring the local bazaars. Stallholders sat wet under the lengths of sacking that hung over them. Rainwater collected in the dull brass bowls on their ancient measuring scales, and scraps of plastic sheeting covered sacks of grain, bags of spices and bolts of cloth. Those who were wealthy enough to have canvas covers battled to keep the collecting pools of rain from damaging the flimsy structures, and more than once I was caught by a gushing spray of chilly water as a stallholder concentrated on making sure that his pole hit the right spot in the pregnant belly of his sagging canvas.

With time to spare, I washed my clothes more thoroughly than they had been in months on the road. I hopefully hung them up to

253

dry in the moisture-laden, polluted air, and repaired them to get a few more months' use. I set up 'Sam's Chai Shop' in my cabin and had the billy on all day, using a mini immersion heater that ran off the ceiling light fitting with an adaptor. Without it I would have gassed myself with the fumes from my petrol cooker, though perhaps by then I was already immune to the effects of carbon monoxide – Delhi's air was so full of it anyway! I made new friends as they arrived at the camp, and lost them as they left. I waxed my bike boots, several times. I wrote letters to everyone I knew. I stood with others, wet and shivering in the post office. I missed Birgit. I ran out of books to read, and lay for many hours in the gloom on the creaky iron bed in my cabin, listening to the sound of rain hitting the corrugated asbestos roof. The guard on the entrance gate to the camp no longer greeted me with his usual cheerful, 'One hundred percent excellent, first class Sah' when I asked if he was fine. In the all-pervading damp his curled moustache seemed to battle to stay in place. I collected padding materials and lined my bike trousers in anticipation of the cold that I hoped I would have to ride through. I made handlebar muffs out of vinyl so I could try to keep my hands warmer and dryer in the midst of Iran and Turkey's winter. Outside the camp, mangy dogs slunk sodden from one pile of washed-out rubbish to another. The ground in the site turned to slimy brown mush, and an air of gloom settled firmly over those travellers who had stayed in Delhi's rain for more than a couple of days. The time passed slowly and still the Iranian Embassy said, "Come back tomorrow."

The only other biker on the site was a Dutchman called Martin, and he was feeling as gloomy as me, but not for the same reason. His trip was about to end, and he was arranging for his bike to be shipped back to Holland. We spent a fair bit of time together over the days, commiserating. Meeting Martin was useful – he told me how much it would cost to ship a bike back to Europe. I'd been so keen to find a way to ride back, or to set Birgit and me up for the next stage of the trip, that I'd not considered doing this. At a pinch, if all else failed, it was affordable, but I still wanted to ride, and Iran was still the prize.

At the post office, mail was waiting for me. My mother had written three letters, which all decided to catch me up at the same time, and a parcel containing two of the fisherman's pocket warmers – Rory had been so pleased with his. I wouldn't be putting them down the front of my trousers though! My sister had also sent out a parcel for Christmas, and that too had only just arrived. She'd been quite wonderful over my years on the road, sending out many of what I'd dubbed 'Red Cross' parcels. They were always full of the sorts of foodie things it was almost impossible to get hold of on the road. Most of the goodies didn't have much nutritional value, but they had real morale value.

On the way back from the post office I'd stopped off to pick up my prints from the developers. I'd still been getting my films developed as I travelled – that enabled me to learn from my photographs, and I could send home the prints in one envelope and the negatives in another - the chances of both getting lost in the mail were slim. My camera had been playing up again as we'd gone through Rajasthan, and I'd been nervously awaiting the return of the prints – I couldn't afford to get the camera fixed if it was broken. As it turned out, they were fine, and some I was quite proud of.

I had my palm read by a guest at the camp that afternoon. He was bald, dressed in full-length peach coloured robes, and reminded me a little of Hari Krishnas in England, but when I asked him he'd said, "No, I am not being a Hari Krishna, I am being Buddhist". After a long look at my right hand, he looked up and said, "This is going to be a very fine year for you." With that he got up, and walked away with his robes dragging on the drying campsite mud.

Then there were more good omens. My Iranian friend Farad and his wife Delbar were back, and invited me around for a giant fruit salad. As Delbar stood cutting the mangoes, pineapples, bananas, pawpaw, oranges, grapefruits and sweet lemons, Farad told me his news. A friend of his had just started to work at the Iranian Embassy, and he'd been to see him to ask if there was anything that could be done to help my application through – he was waiting for news. And before I went to bed that night, my palm-reading guru gave me a gift.

It was a beautiful copper plate that was engraved with Sanskrit. "This is for use when you meditate", he said. "For your good luck to come true, you must meditate for one hour every day. Begin tonight; there is an official who should be in your thoughts."

The next day Farad went back to the embassy for me and returned with amazing news. "My friend says you will have your visa in a week." That night I sat down to write to Birgit to see if she would like to join me for the trip back. I suggested that we should meet in the city of Bam on the Iranian side of the border with Pakistan.

The rains had now disappeared, and as they left, more travellers appeared on the site. Pete and Sashi were the most mix-matched pair I'd met. Pete was a small, skinny German guy whose favourite outfit was a full-length, one-piece sage-coloured leather jump suit, which he topped off with a black leather beret. The finishing touch was a knife with a thirty-centimetre blade, carried in a black sheath. Pete had bad teeth, and the patchy stubble on his skinny chin looked as if it belonged more to an adolescent than to a thirty-year-old man. Sashi was Indian, 22 years old and simply stunning to look at. Every element of Indian beauty had collected in her face, which was framed by long, sleek, very shiny blue-black hair. Her tall tanned body, which she clad in tight faded denim, was equally perfect. She told me that she had been Miss India, and been a Miss World candidate. Sashi was a sign of changing India. At one time she would have been ridiculed and would have lost face by taking part in something as controversial as Miss World. But her Delhi-bred upper class family had supported her. She had achieved fame, and as a result she had become the managing director of her own business. Her family didn't like Pete though. "They want me to be marrying a 'good' Indian boy." She told me. "But I am not having it. Western men know how to treat a woman as an equal, and this is what I'm wanting. I am a new Indian. Life is changing here and I am doing everything I can to make that happen. But it is soooo slooow. Sometimes Pete and I are being outrageous, are you wanting to come to watch?"

I followed them into the centre of Delhi, to Connaught Square. "Bring your camera." Sashi had said with a mischievous grin. "We want you to take pictures of how the people react to us." The two of them held hands as we walked through the streets, and then settled down in the park, kissing and cuddling as they lay. And yes, people were shocked, especially older ladies who were waddling past in their saris. One, with a wide nose that was so long it must have dipped into her chai, stood staring at them from a just a few metres away. Her face, a contour map of wrinkled parchment, was bleached of any sign of life, other than outrage. She stood with miles of vivid rich purple sari wrapping her heavy body; her fingers weighted by fat gold rings. With her tree-trunk like legs spread slightly apart, and her sun-spotted hands on her wide hips, she burned a long, steady, intense look at the two of them. If they'd seen her, Pete and Sashi would have shrivelled up and died from its sheer anger.

The men looked equally horrified, or were obviously envious and excited by what they were seeing. When the police turned up, I thought Pete and Sashi were going to be arrested, though nothing they had done was anything out of the ordinary in England and in fact it was quite tame. Nevertheless, the police tried to arrest Pete – not because he was leading a good Indian girl astray, but because of the size of his knife. He told me later that he had been wearing this knife for months and there had never been any trouble with it before. When I thought about their behaviour later, I wondered if Sashi's way to force progress might backfire on her and her peers.

If I needed it, this was a simple reminder to me that times do change, but that everyone is different. Just two days before, I'd been chatting with an Indian girl on the site. She told me that she had no problem with arranged marriages and that she felt safe in her culture. Her parents knew her better than anyone else did and as she respected them, she had no doubt that they would find her a man she could be happy with. They were not only looking for the right man for her to marry, but also for the right family to marry into, and it was important to her parents that she would be accepted by her new family and not be treated as some sort of slave. "Some mothers-in-law can be very formidable in India," she said. "I think that we Indians grow up with a

257

very strong sense of identity. Our families give us this. Because this is so, I'm thinking that we children are not having to challenge our parents."

The next day, the man in the room beside mine left to go home to England, and left me with two presents. He'd obviously decided that I was lonely, as the gifts were two books – 'How to Meet and Influence Girls', and 'Women's Erotic Fantasies'.

On Wednesday 25th January I got togged up in my best clothes, washed and tied back my hair and trimmed my beard before setting off yet again for the Iranian Embassy. The guards greeted me this time with curt nods of recognition and waved me through without checking my papers. Inside, for a change, there wasn't a queue, but still no visa. "Come back on Monday."

The delay was becoming a severe problem. Dirk and Jens had turned up on the campsite and made me an offer that was too good to refuse. I could ride in convoy with them across Iran, and sleep in their bus at night. It was a good deal for them, as the money I'd have paid for accommodation would go into their fuel tank, and it was a good deal for me, as I wouldn't have to chase around looking for places to stay at the end of a cold hard day's riding. Not only that, but both Dirk and Jens were bikers, so if it got too cold they could do a stint on Libby. I had to think hard about the latter point, as I'd not let many people ride Libby before, but decided to keep the option in mind, just in case, and at that time I'd no real concept of how cold it was likely to get. But this was all academic if I couldn't get a visa for Iran, and I couldn't expect Dirk and Jens to wait for me. That night I wrote to Birgit to tell her the bad news.

The new delay meant there was a chance to sort out Libby's steering head bearings. The weather had been too bad for stripping the bike down before, but as my luck would have it, Dirk and Jens were experienced at dealing with this sort of problem, and they had the tools.

In the night of Sunday 29th I had a nightmare so bad I fell out of bed and hurt the wrist I'd broken in Namibia, twisted my back and banged my head so hard it had a lump the size of the proverbial egg. In the morning, the Iranians told me to, "Come back on Wednesday." As

I walked back through the hazy winter sun, I knew that I was screwed. The option to go with Dirk and Jens had sounded so good.

They weren't around when I got back but Christian was. He was a biker who had just turned up, and we got on together straight away. As one does, we got to talking about our bikes and how they'd been doing. The conversation meandered towards my steering head bearings and Christian said, "You have time now. I know where to get good bearings cheap and I know how to do it. Let's make it happen." Using Dirk and Jens tools, Christian did the job in a jiffy, and Libby felt as if she had been given a new lease of life. The bearings must have been wearing out for some time, but as it had been a gradual process I hadn't noticed how bad they were getting until the desert. I kept the grooved bearing ring as a souvenir.

On the Wednesday the Embassy told me to, "Come back on Monday." By Saturday I was feeling incredibly down. I was missing Birgit, and the longer I stayed hoping for a visa for Iran, in spite of the low cost of living, the more I was eating away at the funds I'd need to follow any other option. Catch 22. I don't ever normally get depressed, but this situation was getting me down. I was stuck and I was beginning to feel like I wasn't in control. I wasn't free and after so long of being just that, it was a shock that hit me hard enough for my, 'it'll be OK' attitude to slip. Then Swiss Bruno arrived, which cheered me up, and I told myself not to be so defeatist.

Bruno had ridden across Russia, and China! He was the first person I'd heard of doing this and I admired him tremendously for making it work – no one was supposed to be allowed or able to do this. Bruno's example gave me just the kick I needed – I was not going to let Iran defeat me. Something would happen if I kept my eyes and options open enough, but I had to do something, anything, positive. So, I sat down to have my first go at writing an article for a bike magazine.

I was lucky to have been able to do a trip like this. I knew it. It's not often that someone in their mid-thirties finds that they have a big enough bank balance to stop working and ride across the world, and just as important, no real responsibilities. I'd had three years of adventure, living my dream. By writing an article, maybe I could share a little of the fun with fellow dreamers who, for whatever reason, were not able to make it happen. I also wondered if writing might bring in the money I was going to need to get to South America. With new purpose, the days passed quickly, and I began to feel more optimistic again.

Meanwhile, Dirk and Jens had been wheeling and dealing. They hadn't managed to find any passengers to travel back across to Europe with them, so had come up with an innovative alternative. As usual, they were skating close to the edge. They had smuggled goods in full view across Eastern Europe and the Middle East, and had sold them on the way, and were planning to smuggle carpets back into Germany. But, they needed to top up with a lucrative boost of ready cash to buy diesel, and more carpets. The two of them had also been looking for old British bikes to buy and smuggle back to Germany to sell, but they'd only found one cheap enough to make that into a good deal. However, some contacts they'd made along the way had come up with a better option.

India was still a relatively closed country as far as imports were concerned, but it was opening up fast in comparison to Pakistan. Developing countries are inevitably stuck in a cleft – with foreign exchange in short supply, they have to limit imports. With that in mind, many countries place import bans on particular items, with the hope that they will be able to deal with shortages internally, perhaps even develop a home industry for the items. The problem is that this can take time and with some things, the knock-on effect to other vital industries, or survival itself, can be harsh.

Dirk and Jens had been told that one such ban Pakistan had in place was for tractor ball bearings. It was completely impossible, unless you had real money, a position of power and considerable influence, to buy new bearings. Vast areas of Pakistan are given over to agriculture, but most of the land is still farmed with age-old methods on a small farm basis. For the country to advance, it needed to be able to use more modern equipment - tractors allowed more food to be produced and a better – fed people meant less poverty and assisted healthy development in all directions. But tractors need bearings.

A group of dodgy businessmen in India had set up a system whereby bearings from Indian tractors would be collected up at servicing time. These knackered bearings would be cleaned and re-greased and, though very worn, I was told that they were gratefully received by farmers who ran the risk of missing planting seasons due to a broken-down tractor. The difficulty came with 'exporting' the rejuvenated bearings to Pakistan. Not only was the import ban in place, but the suspicion between Pakistan and India was so strong that anything like this had to be done quietly, and preferably by foreign nationals. I tussled with my conscience about having anything to do with the plan, and decided that as I wasn't directly involved and wasn't gaining financially from it, I should do and say nothing. Still, every time I thought about the risks involved, my pulse beat a little faster.

In the late hours of Sunday night, a truck eased quietly into the Delhi Tourist Camp. It parked in the moon-shade that was being cast by the tree next to Dirk and Jens' bus. With one man on watch, and all other eyes peeled, heavy, greasy brown cardboard boxes of second-hand Indian bearings were moved with practised ease, to be stored in the cargo holds under the bus. Hardly a sound was made. Bare or sandaled feet pitter-pattered across the beaten earth around the bus, and a heavily greased cargo door groaned gently as it was opened. The muted sound of many hands grasping and passing the boxes eased out into the night air. It was blended within a few metres into the mix of the other sounds of the city at night. The only other sound came from the man in charge of the group, muttering brief, quiet commands to his men. I just hoped that the ball bearings story was true and that the guys weren't being loaded with something completely different!

In the morning Jens came with me to the Iranian Embassy. The guys had come up with the idea that perhaps they would be allowed to 'freight' the bike across Iran on their bus. It had a massive roof rack, and if we could hoist the bike up, it should be strong enough to cope. Our plan was that I'd only freight it across the two borders but we weren't going to tell them that! This time I was greeted with a smile by the visa officer: "Mr Manicom, it looks as if there will be no problem with your

261

visa, but you will need to come back next Monday." Dirk and Jens would have gone by then. I asked the official if there was anything else at all that could be done. "Not here," he said, "but you could get your visa in Lahore or in Quetta. We can telex them when we get the permit."

Impatiently, I decided to risk it. I faxed Birgit to let her know that I was on the move, and on Tuesday 7th of February, Dirk, Jens and I headed for Pakistan.

Riding with such a big vehicle was a completely different ballgame from riding solo or with another bike. Before, I'd felt like a minnow in a pool of sharks, but now I felt like a minnow with a protective whale as my companion. I rode in front, asking directions as we went. Where I'd usually been able to stop to ask directions wherever I'd wanted – now I had to stop wherever there was space for the bus to wallow into. With the weight of all the ball bearings on board, the bus could only wallow and the guys had been weaving an erratic path around all the potholes. They didn't look out of place though. Every other large vehicle was overloaded and following a route best suited to itself. In a strange sort of way Dirk and Jens looked more at home on the road than they had before. The fact that I had to take potluck with whoever was available to ask where we did mange to stop, shook me out of the air of complacency that I'd allowed to form the longer I was in India. I'd become used to doing things in a particular way, and travelling with Dirk and Jens was going to set me new challenges – it was time I had a shake up.

I thought about the time I'd spent on the Delhi Tourist Camp. On reflection I realised that it wasn't such a bad place, and the people I'd met there had made it quite special. It was sad to think I'd probably never meet any of the travelling friends I'd made there, ever again. We had all swapped addresses, but life when you are travelling just doesn't help people to keep in contact, particularly if you are too busy having adventures to spend time writing to anyone other than family. I also felt that manufactured 'reunions' went against the ethos of free travel, so if I met anyone again, it would probably be on the road, because it was meant to happen. If it did, I knew that it would feel as if we had only just parted. Kindred sprits don't need more than a few seconds to reconnect.

The Grand Trunk Road is a strip of asphalt steeped in history, and blood. The blood comes by the bucket load, not only from that history, but from the sheer number of accidents. When I'd told people I was planning to ride along the Grand Trunk Road, not one person failed to warn me of the risks. Indian motorcyclists warned of the almost dreamlike nature drivers took on board when they hit this long ribbon of road, which wends its way from the north of Pakistan to the east of India. "The drivers care for nothing when they are on this road, you must have great care!" They'd said. The more stories I heard, the more I began to think that the violence that seemed to live on this road was somehow instigated by the spirits of the many people that had died along it. Perhaps there was something in the air – perhaps the dead still patrolled – almost anything can be a reality in this unique country. Despite this being my third visit, I still thought India was amazing, but didn't have a cat's chance of understanding it, or the things that happened.

The Grand Trunk Road's death toll during partition was mind blowing. After the end of WW2, Lord Louis Mountbatten was made the Viceroy of India and ordered to hand India back to the Indians, but the handover turned into a bloodbath. For thousands of years, the sub-continent had been an eclectic mix of religions, the biggest groups being the Hindus and the Moslems, who, according to history, had lived relatively peacefully alongside each other. But Muhammed Ali Jinnah, the Moslem leader, believed that after the Raj had gone, the different religions would no longer be able to live in peace together. Against all the hopes of everyone else, he insisted that the land should be split – Pakistan for the Moslems, and Hindustan (as he called the remainder of India) for the rest. His plan involved uprooting the many Hindus in the soon-to-be Pakistan, and the Moslems in Hindustan. Millions of people would be forced to migrate, but no one knew how this could be accomplished.

Fear and uncertainty ruled. Mobs took to the streets and families that had lived alongside each other for generations, attacked and killed each other. Hundreds of thousands migrated to the east and hundreds of thousands of others moved to the west, in 200-kilometre columns of refugees. The people carried whatever they could from their homes; they carried their children and led their animals. Many attempted to flee along the Grand Trunk Road, some crowded aboard trains, packing them so the roofs were covered in people too. The Sikhs were left in the middle of this chaos, and no one knew where the borderline would be. A senior civil servant named Sir Cyril Radcliffe, had been given just 36 days to draw the line on his map which would separate the two new countries, and he had never been to India before!

Panic ruled the fear, which bred violence. Children were slaughtered, whole families wiped out – one million people died and whole communities were extinguished. The refugee trains were attacked and set alight – the bars on the windows combined with the panic and fear to ensure that many didn't manage to get out. They were burnt alive. Rape was common and for many families this was the end of all honour – they would kill their own daughters, sisters and wives. Ghandi was against partition, but felt that he could not join with the Hindus in making this statement, as if he did, then none of the other religions would listen to his words of peace and calm. He retreated into fasting, with the country falling into civil war.

Mountbatten, faced with the growing disaster, elected to pull the British rulers out, a full ten months early, but this helped no-one. On August 15th 1947, after 150 years of rule, the Raj ended with a horror that no one had foreseen. The British had completely failed to prepare for partition, and they left human misery and confusion after they had gone. There had been so much hope for the freedom to come, but both Jinnah and the Hindu leader Nehru had also failed to prepare for the disaster. This failure at such a desperate time sowed the seeds of the animosity between the two countries, which is still strong today. Memories are long, and fear of each other combines with deep-rooted suspicions. So now we have two nuclear powers facing each other across a strip of no-man's land, and they snap at each other like terriers on leashes.

When people had asked me where I was heading along the Grand Trunk Road, I soon learned not to say, 'Pakistan'. I quickly became tired of being told by Indians how dangerous and deceitful the Pakistanis were. I'd grown weary of being warned that I would be murdered. I'd had enough of being told that I would be run off the road by drivers in Pakistan. Didn't Indians look at their own roads? I was worn out by the hatred and suspicion that remain so strong after almost a lifetime.

In a way, this was the time-old tale of one village always warning that the villagers in the next place along were robbers, people with no sense of honour or hospitality. Of course the next village along never was such a place, and the villagers there said exactly the same thing about the people where I'd just come from. They seemed in awe that I had survived that dreadful place, and had the same fearful intensity about the people of the next village along my route. But this time the fear, anger and suspicion were caused by the painful memories of those still living. Now there are more Moslems living in India than there are in Pakistan, but still the fear and suspicion bubbles in the background. It surfaces from time to time, as it had in Nepal Ganj.

Moslems seemed to be quietly discriminated against by Hindus, which was odd. Hindus seemed in so many ways to be open and receptive, with a tolerant religion, but in India, Moslems almost seemed to be treated as second-class citizens. Even in a country with such a strong caste system, surely people who were being disadvantaged would eventually rebel? With the intensity of the partition hatred as evidence, I suspected that if the Moslems in India ever did start to fight back en masse, it could be very bloody indeed.

I also suspected that as India grew in economic strength, then the caste system would become a stumbling block for the nation. The upper castes would become richer, and though the poor would too, on their shirt-tails, the wealth gap would increase. This would cause another level of resentment that could shatter the country, if it was not managed with intelligence and open minds. In England, the class system was the closest to the caste system that I could find. Perhaps the similarities between the two had been one of the reasons why the Raj had done so well in India. It had taken the devastation of the First World War to shatter our class system, and I hoped that no such violent destruction would be needed to break down the caste system in India.

In a land where so many seemed to be governed by fate, and to identify themselves amongst the masses by religion, clan, caste or family, I chewed over the thought that increased wealth could cause people to lose themselves. If there was a rapid change, then the very things that normally held back passion and violence, in an ever more overcrowded land, could be lost. I wondered if the morals of life that had been steeped into the people of India for so many generations, would be lost, with disastrous effect.

It had taken the British hundreds of years to work their way out of their own Middle Ages, but it looked as if vast swathes of India were going to do that in less than one generation. For a very small number of Indians, this culture change had started with their grandparents. For a slightly larger number of people, it had started with their parents, but the most dramatic culture changes were happening in the lifetimes of the young. But there was both a cultural and an industrial revolution going on.

Would the culture change to the pure worship of money and 'me first', as so much of the western world seemed to have done? What would happen to those who were not able to leap on board the roller coaster of development that seemed to be changing the face and soul of India? Perhaps my thoughts were extreme – the opportunity to learn from the many mistakes others had made was there. It was quite possible that greed and the strong desire to obtain security would not place blinkers upon the decision makers. It was quite possible that the ordinary people's desire to pull themselves out of poverty, would

 make a rush forward, but would then settle, and development would go forward gently and positively. Perhaps it would do so in such a way that instead of anarchy, the changing times would bring peace, health and safety to

all Indians. I rode on thinking that Indian politicians were going to have to be very special people to have enough skill and foresight to guide the nation through the coming years.

For me, the concepts of prejudice against the Moslems, and the caste system, just added to my confusion over whether I loved or hated India. It was hard sometimes to see the people that had been so welcoming and open with me as those who could turn into vengeful, bigoted murderers. But I'd seen a similar sort of thing, from a distance, with the troubles in Northern Ireland. Countries in Africa too had shown me some of the dire results of prejudice and revenge, and I struggled to reconcile this with the Indians' attitude towards life. People seemed to be grateful for what they had, and to hold a strong awareness that there was always someone who was worse off. I hoped that this appreciation would not change as the country developed.

In the west we seem to be so different, striving to have as much, or more than, the next person and rarely appreciative of what we already have. Perhaps we have the ability to control more of our future, and maybe it's this that makes the difference. I thought that in India, as many were not in control of their destinies in any real way, they could only react. Maybe that explained the strong belief in fate. The power of faith and a strong belief that things would work out could mean that they worried less about life – Indians certainly smiled a lot. It was just another thing that this complex country gave me to ponder.

We were heading up into the Punjab. This area suffered the most from partition, but today it's one of the most prosperous states in India. It doesn't have any natural resources other than agricultural land. It's the politically battered, hard-working people who have brought success to this part of India. The Punjab is the homeland of the Sikhs, and though they were devastatingly hammered by partition, their no-nonsense approach to life has allowed them to emerge with their heads held high. In every sense, the Sikhs stand out. Religion forbids the men to cut their hair, and as a result many sport beards that ZZ Top would be proud of and their head hair is usually wrapped away in a turban. They also seem to be tall, and bulky or muscular – a combination makes them stand out in a crowd. The women dress in a very individual style too, wearing an outfit called a salwar-kameez, a long, flowing shirt that falls almost to the knee, and partly covers baggy trousers that fasten close around their ankles. I never saw a salwar-kameez that didn't more than rival the bright colours of the Hindu women's saris. As the Dutch historically make jokes about the Belgians, and the British about the Irish, some Indians make jokes about the 'dumb' Sikhs. It's something I never really understood as Sikhs are some of the most adaptable and able people in India, but perhaps Indians felt comfortable making jokes about them as they were on safe ground, or maybe it was envy.

But there was no time to stop and learn more. Dirk and Jens were on a roll, and wanted to get the border crossing over as fast as possible. The sooner they made it to Lahore, the sooner they could get rid of the evidence and the sooner they would get paid. We were all nervous about how it would be. Both of them worked hard at looking calm, and they would need to be past masters, combining calm with confidence if they were not going to get caught by acting suspiciously at the border. We were tested that first night – we had pulled off the road at a deserted spot to sleep, and the police came banging at the door.

We'd pulled off the road to a place where there was no chance that any passing traffic could hit us, but as usual an audience appeared from nowhere. Once we had settled down with curtains drawn, and Libby's bike cover tied into place, they soon eased away. However, somehow we'd managed to either offend someone, or they were afraid for our safety and had reported us to the police. The turbaned, khaki-clad officer pounded on the door of the bus so hard that I wondered if he would break the ageing hinges. As Dirk pulled on his jeans, the banging continued, and when he opened the door, the officer swept past him into the bus. Jens and I were in our sleeping bags, doing our best to look innocently half-asleep. Dirk talked calmly, firmly and at speed. "We have one headlight that is broken. It's too dangerous to drive on in the dark. We can fix it in daylight in the morning." The officer had a good look around, waggled a large finger at Dirk in admonishment, and then stomped back down the steps, leaving three guilty hearts racing with relief. It seemed that the officer was convinced that we were just harmless travellers who had parked up for the night on his patch. He'd been doing his job, no more.

Normally I like to cross borders first thing in the morning. The officials are still fresh and haven't been jaded into bad temper by a day's worth of heat and hassle. Sometimes they were still half-asleep and wanted to concentrate on their first coffee or chai of the day, more than they wanted to hassle me. I'd also found that with a whole day to play with, if necessary, then I'd be less likely to be harangued into a corner where I'd end up paying baksheesh to escape. But Dirk and Jens had decided that, with their suspicious load on board, it would be better to arrive at the border just an hour before it closed. They hoped that the officials wouldn't want the hassle of us hanging around overnight, and would pass us through in a hurry.

Dawn came with a chill fog. Just this short distance north and it was already time for an extra layer of bike clothes to go on. Riding the Grand Trunk Road in the hazy morning light allowed my imagination to run. It was encouraged by the swirling mist as the gentle breeze, or the draft from passing Tata trucks, floated mysterious shapes dancing on the road in front of us. We shared the road with turbaned bicycle riders, turbaned scooter riders, turbaned tractor drivers and turbaned truck drivers. Sometimes the first indication that there was anyone else there was the bright colour of a turban appearing out of the gloom. The roadsides were lined with wrecked trucks and tractors, some of the latter were lined with bullet holes. As the mist cleared we could see that many of the tractors out in the fields had been armour-plated, making them look like they belonged more in a Mad Max film than in rural Punjab. But we were moving ever closer to the border and this made me wonder if they belonged to members of the Punjabi Home Guard. The road became more and more unkempt.

The approach to the Indian side of the border was lined with tanks and half-tracks that were dug in under camouflage netting. Soldiers stood guard at concrete bollard checkpoints, but we were just waved on through. The serious looking soldiers smiled at the sight of the bike and more than a few waved as I rode past. We were late, and the border was due to close in just thirty-five minutes. The Indian officials were impatient, rude and brusque. They couldn't wait to get rid of us, and even the moneychangers and soft drink sellers were shooed away. With amazing speed, we were suddenly out of India.

The Pakistani side was much mellower, but just as easily negotiated. The officials stamped the papers where they should and the only queries they had for us were, 'Did we have money we'd like to change with them, and 'Perhaps you have a bottle of whiskey for us?' We had passed through both sides in just under an hour! Perhaps my theories about border crossing timings had been completely to cock. We didn't hang around to find out.

Chapter 15

Living on the Edge

'As the traveller who has once been from home is wiser than he who has never left his own doorstep, so a knowledge of one other culture should sharpen our ability to scrutinize more steadily, to appreciate more lovingly, our own.'

Margaret Mead

If it hadn't been for the skin colours of the people, it would have been like riding from India into parts of Africa. The villages that were strewn along the roadside for the twenty kilometres to the city of Lahore were incredibly poor. The mud houses, surrounded by rubbish-strewn dirt yards, were a complete contrast to the neat and clean houses of the Punjab. The road was beaten up, but it had been on the Punjabi side as well – almost as if neither government was prepared to spend more than the absolute minimum on any road so near to the border.

Dirk and Jens knew which way to go, and after such a long day's ride, I was happy just to tag on behind. For most of the way my view  was the flashing red brake lights of the bus. The traffic was manic, and there was an air of tense concentration from the drivers. Movements were impatient and abrupt, but there was a reason. We'd not realised that we would be riding into a Pakistan in the throes of Ramadan, and as no one was allowed to eat or smoke in the daytime, everyone was rushing home with a level of fanatical determination I'd not seen since passing through Egypt during Ramadan.

The guys had to deal with offloading the ball bearings and I had to chase the Pakistani AA to renew my carnet, which would now expire before I could get to Eastern Europe. Iran in particular, if I was lucky with my visa, would want to see it. If I had no luck getting the visa, then I'd need the carnet to get the bike into Africa. It was going to take a large chunk of my remaining budget, but the delays in Delhi had given me no option, and I'd not been able to sort it out there because the UK RAC office hadn't come back to me about

271

the extension as fast as I'd hoped. That wasn't their fault though – I'd made life complicated for them.

As insurance in case I wasn't able to get the visa, I'd asked the RAC if Dirk and Jens could be put on the carnet. That way, if the worst happened then they would be able to take the bike through Iran on the bus, which gave me the option of being able to fly from Pakistan to Turkey, where I could meet them for the rest of the ride. It all seemed an awful lot of bother to get across one country, but the strange thing was that as the level of hassle grew, so did the value of the prize. With the stakes raised in my mind, I knew that if I failed to get a visa after chewing around all the options for so long, then I was sure to feel even more disappointed. I was trying hard to be level-headed and realistic, but at the same time I was determined to succeed, somehow.

I had a shock when we'd arrived at the hotel. Libby smelt strange. The usual scents of hot engine and warm rubber had been replaced with the greasy smell of baking hot oil. The back of her gearbox and drive shaft were covered in a blackened slick that had soaked up a fuzzy brown crust of dust. The gearbox was almost empty of oil, and if I'd ridden much further, I'd have done real damage. It looked as if the seal where the shaft fitted through into the gearbox was the cause of the problem – the shaft casing was full of oil when it should have been dry. If it was the seal, then I was in trouble. I was still carrying enough spare parts to keep several BMWs on the road, but this was one of the few spares I no longer had – I'd given mine to another biker who'd been stuck, and I'd not spent the money on replacing it. Sod's Law.

We parked up in the large car park belonging to a swanky Lahore hotel, as per the instructions the smugglers had given to Dirk and Jens. The hotel allowed overlanders with large vehicles to use their car park to overnight on, and the use of a shower, but it was expensive to stay there in comparison to the usual cheap hotels I'd been using. The staff of the hotel didn't look too impressed at my now filthy, oily bike. All I could do was to place a sheet of scrap cardboard under the offending parts of the bike, to avoid staining their car park. Pakistan may had have a ban on tractor bearings, but the oil I managed to find was a brand I recognised, and the bottle was still sealed. I smeared the rim of the possibly damaged gearbox seal with silicone, let it harden off, and filled up. Problem solved, I hoped, but it felt more as if I'd just put a sticking plaster on the problem.

Nothing much happens in Pakistan on a Friday because for Moslems it's the holy day, so we had no choice but to sit and wait for the AA to finalise the new carnet. The Automobile Association of Pakistan dealt with all carnet issues for overseas motoring organisations such as the RAC in the UK, and the fax about Dirk and Jens, which my mother in the UK had been chasing the RAC to send the AA, still hadn't arrived. Mum had been brilliant while I'd been on the road. For someone who doesn't like bikes, and knows next to nothing about them or what is involved with long distance travel on one, she'd done a pukka job with the admin. There'd been quite a few times when, without her being active at 'base camp', I'd have had a far harder life out on the road. In fact my whole family had rallied round and their support had underlined to me, yet again, how lucky I was to be a part of a family that cared. At one time my attitude had been that simply, my family were there, as they always had been. I liked and got on well with them all, but took them all for granted. Though so far away from them, they had influenced my life and I'd come to feel far closer to them than ever before.

This feeling helped me to understand the importance of family to people in so many of the third world countries I'd been travelling through. I'd seen parents starving themselves so their children could eat. A mother in a hill village in Thailand had fed her family, keeping nothing for herself. I'd seen parents dressed in ancient and much-patched clothing, so their children could have decent clothes to go to school in, or simply to be warm enough. A man in Nepal strode through bitter winds in thin clothes, whilst his children tagged along beside him, wrapped up in Yak wool sweaters and padded trousers. His shoes had been falling to pieces, but they had worn neat little leather boots. I'd seldom seen such levels of sharing and understanding between family members, and I'd become quite comfortable with the system which meant that in many countries, jobs would go to family

273

members – care and survival were the priorities. On a grander scale, some of the extreme loyalty to family members disadvantaged others, and even whole countries. This family-first priority is something most of us in the West seem to have forgotten. Our ancestors would have understood though.

Dirk, Jens and I had plenty to do. We were waiting for the Iranian Consulate to open, and I needed money from the American Express office to pay for the carnet. I also wanted to pick up any post that might be waiting for me in Poste Restante, and Dirk and Jens had only been able to offload half of the tractor bearings. As with many big cities, much as I'd rather steer clear of them, they are inevitably the best places to get things done. The relevant offices are always spread through the streets, but that doesn't bother me because it's an opportunity to see a side of a city that many others wouldn't.

In spite of the repercussions to all involved if they were caught, unloading the tractor bearings was quite a funny thing to watch. The plan was that if the police arrived, I would be just another traveller  who happened to be in the same place as the guys. If they were arrested, then I would do all possible to get the German Embassy involved, and I would contact Dirk and Jens' friends in Germany. If they were incarcerated, then I would keep them supplied with whatever they needed. It seemed to be a good plan to me, especially as I didn't fancy the sound of a Pakistani prison. And as I wasn't gaining anything directly from the smuggling, it didn't feel as if I was chickening out.

Towards the end of the day, a small van appeared and parked next to the bus, but nothing happened. We all held our breath. Then, as the mullah started to call everyone to prayer, the doors opened. Three men emerged, darting glances from side to side. One was as thin as a rake and as bald as a billiard ball; the next was squat and broad shouldered, his hair was cropped close, and he sported an enormous moustache which made him look quite villainous. The third man, who was obviously the boss, was so well-groomed that had he been in India,

I would have thought he was there to audition for a Bollywood movie part. He wore white trousers, white shoes, a tight crisp white shirt that was unbuttoned to his navel and he had a small cap on top of his mullet hairdo. I decided that he had styled himself on the smouldering looks of Sultan Rahi, who is one of the few Pakistani movie heroes. Around his neck he had a large gold chain from which a medallion swung, and a waft of some sort of exotic spicy aftershave followed him out of the van. It was so strong I could smell him on the breeze from metres away. His cohorts by contrast, smelt of a mixture of tangy food spices, freshly smoked cigarettes, and sweat.

When the lawns were covered in robed men, all kneeling towards Mecca and away from the bus, the transfer began. The boxes were heavy and it was a slow job, but no one seemed to notice what was happening. As soon as the prayers stopped, so did the transfer and everyone took on expressions of pure innocence. The man with the moustache did not succeed as he tried to contort his face into what was clearly a totally unnatural expression for him. With the comically clandestine behaviour of the three men it would have made a perfect sketch for a Buster Keaton comedy, and I half expected the Keystone Cops to come bumbling around the corner at any moment.

My fax from the RAC came through to the hotel shortly after the smugglers had eased out of the car park, still looking over their shoulders as they went. Great news! The fax confirmed that the AA could add Dirk and Jens to the carnet.

Afzaal latched onto me on the Sunday afternoon. I'd been taking a stroll through the city centre and he'd been watching me from a café table. "Come and drink coffee," he cheerfully called across to me. In India this would have been the start of enthusiastic over-persistent curiosity, but I'd heard that things didn't happen the same way in Pakistan, and this was the perfect chance to find out. Middle-aged, Afzaal was dapper, but in an odd sort of way. His cream linen jacket sleeves were too short, but his shirtsleeves far too long and the collar looked a little too tight. His trousers were immaculately pressed black cotton, but also too short. His red socks matched his

275

red tie perfectly, but it was almost as if he had a body that no tailor had quite managed to understand.

Afzaal knew his coffee though, and for the first time in an age I had one that tasted like the real thing, and not a watery, beige-coloured instant coffee. "I run an air conditioning shop," he said, "It's my own business and that means I am free to make you an offer. You are a visitor in my city and I would like to help you. Sometimes things take too long to do here and you must be out exploring, not sitting in wrong offices all over the place. You must have things to do here and things to see. Let me help you. We can go everywhere on my scooter. I know all the short cuts, and if you need to buy anything, I can get you a very good price." Maybe it was true about Pakistani hospitality.

Meeting with Afzaal gave me the chance to ask why I'd seen so few beggars on the streets. It was a bit of a culture shock after India, beggars had been the norm and many of them had looked quite pitiful. I'd had guilt pangs every time I'd walked past one without putting some money in their hands. Afzaal replied to my question, "We look after our own. It's our culture. It would be an insult to our religion to see a person having to beg."

On the Monday morning Afzaal turned up at exactly the time he said he would. I'd got so used to everything happening late, or at best sometime that's roughly right, that I was almost late myself! He took me straight to the Poste Restante, where there was a mountain of wonderful mail for me. Then he took me to the Amex to get money, which was very handy as the office was a long way away from where we were staying. Then to the AA, which had been closed on the Sunday as the manager was a Christian. After an hour of bureaucratic messing around, and a couple of cups of Pakistani chai (which tasted quite different from the Indian variety) I had my amended carnet in my hand. The new dates were authorised and so were the guys. That left the Iranian Consulate to visit. Afzaal really did know the short cuts and I grew to like him even more when he showed me that he didn't feel the need to prove himself by riding his scooter like a nutter.

But when we got to the address the Iranian Embassy in Delhi had given me, we found a 'Closed and Gone Away' sign hanging from the gates. It looked as if it had been there for quite some time and didn't say where the Consulate had gone away to. I stood feeling totally let down for a few moments, now convinced that in another life I'd been a yo-yo!

But Afzaal had a plan. "I know," he said, "we can go to the Iranian Cultural Centre. They will know what to do." Moments later we were back on his scooter and heading through the streets at a rate of knots. It was almost as if he had decided by this time that I wasn't a liability on the back of his scooter. Chickens scuttled from under the scooter's wheels as Afzaal took us twisting and turning through the back streets, his scooter making that particular whining, buzzing noise that Vespas are famous for. No Indian-made Bajaj scooter for Afzaal.

The Cultural Centre was closed and the phone book offered up no alternatives. If I'd been thinking straight I would have phoned the British Consulate at that moment, and asked them if they had an address. But I wasn't, so I didn't. Dirk and Jens wanted to leave in the morning, so that would leave me with the Iranian Consulate in Quetta as the last chance.

Before Afzaal and I parted I gave him a contact address for me in the UK, and told him that if he was ever there, then he should look me up. "I'd like to return your hospitality." I told him. I could show him around, and it would be my turn to buy the coffee. He grinned at me and said in his slightly stilted, precise way of talking, "Sam, it's been a pleasure to meet you. I am just embarrassed that we did not manage to sort things out for you with the Iranians. I think they are a silly people to close their office, and not to tell people where to go. Whatever you do, do not ride the road between Quetta and Taftan on the border on your own. Here are many dangerous people in the villages on this road. Go in peace. Salaam."

In the night it rained, very hard. The roads were flooded, and once we'd got going I'd no way of knowing what was under the surface of the long stretches of water, some of which were ten to fifteen metres long and frequently stretched across both sides of the road. The asphalt that I could see needed work rather badly, riddled with potholes and rumpled by heat and truck tyres. Even worse, there was a manhole cover thief around, and sometimes, because of the low angle of the light and the wet road, I didn't see when they were missing until the last minute. There was no way of telling if any had disappeared under the sheets of water. Dirk and Jens were taking pictures of me and trying to encourage me to ride fast through the mini lakes. They wanted dramatic water spray shots, which was tempting, but resistible.

With the rain the temperature had dropped again, and even though we were heading south I kept my rain gear on. It helped with the cold, and I was concerned about the dark and pregnant clouds that hung right across the sky. The guys were almost completely protected from the elements inside their bus, and that meant being on the road was relatively easy for them, but I was far more vulnerable in just about every way.

Most of the towns we passed had ring roads and where I'd normally have ridden through the middle, the size of the bus encouraged us to travel the outskirts. It seemed that there was a very clear trade-off between the two ways of travel. I had more flexibility on the bike, but they had more security and protection.

We shared the roads with trucks carrying loads twice their width, buses with roof racks piled high with goods wrapped in brightly coloured plastic bags, gleaming black sit-up-and-beg bicycles, Pakistan's version of the three-wheeled scooter rickshaw, and pick-up trucks that operated as taxis. If you could somehow clamber on one of the pick-up taxis, then it would take you. My record sighting was one with nineteen people and their luggage aboard. Its leaf springs must have been completely flattened under the weight.

Pakistani trucks are works of art. In the olden days the driver's ancestors would decorate their camel harnesses and blankets with jewels, mirrors and embroidery. These were a family's pride and joy, and a highly decorated set of hooves showed how successful a man was. In modern times a highly decorated set of wheels does the same. Most of the trucks seemed to be old British Bedfords, though it was only the bulbous nose bonnets that made them recognisable. The rest of a truck would have been highly modified – sometimes bizarrely. The load bed walls were extended up to double height, and over the roof of the cab the drivers built a sharply curved boxed-in area, which made the trucks look rather as if they were wearing multi-gemmed tiaras. Other than the bonnet, if the truck had a surface it would have been painted with bright colours, or had mirrors glued on in mosaic patterns – the wealthier drivers even stuck highly polished semi-precious stones into the pattern. But for all the love that was lavished upon the trucks decoratively, they were always thoroughly over-loaded and the drivers did so with an enthusiasm that resulted in many a highly decorative heap smashed up by the roadside.

To make a decent living, the drivers did over-long shifts, and that, combined with poor roads and overloading, meant accidents were inevitable. I always treated trucks with due respect, but the main difference between Indian and Pakistani truck drivers was that not one in Pakistan tried to run me off the road. Driving was a much more democratic affair, and there were even signs of gentlemanly respect shown between road users. The only people who seemed to ignore the respect rules were bus drivers, whose style made them professional road demons in my mind. In spite of which, the new rules made riding much more fun and far less exhausting, and the latter was important for me as over the time I'd been stuck in the Delhi Tourist camp, my riding muscles had got out of trim and I was struggling a bit.

The road signs were brilliant. Directions and town names were clearly marked in both Urdu script and in English. Often the signs were on whitewashed milestones which stood by the roadsides as if they were monoliths left by some past civilisation. And that was true in a way – the Raj erected most of these milestones.

Half way to Quetta, disaster struck the bus. One of the front suspension coil springs snapped into three pieces. There were no other vehicles in Pakistan with springs like this and the guys knew that for certain. On their way across Asia they had been looking out for the opportunity to buy cheap spares for the bus, but they'd found none in Pakistan.

Availability of spares in a country like Pakistan is an issue for everyone though. Because there frequently aren't any, people have learned to make parts from scratch, and to mend things you aren't supposed to be able to, with almost prehistoric tools. Our luck was in. We were on a main truck route, and that meant that craftsmen were never far away. The roads on the outskirts of towns and villages were lined with scruffy corrugated iron and sacking covered stalls that did everything from puncture repairs to servicing. A welder had set his business up just a kilometre down the road from us. The guys managed to hobble that far with the dip on the one side of the bus making it look as if it were a drunk staggering home on a Saturday night.

Once Dirk and Jens had stripped the broken parts out from their fixings, the welder could get to work. He took three six-inch nails from a box of rusting bits and pieces, which he cleaned until they gleamed, and then did the same with the springs by first burning the layers of paint off. As he dug a pit in the sandy verge to the road, I wondered what on earth he was up to. He roughly curved the nails to the shape of the spring – by this time a crowd had gathered to watch. Within minutes he had welded the nails to the broken spring, and placed it in the pit, which he rapidly filled with sand. Dirk and Jens knew what he was up to. Because the welder had no way of knowing how close in metal type his nails were to the spring, it was important that the repair cooled slowly and equally – the sand pit helped that to happen.

For some reason that none of us could work out, the crowd turned quite nasty on us. Dirk and Jens had a big time problem with getting the welded spring fitted back on the bus. At almost every turn, someone was deliberately and aggressively getting in the way. It was all I could do to keep them backed off, but as soon as I went to ease one part of the crowd back, other guys would come in behind me. It was actually quite scary.

I'd discovered a trick in India that helped deal with crowds. When I had a puncture, there would always be plenty of men who were only too keen to help or to offer advice. Mostly they just got in the way and added to the hassle level, and I knew that it would be just too easy for tools and other belongings to go missing. They also knew nothing about a bike like mine – it certainly wasn't a 'double-engined, diesel, automatic'. One day I had the idea of recruiting one of the crowd to help. I chose the man who was being the biggest pain and took him by the hand. With a big stick I'd found at the roadside, together we drew a line in the dirt at roughly a metre and a half away from the bike. We made the line go in a circle right round it. As we did so, everyone edged to the other side of the line, and hovered there, waiting to see what I was up to. I gave the man the stick and asked him to make sure that people did not step over the line. If he helped me I'd give him a ride on the bike.

The man took the stick, and not a soul crossed the line, mainly because the first two that tried had been so harshly beaten back by him that I'd begun to regret giving him the stick. We could have done with a handy stick for the bus work though, but I doubt whether it would have had any effect on this particularly nasty crowd.

Eventually, the work was finished and we carried on, though the damaged spring meant that the guys were forced to drive slower, and we averaged just forty kilometres an hour. This wasn't a problem for me because it meant that instead of having to be aware of where they were all the time, I could take in the scenery. If I wanted to, I could blast off up the road and just sit somewhere interesting or pretty, waiting for them to arrive. The next time we stopped together, a truck pulled up next to the bus and the driver leaned across. With a friendly smile he passed over a handful of oranges, and then pulled away with a cheery wave. It made up for the hassle of 'spring town'.

As we headed further into the dryer south I began to notice the effects of over-irrigation on the fields. I'd read about this, but never seen it. This area had fertile soil, but the rain fell too erratically to allow crops to be grown. So the farmers had dug boreholes and used the water pumped out for irrigation. The water was brackish and combined with all the minerals in the soil to increase the salt level drastically. Each field had a crusty salt rim around the low earth walls that patch-worked the landscape. The top of each ridge and furrow was whitened as if a heavy frost lived on through the sunshine. I wondered how long

281

the farmers would be able to eke a living out of the land before it became too salty to grow anything at all.

The road now swung us north and on up into the desert province of Baluchistan. At the junction, I sat for a moment looking at the other branch of the road as it headed further south towards Karachi. In a few days' time, if I'd not been successful with the visa, I'd be heading down this road to catch a plane to Turkey. I've seldom looked at a stretch of road before, and hoped that I'd never see it again.

The highlight of the run north was the Bolan Pass – it felt as if I was riding through a combined history and geography lesson. The pass is a series of long narrow valleys and gorges that split the central Brahui Range. We'd been skirting the southern edges of the range in our loop southwards through the Sind from Lahore. For centuries this magnificent 100-kilometre pass has been a major route from Persia and Afghanistan to India. It rises to 1,792 metres, and not only holds a road but has been mastered by a railway track that's considered to be one of the world's great train rides. Both the track and the road loop their way through steep-edged rocky gorges that would have been a challenge to any engineer. The track was built in the days of the Raj and it goes through seventeen tunnels, while some sections of the track are as steep as 1:25. In those sections, 'helper' engines are required to get the trains up and down the gradient. The road is frequently steeper and the bus struggled up in low gear, grinding and bellowing smoke with the effort. Libby purred as if she was enjoying the change.

Just before Quetta the road turned into immaculate asphalt, which made the ride into this busy city far easier. The city was bursting at the seams – with the civil war with the Taliban going on just a few kilometres away in Afghanistan, a massive number of refugees had descended upon it and an estimated 80,000 were living in and around the city. The first thing I noticed was that even though there were supposed to be so many refugees in the area, no one looked hungry or poorly clothed, maybe the effect of traditional Moslem hospitality, plus the fact that many families had relations on each side of the border. Perhaps in the refugee camps I'd have seen another story altogether.

People in this part of Pakistan dress quite differently anyway, but even to my inexperienced eye I could still see the difference between the Pakistani men and the Afghanis. Most of the Afghans had great bushy beards, whereas the Pakistanis seemed to favour closely trimmed beards or were clean-shaven.

The name Quetta is actually a bastardisation of the Pushtu name 'Kwatta', which means fort. The city, which stands at 1,675 metres, has been a crossroads for thousands of years, but most of the buildings show no real sign of its history. It's also on an earthquake fault line, and in 1935 a massive 'quake pretty much shattered it. The streets in the rebuilt city are mainly wide and well organised, but as we rode in I had no sensation of the place being sterile or out of keeping. The streets bustled and everything had its edges rounded off, or battered and worn by normal life. The gutters were rubbish-strewn, and under red and white circular 'no parking' signs the kerbs were lined with ramshackle stalls selling everything from neat piles of oranges, to videos and TVs. Clusters of electrical wires hung from one side of the dusty streets to the other, and donkey carts jostled for space with vividly decorated rickshaws and buses that were so heavily decorated I wondered how the drivers managed to see through the windows.

The night was cold, and the combination of that and the fear I wouldn't get my visa, meant that I hardly slept. At 9am I was standing first in the queue at the Iranian Consulate. No security check was done on me at all and when the door opened, I was shown straight to the counter. I set into a lengthy description of my situation to the man behind the counter, who happily spoke good English. He had received no fax from Delhi about me. My heart sunk. I now had ninety-six hours before the day my Pakistani visa expired, and Dirk and Jens expected to be at the Iranian border at just that time.

I scuttled across the city to find the post office. The Consulate had told me that I would have to fax Delhi, and I didn't feel very optimistic – there had been plenty of time for the permit to get there. Five hours later I was back at the Consulate, stood in the queue, and luckily got to the same man. No fax had been received, and then he told me the really bad news. "We are now closed for two days, so you will have to come back then."

My options were now finally running out but I started to feel philosophical about the whole thing. If there was no answer from Delhi in two days' time, then I had a day left to scoot down to Karachi. If it was good news, then we would have to scurry 700 kilometres across the Baluchistan desert to the border town of Taftan. The guys had told me the road was dirt for big sections, but wasn't too bad. Other bikers in Delhi had told me that it was grim, that much of the surface was loose sand and gravel, that there were almost invisible potholes and that where there was asphalt, hidden around corners were speed bumps thirty centimetres high. They also warned of roadblocks that the villagers put up across the road. There were no trees in the desert, so the roadblocks consisted of rope strung from one side to the other, at chest height for a biker. A Danish biker I'd met on the road in Nepal had started off with two friends. He'd lost them both on this road. The first had hit a speed bump and had smashed his bike irreparably. The second had been forced to swerve to miss a rope he'd seen at the last minute. He'd shattered an arm and broken his collarbone. Eventually he'd been flown back to Denmark.

I sent another fax to Delhi, pleading with them to send on the permit with all haste, explaining that my Pakistani visa was about to expire, and that the Consulate was going to be closed for two days. I attached a photocopy of my passport and carnet to prove that I 'had' to go overland. This time I addressed the fax to Farad's friend rather than to the 'Head of the Visa Section'. I faxed an update to Birgit at the same time, and was amused to see that it cost considerably more to fax India than it cost to send a fax to Germany.

My journal for the next day: 'Cleaned oil off the gearbox and shaft – doesn't look too bad, oil level doing ok. Let the lad from the hotel wash Libby – did an awful job but looked pleased at the money. Fixed the broken indicator. Fixed the brake light. – D&J being very helpful as always. Upset an Afghan who wanted to slash my face for insulting him – he calmed down over a cup of tea. Ian and Caroline arrived – good news, they have survived so far, and have GOT THEIR IRANIAN VISAS. Hope for me yet.'

When they'd not been helping me with the bike and with working out how we were going to get it up onto the roof of the bus, Dirk and Jens had been out buying carpets. The two of them had made friends with a local man when they had been through the last time, and Isaac was delighted to help them do their shopping. He was great news, as he knew where to find carpets that hadn't been mass-produced for tourism and export, and the guys only wanted traditional hand made carpets. On day two of the wait, I tagged along with them.

Isaac took us down dark, chilly alleyways and into what looked like private homes. Most carpet sellers seemed, as with the firework man in Varanasi, to double their musty-smelling workspaces with their living space. Most of the merchants seemed to be Afghans rather than Pakistanis, and some of them looked decidedly affluent, though their surroundings were basic and simple. Most of the merchants were wearing traditional Pakol hats, made with really coarse wool. From a distance, these looked like they had been made from layers of pancakes, but close up I could see that under the pie-crust top was a sort of inverted tube that had been rolled up to make a sausage thickness rim. The hats looked warm, but must have been quite itchy to wear. The colours of choice seemed to be beige or grey, with a few more flamboyant characters choosing vivid blues.

I too bought a carpet – they were too tempting to resist. I rather liked the idea that I'd be riding with a hookah pipe and a carpet on the bike. It wasn't a logical thing to do, but I'd had enough of being sensible at that moment. My carpet was in fact a camel blanket, and laid out, it was in the shape of a very fat-bottomed 'U'. The tongues would have had leather straps attached, so they could be fastened around a camel's neck. Hand-woven and stitched with all sorts of geometric designs, it was the unusual shape and the combination of the reds, blues, blacks and creams that sold it to me. The grey-bearded merchant was dressed in a collarless knee-length shirt, baggy matching pale grey cotton trousers, and a burgundy woolly cardigan.

Over those he had a beige waistcoat and turban, and he didn't have to say a word. He just watched me with a smile from his grandfatherly face, until it was time to bargain over the price. He was a haggling master and though I tried every knack I'd learnt in Africa and Asia, I'm sure he still got the better of me. I was quite pleased with myself that I'd not been too bothered though. The carpet was mine, and I'd enjoyed the whole experience.

That night Isaac invited us all back to his house for dinner. We'd no doubt that he'd been able to take a commission on every carpet that had been sold, and this seemed to be his way of saying thank you. Dirk entered the breezeblock bungalow first. As the more outgoing of the two it was natural that he should. He was followed by Jens in his capacity as co-owner of the bus and co-buyer of carpets, then by me as the friend, but guest traveller. We sat cross-legged on the carpet and Dirk was invited to sit next to Isaac on cushions against the wall furthest away from the door. The only other furniture in the room was a low table which sat against one of the rough rendered walls, and a TV with a video player that stood on wrought-iron legs. The table held a brass bowl full of oranges and a set of photos of Isaac's children, though there weren't any photos of his wife. The children came in to introduce themselves briefly and respectfully, but the only time we saw Isaac's wife was when she brought in bowls of water to wash our hands, and then bowls of rice and stems of goat shish kebab. She kept her eyes pointing downwards at all times, and Isaac ignored her.

I wished that Birgit had been with us in the house. We'd seen very few women out and about in Pakistan, and those we had seen were robed. In Quetta the women mostly wore full Islamic clothing and their faces were rarely seen. If Birgit had been with us at that moment we might have had the chance to learn more about life for women in Pakistan. As it was, Isaac's wife was almost ghost-like.

I slept well that night, helped by a full stomach and a fatalistic attitude. In the morning I was going to be lucky with my visa, or I wasn't. It really was as simple as that. I'd made my alternative plans and had done everything possible to make things work. There was no point in worrying further.

At the Consulate I was greeted with a smile and a firm handshake that spoke of success. The man behind the counter stood to greet me. He beamed and announced, "Mr Sam, your seven-day transit permit is here." He did so with a level of pride that made it seem as if he had been working furiously over the past two days to get me the thing. He couldn't have been more pleased than I was though, and when I walked out of the office two hours later, to the amusement of the people standing in the queue, I couldn't resist doing a little jig. The world had suddenly turned into a very positive place to be.

But before I went back to the bus, I had to go to the railway station. On the way up to Quetta, we'd stopped at a level crossing where a small, square, whitewashed house stood surrounded by kilometres of scrubby desert bush. The walls of the building were topped with white-painted domes and a couple of mini-minarets. Its slightly rusty, pale green metal door had four large wrought-iron diamond-shaped panels fixed to it. The panels enclosed feathered curves of iron which matched the peaks and domes of the roof with simple elegance. It looked more like a tiny mosque than the living quarters for the men who looked after the level crossing. They had all come out to see what was going on when we stopped, and kindly posed for me to take photos. I'd promised to send them copies of the shots when I got them developed in Quetta, but the postal address they'd given me hadn't been complete. I was heading for the station to see if, on the off-chance, there might be a train running through that level crossing.

The platform manager couldn't have been more helpful, and pulled me down the platform towards a large noisy diesel engine that looked as if it was about to head out of the station. Behind it stretched fifteen carriages and trucks. The driver was leaning with one elbow out of a side window. From what I could see he was clad in a white baggy desert robe, that wasn't quite as white as it should have been. On

287

his head he wore an embroidered cream pillbox hat that had a small 'v' shape cut out of the edge. He was several days unshaven and had a weathered face, from which his crease-edged eyes looked steadily down at me as the manager shouted up my request in Urdu. Yes, he knew the crossing, yes he knew the men and yes of course he'd take the pictures down. But not until I'd shown him the shots. "These men will be very happy," he said, laughing at one of the shots. The picture in question was of the only man who'd been unable to smile when I'd taken it. Aziz was the boss and had obviously felt that it didn't suit his position to smile.

Back at the bus, Dirk and Jens had decided that they weren't ready to go. They still had room for carpets and Isaac had told them of a place they hadn't been to. The final deciding factor for them was that some friends had just turned up, and that meant a party was in order. I was faced with a choice. Ride on my own and meet up with them on the way somewhere, or wait, enjoy the party and do the two-day ride with them. If I chose the latter then I'd actually be arriving at the border on the day my visa expired, and that would be leaving no time for anything to go wrong. I went for the party.

Chapter 16

Ice and Red Mist

'We live in a wonderful world that is full of beauty, charm and adventure. There is no end to the adventures we can have if only we seek them with our eyes open.'

Jawaharlal Nehru

The party was fun, but it didn't feel as if it had been quite as much fun when we hit the road at six in the morning. It was bitterly cold, but as a bonus, under a still dark sky we were able to ride nearly deserted streets out of the city.

I filled up with fuel at the last possible petrol station on the western edge of Quetta. I was really happy to find that the PSO station had two grades of petrol. Most of the stations I'd come across pushed 80 octane fuel, and though Libby worked OK on that, the 87 octane that this station had was going to make a difference. My bike had a 43 litre fuel tank and that, at a steady and gentle speed with good quality fuel, could give me a range of 750 kilometres, though with the road to Taftan being 700 kilometres long even that was only just going to be enough. The bus, with Dirk and Jens aware of the distance but going gently because of the repair to the spring, seemed most happy to be sitting at between sixty and seventy kilometres an hour, on good road. That suited me fine, but I'd no idea where I was going to be able to get fuel along the way, and if the road really was in a rough condition then Libby was going to suck it up at a thirstier rate. We'd heard tales of fuel shortages in Nuskki, Dalbandin and Nak Kundi, which were the only real towns on the road west. In spite of the stories, we'd also been told about locals who sit by the roadside selling petrol out of glass bottles, and every litre I could get into Libby could make a real difference. Stupidly, it didn't occur to me to buy a fuel can and ask the guys to carry it for me.

I was going to miss Quetta. Though our time there had been so tense with uncertainty, it had been a fascinating place to stop for a few days. What was going on over the border in Afghanistan with the Taliban produced an edgy feeling. Guns had been the norm and suspicion was in just about every first look we'd been given by the people. But the mix of cultures, and the strong feeling of life being lived to the full, had outweighed the tenseness. As I glanced in my mirrors I hoped that someday I'd be back.

Taking one last look at the soft browns of the mountains surrounding Quetta, one of which was covered with snow, we eased on through the foothills in the clean crisp dawn colours. The road was good and I felt great. A new adventure was beginning, and I was really conscious that I was riding through an area steeped in history. This area of Baluchistan has a landscape intrinsically hostile, and its climate makes no concessions for the traveller. Even though so bleak, it has been inhabited since 7000BC, and until it was captured by Alexander the Great it belonged to the Persians. But the region has always been a problem for rulers. It's so hard to travel through that many 'conquerors' controlled it pretty much in name only. The people who live there are called the Baloch but no one really knows where they originally came from. There are all sorts of stories, including that the people came from Syria or Babylon, or are even one of the 'Lost Tribes' of Israel. Modern experts think that the people migrated from the southern edge of the Caspian Sea. Wherever they came from, the people have a reputation for being fiercely war-like and travellers are warned of the risks of passing through the region. With the troubles over the border in Afghanistan, this reputation was simply enhanced.

I found the speed bumps I'd been warned about and yes, many of them were unmarked. They were frequently in illogical places, and very steep. They were also on either side of the railway where the road meandered back and forth across the tracks. Hand painted warning signs on black and white striped poles let us know about those, at the last minute. The bus was forced to gently edge up and down each one, and as it did so I renamed them. They weren't speed bumps at all – 'Speed Killers' seemed far more appropriate. If I'd not been riding gently I could have come a real cropper, but the road was pretty good as it looped through rolling hills and scrubby, rocky bushland. The deep blue sky to the north of us had low-lying wispy horizontal trails of thin white cloud painted across it. In the distance, a layer of indigo craggy hills seemed to be floating on a bed of soft white mist. The crisp air tasted fresh and clean, and as the hours eased on by we passed not a truck nor a car.

The PSO station at Nuskki had diesel but no petrol, and a kilometre out of the town I had a blow out – the front tyre had picked up a nail. I'd been trying really hard to steer clear of the piles of rubbish strewn across the road near the petrol station, but it had been like tiptoeing through a minefield. Dirk and Jens put the kettle on and left me to it.

All went well until I wanted to inflate the tube. In Thailand I'd junked my ancient and no longer functioning foot pump in favour of a small air compressor, which ran off the bike's battery. I'd used it in India and had been really impressed. It had been very nice not to have to jump up and down on the foot pump pedal, but in the midday warmth of the desert, the compressor wasn't happy. It grumbled at the amount of pressure I had to keep putting into the tyre to try to get it to pop out onto the rim, and all of a sudden a wisp of smoke from the compressor was followed by a flame, and the thing self-destructed. It was a pity, but I wasn't worried. I was carrying something called a Schrader pump, which could be fastened to one of the bike's cylinders, from where it took compression to pump the tyre. I'd never used it before because I'd heard stories that the petrol-laden air it pumped would melt the glue on any repair patches. But this time I'd put my last brand new tube in, so that shouldn't matter. With everything connected, I started Libby's engine. The pump was pumping, but with the bike's engine getting decidedly warm, running on the spot with no air passing over the cooling fins on the cylinders, I was in trouble.

Jens took pity on me – I hadn't realised that the guys had a giant air compressor in one of the holds on the bus, and as a motorcyclist pulled to a halt to watch from his turquoise Russian Ural, Jens took over. Seconds later – BANG! But it wasn't the tyre popping out onto the rim; it was the whole tyre shooting off it. Jens had accidentally over-inflated the tube, and badly damaged the tyre. When we replaced the tube with the old patched one, and got the tyre back on the wheel, I could see that I'd be riding with a blister on the side that would only just pass through the forks. But there was no choice and we set off with me feeling very nervous. I'd no idea how much of a risk I was taking riding the bike like this, but had a very good idea of what could happen if the tyre came off at any speed.

The first stretch of rough road appeared in front of us, three sections of gravel that were roughly ten kilometres long. They were fine to ride and I felt a little heartened. If this was the worst the road had in store for me, the ride was going to be a doddle. But at Dalbandin, after finding they had no fuel, the road turned worse. To make life even harder, it was now dark and Dirk and Jens wanted to keep going. Soft sand patches had the bike squiggling from side to side, and with no warning of where they were, the riding became quite scary. As I hung on white-knuckled to the handlebars, I kept repeating to myself, 'I'm going to Iran, I'm going to Iran, I'm going to Iran.' If positive thought power was going to keep me safe, then I was going to overdose on it! When we eventually stopped, it took me nearly three hours to get rid of the adrenaline that my body had conjured up.

In the morning, the last 20 kilometres to the town of Nak Kundi was loose gravel, and in the dust as the bike fish tailed along, I felt as if I was back in Africa. Except when there are corrugations, this sort of gravel is fun to ride and you can do so at quite a speed, so long as you have the confidence that the surface isn't going to change suddenly. It didn't, and in Nak Kundi I bought the last two litres of bottled petrol the stall had. We were almost at the border, and though my visa had officially expired that day, I felt sure that if I played dumb then I'd have no problem. The last kilometres went with a wobbly-wheeled rush on an excellent asphalt surface, and then there it was – the town of Taftan – and my fuel had lasted.

The customs post was totally unmarked and the village dirty. There was only one building of consequence, and that was a guesthouse. The rest were all mud-brick and plastic, and the place seemed like a rather ignominious end to an interesting and friendly country. Other than its colourful trucks and buses, Pakistan could not claim to be flamboyant, but for me as a man it had been an easy, colourful and attractive part of the world to travel through. I'd enjoyed the challenges of India, and Pakistan, though so different in so many ways, had been equally enjoyable. As I stood looking back out over the road into the country, I promised myself that one day I really would be back. The next time I'd allow more time and I'd get my seasons right. I was keen to see some of the north – winter was definitely not the time of year to be trying to do that on a bike.

Pakistani customs were friendly and efficient, and the moneychangers hassled with forceful enthusiasm. They'd nothing to lose except the chance to change the last of our rupees. They did so with the worst rate I'd come across so far, but at least I'd have money to get into Iran with. That gave me a mental comfort zone which would help take the pressure off if the Iranians were going to be difficult. The immigration officers were friendly and polite, and not a word was said about the fact that I'd left leaving until the last possible minute. Though that wasn't exactly true – we had a whole hour left before the offices closed.

I was tense as we rolled the few metres across no-man's land to Iran. Things could still go wrong, and I wasn't counting any chickens until I was actually in and riding free. I was also tense about being in Iran at all. I'd been brought up on what the western media had to say about the country, a place full of fanatics and religious zealots who would hate me, because of where I came from and the politics of my government. But in real life, on both sides of the border, men scurried back and forth loading trucks and throwing brightly coloured bundles up onto the tops of buses. The Pakistani buses were flamboyant, and the Iranian equivalents looked tired and boringly efficient in comparison. The men looked just like ordinary people who were making a living in a harsh climate.

The Iranian immigration officers didn't start things off too well for me. They didn't like my British passport at all. One officer looked up at me and said, "How you get your visa?" The tone of his voice was a combination of dislike and disbelief. Dirk and Jens had no problem at all, and I heard the same officer say, "Welcome", to them. The attitude was I guessed, down to the fact that the British Government was conducting sanctions against Iran, but the Germans were being a lot more open, and vital equipment was travelling into the country from Germany.

Customs were a lot easier for me to get through, but that had nothing to do with nationality, more to do with size. I had panniers and a bag on the bike to be checked, and check they did, with everything completely unpacked. If I'd been trying to smuggle anything I'd have been in real trouble. The bus fared worse. Everything had to come out and the guys' carpets were all customs tagged and entered on their paperwork. Dirk had a fit when one of the customs officers put his foot through a Plexiglas skylight next to the roof rack. He was furious at the man's carelessness and had to be held back by Jens. I could understand why though; the broken skylight would make a winter run far less comfortable, and there was a good chance that water would get through whatever temporary repair they made.

The first checkpoint away from the border wouldn't let us through. "It is too dangerous for you to be travelling at night in this area," the olive-green clad soldiers told us authoritatively. "You park there. You go in morning." No sooner had we settled down, bodged a repair on the skylight and had prepared dinner, when another group of soldiers marched across to bang impatiently on the bus door. "You no stay here! You go now!" the one in charge shouted at us. His face was reddened and spittle was flying from his mouth as he shouted and stamped his foot like a petulant child overdosing on power. The soldiers with him all had their guns pointing at us and looked as if they were itching to try them out. The head soldier's angry enthusiasm was infecting them and they appeared to be more like a mob than a unit of a nation's army. Most of them looked like teenagers in uniforms they'd borrowed from their fathers, and I couldn't see one who looked as if he was safe handling a gun. In spite of the petulance of their boss, they calmed down with firm but gentle talking from Dirk, who was superb at doing this in times of crisis. "OK. You stay; you leave 7 o'clock. We come back, you no go, you trouble!" In spite of the hassle factor and the aggressiveness of the soldiers, I was glad that they'd spoken some English. The situation could have felt far worse if we hadn't been able to understand what was going on.

We were away before the hassle was due to start in the morning, but I was worried about something else. There hadn't been any petrol available at the border and the nearest town was 90ks away. I rode with fingers crossed towards Zahedan, and I began to get really worried as a strong headwind picked up. Logic said that if I really got stuck, then there would be a solution. The guys could get me petrol from the town, but I didn't want them to have the hassle of doing that. The other option would have been to stop a passing car and ask if I could buy some, but if Iranians were the same as the men at the border then there was no chance of that happening. Instead, I tucked in very close behind the bus  and rode in their slipstream. I'd never done this with a vehicle before – it had always seemed like a mad thing to do. The only warning I'd have that there was trouble in front, would be when their brake lights came on. But the road was immaculate asphalt and there didn't seem to be any other traffic on the road at this time of day, so I risked it and sat in the diesel exhaust fumes of the bus for the next hour. In Zahedan, I filled just over 42 litres into the tank, so I'd had about 35ks left. The next thing I did was to buy a big 40-litre plastic container which I filled with petrol and strapped to the top of the bus. Filling the tank and Libby at Iranian petrol prices cost me less than seven litres would have done in Pakistan.

The guys had some work to do on the bus so I went out on a tyre and inner tube hunt. Now we were on better roads and on such cheap fuel, I knew that they would want to drive faster, and my front tyre had got worse – it was now bulging so much that it was rubbing on the left fork, and just the thought of riding gave me the shivers. Tubes yes, but Zahedan had no tyres that would fit, so I had to risk it. We kept going in a strengthening wind, blasting its way along the base of the mountains with nothing to break it.

The asphalt road cut straight, immaculate and true across the desert. An uninterrupted single white line ran along the centre, hypnotically weaving up and down as the road meandered over small rises and into slight dips on its never-ending journey towards a horizon that was sheathed in dark grey, heavy-looking clouds. Occasional rocky outcrops were the only things that broke the undulating land, whose surface was randomly scattered with wiry, leafless, tan-coloured bushes. Far to the east, a lonely twenty-five carriage train heaved its way as a stocky brown line along a distant parallel to the road. Behind it, the mountains stood as an immense, broken-topped, snowy blue band that split a world of beige and heavy grey. The wind blew cold and insistent, continuing to play its games with the heavy old bus. It played with me as if I were some sort of insignificant ultra-light toy that it could blast away on a whim.

In sombre mood, none of us felt like cooking, so we decided to try out one of the truck stop restaurants. It was no more than a large windswept expanse of heavily rutted, oil and diesel-soaked earth, with a breezeblock single-storey building standing on one side. Only this and the long straight ribbon of asphalt disturbed the desert. An erratically flickering blue neon sign proclaimed something over the entrance. Bright welcoming lights shone out from inside, highlighting Mercedes, MAN and Volvo trucks. The overweight and unshaven truckers stopped talking as we walked in. Their trucks gleamed, but the drivers seemed to care nothing for how they looked. In the corner of the restaurant an old colour TV, with lines that flickered up its screen in irritating jerks, showed a Mullah speaking intensely and enthusiastically about something in rapid fire Farsi. No one was watching. The calm air inside was filled with the rich scent of grilling meat.

A heavily built, greasy-haired man, dressed in baggy grubby beige trousers and an equally rumpled off-white shirt, came towards us with a look that somehow managed to combine trepidation, and indifference. He wasn't sure what to make of us, but whoever we were he wasn't going to lose face in front of his regulars. Dirk mimed eating. The man nodded and indicated for us to follow him. He led us to the kitchen and pointing at the food that was being prepared, shrugged his shoulders as if to say, 'Well, choose.' The cook looked up at us and with a brown-toothed smile pointed at kebabs, rice and a pan of onion tomato sauce. He gave us a thumbs up, and licked his lips dramatically. We ate on his recommendation, and it was excellent.

By the time our food had arrived, the truck drivers had lost interest in us, but the staff of the truck stop had all gathered round to watch us eat. One could speak some English. "I like CDs." he said. "You have magazines; girl magazines?" he added with twitching eyebrows. The other staff laughed at him, but as we hadn't reacted in the wrong way - no we didn't have any girly mags – they pulled up chairs to sit with us. Conversation in an eclectic mix of Farsi, English and sign language bantered back and forth. The guys were fascinated about what we were all doing, and where we had come from. They wanted to compare their lives with ours. We must have seemed rich to them but that never entered the conversation. As always the grass seemed to be greener on the other side, and the one thing they all agreed on was that Iran was a bad place. It seemed to be such a bad place simply because they weren't allowed to drink whiskey. The staff followed us out through the now fierce wind to the bus. They were fascinated with how the guys had kitted it out to be a home, and insisted that we played CDs for them. Within seconds the aisle on the bus was full of men dancing; the bus literally rocked!

That night we camped in the desert. The wind now felt as if it was at gale force, and the only way I'd been able to stay on the bike was by tailgating again. We managed to find a spot right off the main road and well out of sight. The parked bus swayed and jiggled under stars that were superb in the blasting frigid night air. Shooting stars shot across the sky as if some sort of celestial celebration was going on. To the east of us, the dragon-backed mountains still stretched from one darkened horizon to the other. In the west, the bleak desert plain remained stretching out uninterrupted towards another horizon. When

I went out into the sand to go to the loo behind a small outcrop of rock, the wind was so strong that I had problems holding onto my loo paper, let alone keeping it flat enough to use efficiently.

In the morning the wind had disappeared, leaving an unreal calm in the desert. The almost shell-shocked silence of the dawn made me feel that the desert too was recovering from the blasting wind. The wind had left behind a still but bitter cold air, and I was now riding with all my layers on. For the first time I fitted the handlebar muffs I'd made in Delhi, and the difference was phenomenal; behind the muffs, circulating blood was enough to keep my hands warm. As we climbed up through a small range of hills, I rode on the first snow of the journey.

In the town on the other side, all traffic had stopped. I parked the bike and walked to the front of the queue to see what was going on. It was a funeral. There was no indication of the cause, but hundreds of people dressed in black carried coffins through the town. A white-turbaned Mullah on the back of a battered, blue and white Toyota pick-up truck was using a megaphone to exhort the people to do something, but no

one seemed to be paying much notice to him. I couldn't see the women's faces under their black veils, the men looked grief-stricken and some were crying; children walked alongside the adults, confused and uncertain expressions on their faces. Back at the bike I realised that the tyre had slipped and a shiny bulge of inner tube was now sticking out like a black bubble gum balloon between the tyre and the rim. We did the best we could to fix it and I wrapped duct tape around the weakened section of the tyre. It wouldn't last long, but it might help. Jens wanted to ride the bike for a while but I wouldn't let him; the risk was now too great.

We pulled into the city of Esfahan in the middle of the afternoon; we'd been on the move for nine hours. Two traffic police assured us that there wasn't a camping site but kindly guided us to the Amir Kabir hotel, which bikers had told me was good. It was, and with the bike off the road I went straight out on a tyre hunt. If I couldn't find one then I'd have to let Dirk and Jens go on without me. There was no way I was going to ride the bike without a new tyre. If the worst came to the worst, and I couldn't get one in Iran, then I'd have to get one couriered out, and if I was going to be stuck anywhere, then Esfahan was the place to be. I'd heard that I might well be able to extend my transit visa here, though in fact we were all intending to try to do that anyway; seven days was just enough to get across the country, but not to allow us to do any looking around.

First stop next morning was the visa office. The guys had stayed up late the night before and were paying the price. Both looked absolutely shattered and Dirk was actually swaying with exhaustion as he stood in the inevitable queue. I went first. The officer behind the thick glass screen had what looked like three days of stubble on his chin, a look that Iranian men seemed to favour. I explained the situation with my tyre and that it was too dangerous for me to be riding without a new one. "OK", he said. "You can have seven more days. Come back in two hours." I thanked him, and stood to one side to let the guys have their turn. For a change Dirk had lost his ability to be diplomatic, and with a very tired Jens glowering at the officer from Dirk's shoulder, they were not successful at all. "No", the officer said abruptly. "You cannot extend." That put the pressure on. I had to find a tyre today if I was going to stay with them. I left them arguing, with Dirk getting ever more agitated in front an increasingly stony-faced officer.

I searched for two hours and as I did so, learned to like the Iranian people of Esfahan tremendously. Everyone was kind, courteous and incredibly helpful. People went out of their way to direct or guide me to motorcycle shops. Some even took me to them, and on the way explained about the city in broken English.

But shop after shop had no tyre that would fit. It seemed that none of the local bikes had 21-inch front wheels. As I got to the last shop I'd pretty much accepted that I wasn't going to get one, but on the up side I had found the DHL courier office in a side

street. As is so often the way the last garage had a tyre – it was intended for a 250cc trail bike, not a bike of Libby's size, but it would be much safer than the blistered tyre and as I wouldn't be travelling that fast, it would do. I hurried back to the hotel to dump it off before getting back to the visa office for my extension. Dirk and Jens were at the hotel. They'd been completely unsuccessful and were steaming angry with the office. "Go, go, go!" they said. "We'll fit the tyre while you're gone. We have to leave today. We must get to Tabriz before our visas run out. We'll put your gear on the bus. Tabriz is our last chance. Hurry. Take a taxi." I did just that and the car I flagged down was a Pakyan, which is an Iranian made version of the British 1960s Hillman; I hadn't been in one since I was a child. At the visa office the official smiled at me and gave me my extension, marked with an additional twenty days! It felt like the twenty days were his version of a middle finger to Dirk and Jens.

It was mid-afternoon by the time I got back to the bus. I'd not eaten or drunk anything since 7am, and I had a raging headache as a result. Dirk rode Libby so I could eat on the move, but after a 150 kilometres I took over. Now, as well as all my bike gear, I was wearing almost every item of clothing I had. The day was sunny, but very cold, and the wind was adding a chill factor to the afternoon. I used my pocket warmer for the first time and to my delight, it was bliss. I was having a good time. No visa worry for me, no tyre worry, Libby felt great, the road was superb, the fuel was cheap and it didn't matter how cold I was going to get, I had a nice warm bus to sleep in at night. Though I was concerned for the guys, life felt very good.

It was so cold in the night that the bus's diesel fuel froze, increasing the guys' frustration. I think that if I hadn't been with them, they would have driven through the night. Dirk and Jens put a couple of litres of my petrol in the tank with the hope that it would help defreeze the diesel. That and the sun did the trick, but it wasn't until a very late 10.30am before we could get on the move again. We arrived at the Tabriz camping site on the outskirts of the city just after dark. It had been our first full day of snow, and the roadsides had gathered a thin clean layer of pure white, but the road itself had stayed clear. I took it as a warning of things to come.

Most travellers seem to bypass the city of Tabriz, but I liked it. It bustled, and yet again the people were very friendly. There was hardly a sign of anything to do with tourism and that, I supposed, was the reason why people were keen to meet and spend time with us. People came and asked if they could practise their English, but there was absolutely no hassle at all.

The visa office said yes to an extension for Dirk and Jens with hardly an eyelid blinked; seven extra days. Now we headed straight for the carpet bazaar, the guys on a mission. It's right in the centre of Tabriz and is said to be one of the oldest in the Middle East. It's also supposed to be the largest closed one-roofed structure in the world. Historically, the city has been a trade crossroads between cultures and visiting the bazaar was rather like walking back in time. You step down into a darkened world of alleyways, whose vaulted ceilings are whitewashed curves that are punctuated by small domed sections with skylights set into them. These openings throw shafts of light down into the rough floored, but immaculately clean, trading areas. Small open-front shops are set into the walls, hung with brightly-coloured, exquisitely stitched and woven samples of the merchants' carpets. The rough floors are covered with more, and as a customer you are encouraged to walk over the goods to enable you to feel the sheer luxury that only quality can give. It's quite special that the bazaar still stands. Tabriz is yet another of the region's cities that is in an earthquake zone and as a result, it's been badly damaged many times.

An Iranian man had been watching us for a while. "You guys look as if you need some help," he said with a broad New York accent. "My name is Kaveh and I'm a carpet exporter, so I know my way around. No pressure, but if you want I'm happy to take a stroll with you. Sometimes it helps to have inside knowledge. I can tell you about the carpets you are looking at, where they are made and how. I can also tell you which ones are worth buying to sell on. When you are with me the merchants won't over-charge you, too much," he added with a grin.

Kaveh was dressed in neat western-style black trousers, a white open-necked shirt and a blue sports jacket. Unusually for an Iranian, he was clean-shaven. "You're probably a bit suspicious of me, aren't you? It's OK though. If you don't need any help I'll carry on with my own buying. It's just that I know what it's like to be in a strange land. Someone offering help can make all the difference." The three of us liked him instantly; we'd all travelled long enough not to be taken in easily. I thought that if he was a con man, he would have to be very good to fool three sets of instincts.

Kaveh knew the names of all the merchants and politely introduced us to each. Dirk and Jens were after Kilim carpets and Kaveh knew some superb stalls and shops, some of which we'd probably never have found for ourselves. The biggest problem was choosing which to buy. And yes, I bought another carpet. Kilims appealed to my liking for geometric design, and I appreciated the fact that the better versions we were looking at had been traditionally made by hand, way out in the countryside. By the time Kaveh had finished with his lectures on carpets, we could tell the difference between fakes that had been made by machine, and the genuine article.

The women of Tabriz respected the Moslem religion in a most traditional way. I didn't see one woman on the street who wasn't dressed in the long, loose-fitting black robes, with a black headscarf and veil covering their heads and faces. In Esfahan, many of the women had worn brightly coloured headscarves and had kept their faces uncovered. I'd been told that in the capital city, Tehran, the women were able to be even more flamboyant. But here in Tabriz it looked as if the streets were populated by men, and black ghosts. The only way I could tell a woman's likely age was by the type of shoes and stockings she was wearing. If the shoes had a heel of some sort, they more than likely had a young owner. If the shoes had no heel or the stockings that went with those shoes weren't sheer, or were worn with socks, then there was a good chance that the woman was older. I found it hard not to stare as I tried to work out who I was looking at. Older women averted their gazes but younger women would more than often give me a quick straight-eyed stare in return for a few seconds.

The cultural surprise came when an Iranian family Dirk and Jens had met on their way through Tabriz months before, invited us to their home. The house was set inside a tall rough wall, and to get into the courtyard we had to be allowed through giant, solid gates that looked as if they would withstand an attacking army. The courtyard was tiled, and potted plants were artistically placed to soften the almost antiseptic area. Shoes off, we were shown into a living room that had a rug-covered tiled floor, and the family were introduced. To my surprise, none of the women were wearing chadors; but wearing mini skirts that left little to the imagination. They had tight fitting blouses, wore eye makeup, and were dripping with gold jewellery. On the street the men looked as if they were in charge, but in this home it was very plain to see that the women were the bosses. I wondered if all the proud looking men we'd seen on the streets outside would all go home to a territory that was not theirs to command.

I tried a hammam for the first time in Tabriz too. The camping site didn't have any showers and after a few days on the road, I was conscious that I probably didn't smell good enough to be mixing with the people. Hammams are the public bathhouses of the Middle East, and for hundreds of years have been a place where, besides getting clean, people have conducted business or just socialised. They are inevitably ancient and ours was a cellar with vaulted ceilings and blue and white tiles.

The hammam experience is methodical. First of all you strip down to your underwear, though in some hammams you strip naked. The first room is known as the 'warm' room, and in here you lay in hot dry air which encourages you to sweat. You then move on into a hotter room, which I thought was rather like a sauna. You then cool off in bitterly cold water before moving on to the washroom, where you clean off all your dirt and sweat under a fountain of warm water. As massage costs extra, and still nervous about the state of my back, I gave that a miss. After the body wash we went through into a cool room to unwind and ease away some body temperature before heading out into the chill night air. I felt as if I'd never been so clean, and though time-consuming, the whole experience was far better than my usual five-minute duck under a shower.

Tabriz now lay under a light dusting of snow and the weather forecast was for heavy falls towards the border with Turkey. Kaveh told us that the road away from the border into Turkey had had thirty centimetres of snow in the past two days. The thought of riding in conditions like this scared me, afraid that if I fell off the bike then I'd do some real damage to my back. I'd ridden such a long way since it had gone wrong and on most days the pain had been manageable, but I'd also had bad days when the pain had been so grim that even an overdose of paracetamol hadn't been able to cut through it. Those days had reminded me of how I'd felt in Germany, and how long it had taken me to get fit enough to ride the bike again. I was so close to the end of the trip, the thought of riding on snow made me wonder if I should find somewhere to hole up until the worst of the winter was over.

But Dirk and Jens had a plan. Though the spring repair on the bus was standing up to the journey incredibly well, there was no way the bus would cope with Libby on the roof rack. Dirk and Jens hadn't been able to find a replacement spring, but we could get an attachment made locally that would allow me to fix Libby to the back of the bus by her forks, if the snow got too bad to ride. The idea looked decidedly flimsy to me, and I was concerned about how the bike would cope with the unnatural stress on the forks. But it was the only plan we could come up with, unless I gave up riding the bike altogether and arranged for it to be trucked at considerable expense to Ankara.

The last 250 kilometres of Iran went as smoothly as all of the rest. The sun was out and though horribly cold, the snow stayed away. The mountains we were climbing up into were covered in snow but the road was clear. A series of police roadblocks held us up with polite but insistent demands to see our paperwork, and just before the border I found a bonus petrol station, filling Libby to the brim and happy that my eighty-three litres could take me just over 1,400 kilometres across Turkey, which would be a massive saving for my budget.

The border was one of the most organised I'd been to in a long time. The buildings were neat and well painted, and the signs showed exactly were we had to go. The officials were friendly and one asked me if I had enjoyed my visit to Iran. When I replied that I'd had a too short but wonderful time, and that I had enjoyed the company of Iranian people, the officer said, "I am so happy you have enjoyed my country. Please visit us again."

The Turkish side was even more polite, the officials extremely friendly. No, I didn't need a visa after all, and nothing was said about needing insurance, but they did want me to have a carnet, and this I hadn't expected. Somewhere, I'd read that Turkey didn't ask for one, and if I'd stayed in Iran for my full twenty days extension, then there was a good chance I'd not have got into Turkey with the bike – my carnet would have expired by then. Funny, how things work out so perfectly sometimes. Mount Ararat stood off to the north, and it looked absolutely stunning in its snowy coat as the sun started to go down, the colours shifting like a cross between a chameleon and a giant ice-lolly. It started with lemon, and then went to apricot and orange, then strawberry and raspberry, before finally ending up as passion fruit. I knew that I was being foolish with this thought, as this majestic mountain deserves more respect, but it helped to pass the time. Mount Ararat is a dormant volcano and at 5,137 metres high, it's the tallest peak in Turkey, as well as the supposed resting place of Noah's Ark.

As the sun set it began to get even colder, but the guys wanted to get a 100 kilometres of Turkey under our wheels before we stopped for the night. With 200 kilometres to go before the city of Ezrurum, the sides of the road were banked a metre high with dirty-edged snow drifts. Thankfully, though very rough, the road itself was free of ice and snow, but it didn't help me to keep warm when at each army checkpoint I was asked to produce my papers. This meant taking my gloves off and each time I did so I lost any element of warmth they'd managed to build up. By the time we pulled over onto the forecourt of a petrol station I'd more than had enough. My fingers were numbed blue from the cold and I'd no feeling left in the tips. In spite of three layers of socks inside my bike boots, my feet had lost so much feeling that I almost fell over when I got off the bike. I decided at that moment that I never ever wanted to ride my bike in the cold after I completed this trip. That night we slept with the bus engine running, so the diesel didn't freeze again – the sound and vibration making it rather like being back on board the cargo ship from Durban.

It snowed in the night. The road was covered in a fresh layer that had just a few tracks from big trucks running through it. Even the slim blue road signs had a layer of ice and snow collecting along their upper edges. Fifty kilometres down the road, the surface changed from centimetres of snow that had been making the bike feel skittish, to thick ice. We stopped, and when I hammered through the opaque layer it was almost three centimetres deep. I'd imagined that riding on snow would be a bit like riding in soft sand, but it wasn't. Sand has a drag factor which slows you down, making the back wheel fishtail. Though initially an interesting challenge, snow made the bike feel almost uncontrollable. If there was a hole in the road, I couldn't avoid it, and sudden movements were potentially lethal.

I was forced to ride one handed, snow was still falling and it was settling on the outside of my helmet visor, the inside of which fogged up with every breath I took. I had to ride with one finger clearing the snow and another finger hooked inside to clear away the fog. With a windscreen wiper motion I could see where I was going in bursts, but controlling the bike on the ice with one hand was a mini-nightmare. My beard was developing icicles and even though I was breathing out warm air through my nose, my moustache was freezing over. My lungs were burning with the cold and after just an hour and a half of riding, I wasn't sure if all parts of my body were still attached. Enough was enough.

The 'U' shaped fitting we'd had made was already fastened onto the back of the bus at bumper level. The guys gave me a hand to strip off all we could from the bike to lower the stress levels, and we hooked her up. The welder's engineering was spot on – the forks fitted precisely on the outer edges of the bracket, and the front wheel spindle passed through the bracket and forks with the help of Copaslip. To give a little support, we then slung ratchet straps over the bus roof rack and round the handlebars on the bike. It all looked very weird.

The guys had the heater turned up full blast inside the bus, and as I removed my layers we eased out onto the ice again. The bus gently meandered over the slick layer and outside of our mid summer climate zone, the snow began to fall harder. Behind the bus, Libby looked naked, stable and rather lonely.

We climbed through 2,400-metre mountains, and soon the conditions became even worse. The road was treacherous, even for the bus, and with a blizzard in full blow, snow glare became a major hazard. The guys were driving with sunglasses on as we made slow but steady progress, and I was endlessly impressed with how they handled the bus in the conditions. Most other people seemed to have decided to stay at home – we hardly saw anyone else about on the road – and with a short amount of daylight available, we crawled on for five hours into the night. With luck we could get out of the worst of the weather by doing that.

Brilliant, beautiful sunshine greeted us in the morning. It was rather like an old and very valued friend coming to visit. We were out of the mountains and the well-salted roads were clear of snow. We unhooked Libby so we could get cracking. She seemed to have suffered no harm from piggy-backing on the bus, and in spite of the fact that the air was still very cold, I was glad to be back on her. Next stop, the city of Ankara, whose cosmopolitan feel I really enjoyed and after India, Pakistan and Iran it was strange to see girls with legs! On then to Cappadocia – because of the weather, travelling in Turkey in winter wasn't easy, but we were all keen to see this area, and the guys had an added incentive. Kaveh had a carpet shop there and had said that he'd do the guys a good deal on more Kilims.

The name Cappadocia translates as 'The Land of Beautiful Horses', and it's considered to have been one of the earliest areas in the world to have been settled. Communities have been there for as much as 10,000 years. The Central Anatolian Plateau is dotted with volcanoes, and over history the eruptions have created a really fertile soil, and a very soft rock, which has been carved into to make whole cities, some of which extend for fourteen floors below ground level. Sections of these cave cities are still used for storage, but archaeology  has shown that the cities included living spaces, churches (whose walls still display magnificent frescoes), wineries, stables, grain mills and kitchens. The subterranean systems have airshafts, wells and chimneys. It's thought that most of the excavations were done by Christians trying to escape from the Romans in the days before the Romans converted to Christianity. Outside in the valleys, the stone windows of the rooms spread up over the cream-coloured rock faces to look rather like eye sockets from stacked up skulls. 'Fairy Chimneys' stand solo across the valley floors under caps of harder rock; the wind and the rain having eroded the softer rock to leave these elegant, almost mystical towers. Amazingly, the true extent of the cities was not discovered until the 1960s.

Coach accidents are common in Turkey and Kaveh told us not to be surprised – many of the drivers bought their licenses on the black market. We were hustling along towards Istanbul when I nearly became a coach accident statistic, and experienced road rage for the first time. The road we were on looped and curved its way through the mountains, following the contours, with steep drops into gorges to the side. The road in summer would have been fun but to me it wasn't. It had been sleeting, and passing traffic threw up muck from the road so my visor was almost constantly covered in a salty, grimy mush. The surface was slightly potholed, and would have been OK if I'd been able to see the holes far enough in advance. It was manageable – it wasn't snowing and the road wasn't completely iced over – but coaches travelled fast, whatever the conditions. One started to overtake me, easing alongside on a long bend, and then abruptly pulled in. As it did so the back end belted my handlebar. The driver had completely misjudged things and all of a sudden I was wobbling at speed towards the gravelly edge of the road, beyond which was a sheer drop – there was no barrier to slow me down. Instinct took over and I hauled at the handlebars with every bit of strength I could muster. I'm not sure how it happened, but as we bucked and skittered across the gravel, somehow we stayed upright, and though we were just centimetres away from the edge, we didn't go over.

One of the mirrors had been ripped off from the impact, and shaking, I rode back to pick it up. Then pure rage flooded over me. Back on the bike, ignoring the holes, loose gravel and icy patches, I belted off down the road after the bus. I caught it up, and holding the throttle open with my left hand, I pounded on the side of it with my right as I steamed past. I pulled up a couple of hundred metres past the bus, at a ninety-degree angle across the road. The driver was not going to get away with what he'd done!

The coach pulled up at my roadblock, the driver looking both innocent and slightly annoyed at being stopped. The hostess looked frightened. She perhaps had been more aware of my furious banging on the side of the coach. Then I had to laugh. I'd stopped the bike on such a steep gradient I couldn't get the side stand out without the bike falling over. At that moment, other than being able to rather pathetically shake my fist at the driver and yell curses at him from inside my helmet, I was totally impotent. I don't think he had a clue what the problem was and as he drove his coach around me, he looked across shaking his head at the crazy tourist. It was only then that I realised how stupid I'd been. To catch up with the coach I'd been overtaking cars at speed, unable to see if anything was coming up behind me. The realisation of how badly I'd lost my temper was a sobering moment. Moving off, I stood on the foot pegs and looked down into the gorge, where the wreckage of a large truck lay crumpled and rusting. I'd been lucky, twice.

The road conditions changed dramatically once we were out of the mountains. We'd left the worst of the snow behind us and at lower altitude it was noticeably warmer. Just as we got onto the first section of motorway my indicators stopped working, leaving me feeling incredibly vulnerable in the now heavy traffic. I stopped briefly to see what the problem was but with no luck. When Dirk and Jens caught up, I tucked in behind them and let them do the indicating for me.

Finally through Istanbul, I had some hard thinking to do. In front of us lay Bulgaria, Romania, Hungary and Austria. In mid-March they would all have plenty of snow around. The last days of riding had made me acutely aware that bikes and snow don't mix very well. It had been a challenge and I felt good about having made it. I also felt good that Libby piggybacking had worked so well. But did I want any more of it?

The alternative was to split from the guys, and take the longer but lower route round through Southern Greece and then onto the ferry across to Italy. It would be far easier and I already knew some of the roads, having ridden them nearly four years before at the start of the trip. A little voice in the back of my mind kept chuntering at me, 'The easy way is the defeated way.' So far I'd not let much on the road beat me. The challenges had kept on popping up, but with common sense and large doses of flexibility I'd always ended up going where I'd wanted to get to, and I'd had one amazing adventure after another as a result. I'd missed out on China and Burma, but they had been long punts. I'd had a few disasters, but my Guardian Angel had got me safely out of most of those, and she still seemed to be up for it. Did I really want to take the easy way out now? Or was it plain stupidity to risk it all at this late stage of the trip? I knew that we'd be passing through the countries rather rapidly, but at least I'd be seeing new things yet again. I'd be getting to Birgit faster too. Libby was working really well and I'd managed to fix the indicators – damp had got in somewhere and both the bulbs and the fuse had blown. It would be cheaper riding through Eastern Europe too.

So when the guys headed for Bulgaria, I went with them. At the border, long lines of articulated trucks with big blue and white TIR – 'Transport International Routier' – signs, stood waiting to be let through. The roadsides were lined with snow, but the sun was shining and the officials passed us through with handshakes and smiles. After riding Libby through a murky slippery chemical disinfecting dip, Bulgaria lay before me.

Sections of Turkey had felt almost third world and Bulgaria seemed the same, but despite the fall of the Eastern Bloc, still with a sinister Soviet influence. When the houses weren't ramshackle and roofed with terracotta tiles, they were stark utilitarian concrete that looked like square bunkers. The road surface was potholed asphalt, and when we weren't riding through dark forests whose trees hung with icicles and dripped water onto dark sodden layers of fallen leaves, we eased on past land farmed in small plots. Fields were edged with shaggy bushes, and ancient wooden carts stood outside in sleety rain. At the camping site on the coast, the ablution blocks had the basins, toilets and showers ripped out. Once it had been a major holiday destination for anyone in the Eastern Bloc who had been privileged enough to be able to afford or get a permit to go there. The man on the gate told us that since the change in government, people had no respect.

On the Romanian side of the border, army conscripts crowded round the bike in what my thermometer said was -1°C. The teenagers stared with shiny enthusiastic eyes at Libby, their breath clouds mingling with mine. From the list I now had on the side of my panniers, one of the conscripts read out the names of the countries I'd been able to visit. He told me that all young Romanian men had to do national service, and that they all hated it. "Do you smoke dope?" he asked. "We do. Do you have any, or would you like some of ours?" He told me that he felt like a whole new world was beginning to open up for Romanians, with the change of the government. "NATO very good. We are friends now, yes?"

Buildings were again mostly terracotta-roofed or ugly concrete, but some had a classic elegance, and looked as if they would be more at home on the streets of Paris or Vienna. I was also surprised at how many churches there were; their different shapes made a real change

from the domed minarets of Pakistan, Iran and Turkey. The roads were sadly neglected. Strangely, some sections were really smooth, but they could change instantly into a nightmare, cratered surface. Urban roads were the worst, and sometimes the manhole covers were missing. Usually where that was the case, someone would have stuck a branch of a tree in the hole as a warning, but not always. Outside towns I was surprised to see how few shops there were, but I supposed that in the country areas, the people were used to being self-sufficient and would barter between each other. The people I tried to talk with seemed highly suspicious, though perhaps by this time I looked so unkempt from the weeks of hard riding that I appeared too dangerous to be with. Except for the odd Mercedes or Russian Zhil, the cars were mostly beaten up Trabants, Ladas, and Olcits, which looked like some sort of Citröen. The speed limits were a bit of a problem for me; in the bus, the guys were allowed to drive at a max speed of 90km/h, but on the bike, officially I was restricted to sixty. I'd read that Romanian police were allowed to do 'on the spot' fines, so I kept my eyes well open. Village dogs seemed to think that I was being laid on for their entertainment and they would appear in packs from around the corners of houses, rushing towards me yipping and yapping as their legs scrabbled to propel them fast enough to catch me. They never did. In spite of my chilly thoughts about Romania, I couldn't help thinking that the summer sun would have painted a completely different picture.

Another long line of trucks stood waiting at the border with Hungary, the border the guys feared the most. Though not a part of the EU then, they were part of the customs union and as such, customs checks on the Hungarian side were reputedly thorough. With all the carpets, hookahs and samovars they had on board, they were afraid that they were going to get stung for import duties, which would wipe out their profit margins. The night before we'd got to the border, Dirk and Jens had given the bus a meticulous going over. They'd washed and polished it, inside and out. Every piece of kit was stored away neatly and every item they intended to sell on was discreetly hidden. With an exhaustive check, the things would have been found, but they did all they could to make the bus look as if it had never been across the Middle East and Asia. Stickers from those regions were removed, maps were given to me, and German food they still had was put in obvious places, and I was given strict instructions to ignore them totally at the border. We'd meet up afterwards.

For me, this was the last time I'd be crossing a border with any sort of serious check, and as I'd been so lucky with all the previous crossings, I hoped that this one would be simple too. I'd been trying hard not to let Dirk and Jens' nervousness rub off on me, but as I rode the last few metres I felt sure that I must look guilty. I sat with the bike in the row of cars. An officer came out of his glass-walled cabin and clicked his fingers at me, indicating that I should come to the front. Libby, still warm, fired up first time and I eased gently to the top of the queue. The fact that I was queue jumping enhanced the feeling of guilt that I'd not been able to shake off. Behind me on the bike I had all my usual travel kit, a hookah pipe and two carpets. Libby was battle-scarred, with lost paint and dents from every fall off or impact along the way. She was filthy from the wet roads and my bike trousers were covered in grime. What had once been a fluorescent strip on my waterproof jacket was now just a dirty yellow band, and my once white helmet was battered, grime-streaked and fly-splattered. We looked just as if we had ridden across a couple of continents, and in spite of the chemical dip on the Bulgarian border, Libby was probably carrying a little dirt from every country along the way.

I stopped her right next to the official, climbed off and then, after taking my gloves off, I removed my helmet. The official waited patiently while I did this. He seemed a little surprised when I moved across to shake him by the hand. "Nationality?" he asked. "British" I replied. "Oh good" he said. "Now I can practice. Where did you come from, and where are you going?" It was the start of an hour-long conversation in which I'm sure he neglected his other duties while he took me to see the various officials I needed to get rubber stamps from. In a nice way, everything seemed to be happening in slow motion. It allowed me to savour this last crossing. When all was done, he gave me a little salute and said, "Welcome back to Europe. Be careful with the drivers. They are very dangerous you know."

313

Meanwhile Dirk and Jens had made it through the border as well, and breathing a sigh of relief we parked up for the night to enjoy a celebratory beer. As we sat in the warmth of the bus I looked around at what had been my home for so many weeks. It wasn't strange that the three of us, though we hardly knew each other, had got on so well. We had bikes, travel and the route in common, a combination that had worked. India seemed a long time ago and I knew that the ride across would have been very different if I'd been on my own. The weather would have made the journey particularly harsh and I wondered if I would have survived riding the snows of Turkey. I'd be parting company with Dirk and Jens in two days' time, and that thought seemed rather like drawing a curtain across the end of an adventure.

In the morning, the sun was shining in the sky over Hungary, but it was grey and dull over Romania. It felt strange to ride the country's perfect roads. The shops were stocked with things I recognised, and petrol stations were immaculate affairs that seemed rather sterile after Asia. But I knew that the chance of getting a leaf pumped into my fuel tank, as I had in Pakistan, was remote. The higher-octane fuel had Libby singing and the guys pushed the bus along faster than they had in weeks. They were now in the land of replacement springs, though they were determined to make it all the way home with their Pakistani souvenir. Snow lined the fields, but somehow it no longer seemed so cold. The guys' thoughts were turning towards home, family, friends and selling their goods. I thought of Birgit, and ways to earn enough money to get to Africa, then up through the Americas. The clean open road gave me time to think about the last few years. Asia had been full of idiosyncrasies, some of which had made me laugh and some of which had made me almost bubble over with frustration. But I knew that I was a lost cause. I'd developed a raging hunger for the world. I loved being out on the bike and my life was far richer than I'd ever imagined it would be. I'd lived dreams and with perspective, the nightmares had all been part of the adventure. The years had been full of extremes, and each one had challenged, surprised or delighted me. I wanted more!

Libby's thoughts had obviously settled on the land of her birth. Just over the border into Germany, her drive shaft started to vibrate and a nasty whining noise rose up at me over the usual rhythmic tapping sounds of the engine. By the time I was 100 kilometres away from Birgit's home on Lake Konstanz, Libby was telling me she'd had enough. It was almost as if she had waited to go wrong until she was on home territory; she's a bike with class.

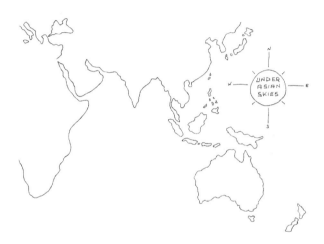

'Freedom is useless if we don't exercise it as characters making choices...
We are free to change the stories by which we live. Because we are genuine
characters, and not mere puppets, we can choose our defining stories. We can
do so because we actually participate in the creation of our stories. We are co-
authors as well as characters. Few things are as encouraging as the realisation
that things can be different and that we have a role in making them so.'

Daniel Taylor

Authors Note

'Under Asian Skies' covers the period from the start of 1993, through to mid 1995.

Since my time riding in this part of the world, disaster, politics and economics have dramatically changed some of the countries. It's also that cultures are ever evolving; they rarely remain static with the passing of time. As is the way of the world, sometimes these changes are for the better, and sometimes not.

At the time of writing, New Zealand has moved on from being a backwater, to some very different ways, but it seems to me that Kiwis still grasp strongly the way of life that is so special and almost unique to them in their peaceful, beautiful land. Australia has vastly slowed its acceptance of immigrants from Europe and has increased the numbers allowed in from Asia – this has added yet another level of rich diversity. China, as we all know, has changed dramatically in far more ways than I was able to consider at the time – it's still not easy to ride a bike through, but some adventurous overlanders now have some great tales to tell about this fascinating complex part of the world. Burma (Myanmar), sadly still struggles on, but things are beginning to look promising. East Timor is now an independent country, but the battle for power continues and the people still struggle. Indonesia has suffered from governmental issues, Tsunamis, and Moslem extremism has reached new heights. But it remains a stunningly diverse and intriguing part of the world. Malaysia has developed strongly on the economic front and is still a calm and beautiful country to visit. Thailand underwent a coup, but the tourist buck still makes a major difference to this fascinating and unusual SE Asian country. India has developed enormously on an economic basis, and my 'on the saddle' thinking time fears are becoming a worrying reality. The country has ever more influence as a world power, but the wealth gap is widening and the stress levels between castes, and Moslem and Hindu are increasing. It seems to me that there are exciting but potentially dangerous times ahead for the Indians. India remains challenging, baffling and hypnotic;

it's quite unique and always an adventure that inspires you. Pakistan has become more unsettled in many ways, stuck as it is between political world awareness and the wars in Afghanistan. The two countries talk to each other, but uneasily, and Kashmir remains a stumbling block. Iran thankfully remains peaceful, has become more open and now has a louder voice in the world. Many more people within the country itself, who at the time I was passing through would not have done so openly, now speak out, but they do so with a glance over their shoulders first. I would have liked to spend more time there, and in fact, I would happily go back to every country I was lucky enough to be able to visit.

For me, it's the people of any country that make travelling such a special thing to do. The one specific thing I hope never changes, is how amazingly welcoming and friendly the vast majority of people were to a visitor to their land. It's easy to forget that we live in an stunning, ever-changing world that's full of remarkable people.

I can't resist recommending that those of you who dream of travel, should make it happen, you'll never regret it. To travel is to adventure. To adventure is to learn. To learn is to make a better world, and to adventure on a motorcycle means having stupendous fun while doing so! Your trip will be unparalleled. Disregard how many travellers have passed that way before – your experiences, observations, disasters and adventures will be unique.

Reviews

Into Africa

'The word-pictures that bring a good travel book to life are all here; Sam's perceptions of people, places and predicaments have real depth and texture, their associated sights, smells and sounds are evoked with a natural ease. Where other author's detailed descriptions can sometimes get in the way, Sam's style is engaging and well tuned. I found myself in the midst of action rather than a mere fly on the wall.'

Overland magazine

'Fantastic book, a must have.'

WebBikeWorld.com

'Into Africa is the journal of a gifted storyteller; a writer with keen observational skills, his flowing narrative alone distinguishes Sam Manicom from his contemporaries. ... This is the book for the beach, for the tube, for the bus and always for the sheer enjoyment of reading it.'

Brennig Jones - Author

'In the range of Motorcycle Travel Books out there, this one pulls no punches. In the gritty bits, you can feel the grit. I liked it a lot.'

Motorcycle.co.uk

'Inspirational Reading'

World of BMW

'I was quickly immersed in the adventures. I felt like I was around a camp fire and Sam was reliving some of his experiences... I enjoyed this book very much.'

Londonbikers.com

'This is a great adventure and a really enjoyable read.

Johnnie Walker - BBC Radio Two

Distant Suns

'A refreshing change'

Motorcycle Sport and Leisure

'Drama, action, passion, disaster and the pure adrenaline buzz of overlanding are all here'

Overland Magazine

'I was thoroughtly impressed'

BMW Owners News USA

'This could easily be Manicom's best book yet! I was riveted right from the very beginning and enjoyed every minute of the 3 year adventure the book details; containing a little bit of everything, from Africa to South America... '

canyonchasers.com

'Sam describes cultural differences, traditions and lifestyles of the various countries they cross, whilst painting a vivid picture of the terrain they cross... A really great read that'll doubtless give you itchy feet...'

TBM - Trail Bike Magazine

'Once again, a superbly entertaining piece of travel writing...'

BM Riders

'Distant Suns has it all: love, good guys, bad guys, beauty, danger, history, geography and last but not least-bikes!'

webbikeworld

'Few travel writers can conjure up sights and smells so provocatively as Sam.'

Daily Record - Scotland

'Author Manicom and his companion are the real thing...'

RiDE Magazine

'Has Sam peaked with his last two books? Not a chance. In fact it's better!'

Honda Trail Riders

Tortillas to Totems

Sam Manicom's fourth book is a gripping rollercoaster of a two-wheeled journey which takes you riding across the dramatic landscapes of Mexico, the United States and Canada.

'You feel it, smell it, you freeze, you sweat, and you see what's before him like you're along for the ride. You are very much there'

ADVMoto

'Any good travel book must involve the reader as well as inspire and Tortillas to Totems does just that with vivid descriptions of the roads, places and people that Sam and his partner Birgit travelled and met. By the end of the book I was definitely itching to get out on the road on an adventure like this – in my opinion, the best compliment one can pay to a story like this. Sam goes way beyond 'we went here and did this...'

The Rider's Digest

'Globe-trotting biker Manicom's a natural storyteller. Although this trip may sound like a standard ride through familiar country, be assured, it isn't.'

Adventure Bike Rider

'Tortillas to Totems is the story of another epic journey covering the length and breadth of North America. You could be his pillion, so well does he describe the sounds, sights and smells of the road. If you like bikes, riding and people watching, Sam is your man.'

Daily Record

'If you want to know why motorcyclists get out into the big world and ride across it then it's all here'

Motorcycle Sport and Leisure

Sam's books, *Into Africa*, *Under Asian Skies*, *Distant Suns* and *Tortillas to Totems* are all available for download as Audiobooks. Recorded in Kite Studios Cambridge and narrated by Sam.

All four books can be found in eBook format

Sam's books are available from www.sam-manicom.com Amazon, and all good bookshops

A request from Sam

I hope you have enjoyed the ride with me through these incredible lands.

The aim of my book is to share the fun, the drama and the unexpected things that are to be found under Asian skies. If you feel that I have done this well I would be very grateful if you'd take a few moments to post a review on Amazon.

Independent authors like me really value this help.

Most of us check reviews before we buy something. Your review will help me to share the huge range of extraordinary things that make the Antipodes, Asia and the Middle East such special places to explore.

Did you know that you don't need to have bought this book from Amazon to be able to post a review?

Thank you for reading *Under Asian Skies*, and thank you for your help.

All the best,

Adverts in a travel book?
Why?

Why are you finding adverts from companies involved in overlanding at this stage of *Under Asian Skies*?

These are all companies who are highly recommended as having excellent equipment and quality service.

I'm enjoying the opportunity to guide you in their direction. If you are planning adventures of your own, be they two weeks, a month or two years, I hope you will find some inspiration on these next pages.

You'll also find some worthy causes that I'm happy to help out.

323

324

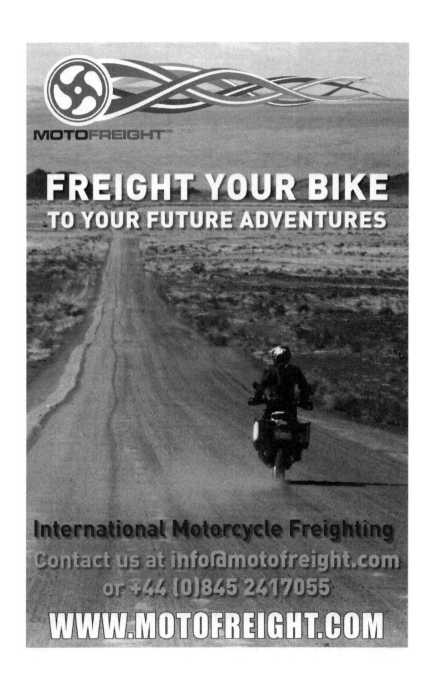

328

ON TRACK. ON ROAD. ON AVONS.

Winding coastal roads leading to open blue sea vistas. Snow capped mountains rising above oceans of evergreens. Imperious fairytale castles silhouetted against dazzling azure skies. Let the world be your backdrop and the open road your stage. And let Avon performance tyres race with your imagination and take you where you want to go. Avon. The great British tyre that's taking on the world.

OVERLAND JUNCTION

Motorcycle Organizations and Equipment Suppliers:

www.gsclubuk.org
BMW GS CLUB UK – Enthusiast's Club

www.ukgser.com
BMW 'GS' Enthusiast's Forum

www.bmw-club.org.uk
BMW Owners Club

www.bmwmoa.com
BMW Owners Of America

www.bmridersclub.com
The alternative BMW Owners Club

www.airheads.org
Airheads Beemer Club

www.advrider.com
The Adventure Motorcycle Forum

www.adventureriderradio.com
Adventure Motorcycle podcast and radio show

www.adventurebiketv.com
Light-hearted but adventure packed TV show

www.jupiterstravellers.org
The Ted Simon Foundation. All adventure travellers have it in them to be reporters of truth in the world.

www.berndtesch.de
Books, survival training, equipment and overland enthusiast

www.motorworks.co.uk
BMW parts and equipment – New and Second hand

www.motobins.co.uk
BMW parts and equipment – New and Second hand

www.james-sherlock.co.uk
BMW parts and equipment – New and Second hand

www.worldofbmw.com

Find out what's going on with BMW here

www.rally-raidproducts.co.uk

Helping you to equip your overlanding motorcycle

http://overlandjunction.com

Connecting riders with adventure & the brands that encourage them

www.touratech.co.uk

Suppliers of an extensive selection of overlanding kit

www.traveldriplus.com

Waterproof bags, tents and loads more

www.kaapstaadmat.com

Touring adventures in Southern Africa

www.globebusters.com

Unique long distance touring across the globe

www.cwmotorcycles.co.uk

Extremely helpful and experienced BMW garage

www.held.de

High quality motorcycle clothing

www.stahlkoffer.com

Hard luggage and accessories

www.blazingtrailstours.com

Royal Enfield adventure motorcycle tours in India

www.wolfmanluggage.com

Touring motorcycle luggage

www.motofreight.com

International motorcycle transport specialists

www.avon-tyres.co.uk

Quality motorcycle tyres for overlanders

Publications and Travel Information:

www.horizonsunlimited.com
The world's motorcycle travel site

www.overlandmag.com
Publication for motorcycle overlanders

www.adventuremotorcycle.com
Publication for adventure motorcyclists

www.adventurebikerider.com
Publication for adventure bike riders

www.lonelyplanet.com
Supplier of superb travel guides.

www.stanfords.co.uk
UK's best one stop shop for travel books and maps

www.backpackers.co.za
The best Backpackers' hostel in CapeTtown

www.africaguide.com/culture/artcraft.htm
A Cultural Discovery

www.uclh.org/about/htd.shtml
Tropical Disease Hospital/Travel Clinic offers pre-travel advice e.g. inoculations

www.adventure-motorcycling.com
Chris Scott desert specialist

www.maf.org
Mission Aviation Fellowship

www.2mororider.com
Inspiring riders of tomorrow

'Stay Alive in the Desert'
K. E. M. Melville, ISBN 0 903909 11 1

❝ When a person travels they discover
who they really are, what they can
achieve and so much more.
The moment a person's senses are
brought alive, an adventure starts to be
a success. The travel bug bites hard, but
motorcycle travel bites deep. **❞**

Sam Manicom

Printed in Great Britain
by Amazon

29897724R00201